Rethinking Rural Literacies

Rethinking Rural Literacies
Transnational Perspectives

Edited by
Bill Green and Michael Corbett

RETHINKING RURAL LITERACIES

First published in 2013 by
PALGRAVE MACMILLAN®
in the United States—a division of St. Martin's Press LLC,
175 Fifth Avenue, New York, NY 10010.

Where this book is distributed in the UK, Europe and the rest of the world,
this is by Palgrave Macmillan, a division of Macmillan Publishers Limited,
registered in England, company number 785998, of Houndmills,
Basingstoke, Hampshire RG21 6XS.

Palgrave Macmillan is the global academic imprint of the above companies
and has companies and representatives throughout the world.

Palgrave® and Macmillan® are registered trademarks in the United States,
the United Kingdom, Europe and other countries.

ISBN: 978–1–137–27548–6

Library of Congress Cataloging-in-Publication Data

Rethinking rural literacies : transnational perspectives / edited by
Bill Green and Michael Corbett.
pages cm
Includes bibliographical references.
ISBN 978–1–137–27548–6 (hardcover : alk. paper)
1. Education, Rural. 2. Literacy. 3. Critical pedagogy. I. Green, Bill,
1952–, editor of compilation. II. Corbett, Michael John, 1958–,
editor of compilation.

LC5146.R48 2013
370.9173′4—dc23   2012045789

A catalogue record of the book is available from the British Library.

Design by Newgen Imaging Systems (P) Ltd., Chennai, India.

First edition: June 2013

10 9 8 7 6 5 4 3 2 1

Contents

Illustrations

Map

Figures

Table

Acknowledgments

B ooks and projects such as this always involve more people than are named in them, as their authors and/or editors. In this case, we want to especially acknowledge the work of Kylie Press, at Charles Sturt University, who not only did the formatting and much else of that nature, but was also diligent in following up copyright matters and other technical requirements. We want, of course, to thank all of our contributors, sometimes for their patience and forbearance as much as their scholarly efforts. There were others, too, whose participation in our various sessions along the way was most appreciated. Finally, we need to formally acknowledge the funding support of the Social Sciences and Humanities Research Council of Canada (SSHRCC).

Rural Education and Literacies: An Introduction

Bill Green and Michael Corbett

This volume explores the relationship between literacy studies and rural education, expressly from a transnational perspective. It is worth clarifying, at the outset, what we are dealing with, in bringing together not only two quite distinct fields of scholarship but also researchers from a range of countries, with contributors from Australia, Canada, the United States, and Finland. First, we see the need to take into account the possibility that there may be quite different *ruralities* in play, but also, conceivably, quite different *literacies*. Indeed, it seems highly likely that there are, across and within national contexts, differing constructions of the rural, as well as different manifestations of rurality, depending in part on geography but also on culture (Donehower, Hogg, and Schell 2011, p. 10). Second, what counts as literacy, and also literacy studies, needs to be (re)articulated, and made explicit. This is because there may be distinct affordances in different scholarly cultures and different educational systems, from primary schooling right up to graduate work and beyond. Different things are imaginable or intelligible, according to standpoint, and acknowledgment of the now thoroughly globalized nature of academic inquiry, including that associated with both literacy studies and rural education. Hence, there are different rural imaginaries evident across this book, and divergent experiences and histories, *despite* important commonalities and connections. Literacy is also variously understood and realized, with some of us working with a more constrained view of literacy, at least semantically, as referring to more or less recognizable textual practices, while other uses are more, as it were, metaphorical, or at least more open-ended and adventurous. That range is only to be welcomed, it seems to us, partly because it conjures up possibilities for new realizations and articulations of literacy, rurality, and education, but also because it helps in rethinking the familiar, *including* the literacy practices of the school, and thereby in enriching both praxis and inquiry.

As indicated, the book explores the intersection of contemporary research in literacy/literacies education from the perspective of the multiple understandings of rurality that globalization opens up. Notwithstanding the rich development of literacies research in recent years, particularly under the banner of the New Literacy Studies (NLS), there is a notable absence of work addressed specifically to the intersection of rural education and literacy studies, as fields of research and praxis. The book brings together scholars from these two distinctive fields to explore various issues within an emerging nexus of concerns about literacy, rurality, and education. It takes an explicitly socially critical interest in matters of equity, disadvantage, and social justice, as well as with regard to its own terms of reference—"literacy," "rurality," and indeed, "education." Hence the very notion of "rural literacies" is thematized *and* problematized.

There is much value, at this particular moment in history, in providing scholarly insight into the role and significance of literacy practice and education in and for rural society. We might begin by defining rurality (albeit provisionally) as the ecosocial world beyond the Metropolis, recognizing that this definition itself needs to be interrogated. While it has recently been announced that, for the first time, more people across the world are living in cities than in the country (Davis 2004; Schafft and Youngblood Jackson 2010, p. 1), that does not mean that rural life should be assigned to the past, or viewed now as more or less irrelevant. For a whole host of reasons—environmental, economic, political, and so on—rurality needs to be kept on the agenda and it is hoped that this book makes its own innovative contribution in this regard. Attention to reconceptualized rural literacies has, therefore, larger (global) ecosocial significance.

The book builds specifically on recent work by Donehower, Hogg, and Schell (2007), whose pioneering book *Rural Literacies* raised questions concerning sustainability in rural communities. They looked at literacies as a window for conceptualizing positive social change that gets beyond preservationist nostalgia and promotes forward-looking transformational thinking. The approach is to confront established stereotypes about rural people and to support them in recognizing and strengthening their literacies, while at the same time supporting a general broadening of the frame of what counts as literacy. This expanded view of literacies is linked to rural social development, the reconstitution of rural places in the face of global change forces, and productive thinking around sustainable futures (Woods 2007). It has implications well beyond the rural sector, moreover, as Donehower, Hogg, and Schell (2007, p. xi) assert: "[R]ural literacies are not something for only rural people to pay attention," since, "rural should not be seen in opposition to urban but as part of *a complex global economic and social network*" (emphasis added). Hence, the book can appropriately be seen as a *complement* to the now burgeoning work addressed to urban education, to questions of place and space in education, as well as to rural education per se, and more generally to global studies in education.

Further, *Rethinking Rural Literacies* works with and yet seeks to go beyond Edmondson's (2003) account of three distinct "*rural* literacies": (1) a "traditional" rural literacy; (2) a "neoliberal" rural literacy; and (3) a "new" rural literacy. While seeking to contextualize the first two of these, then, our book provides a further basis for thinking about the third, a new or still perhaps emergent "rural literacy," to be understood with specific regard to notions of globalization, sustainability, place and space, mobility, representation, and post-rurality.

Conceptual Framework

The book's overall theoretical orientation draws on three principal strands of thinking. First of all, it is located broadly in the idea of *place-conscious education* (e.g., Gruenewald and Smith 2008), particularly as this applies to literacy education (Comber, Nixon, and Reid 2007; Thomson 2006). The broad argument in place-conscious education is that while educators have long understood the importance of context to learning, we have tended to value more the abstract, the generic, and the imagined "fairness" of allegedly objective forms of standardized pedagogy, curriculum, and assessment. Place-conscious educators contend that the most powerful forms of learning engage people in real problems and issues, beginning in their particular, nonstandard communities of practice.

Second, the book is informed by and situated in the context of the New Literacy Studies (NLS), as elaborated further in chapter 1. The NLS framework understands literacy as a social practice through which differently placed agents engage in different kinds of literate activity based upon their social context, the contingencies of work, established family textual practices, personal networks, interests, and inclinations. In this framework, literacies are *multiple*, rather than singular. Projects inspired by the NLS investigate the ways in which ordinary people are literate, rather than trying to understand the extent to which individuals possess particular decoding/encoding or other abstract skillsets assumed to be the foundation of literacy. Rather than evaluating individuals on an abstracted and generic level of mastery of decontextualized literacy skills, the NLS investigate how people use their situated literacy skills and knowledges in practice. This view of literacy as social practice focuses not just on print, but also on sound and image, and digital-electronic resources more generally.

In this regard, we also want to highlight the key connection between textual practices and life practices—"literacy" and "life"—in the sense that we see literacy as a set of connected political, economic, social, spatial, and psychological practices. So we wish to expand narrow ideas of literacy toward questions of "reading and writing" political, ecological, and economic practices as well. We see these forms of what Freire and Macedo (1987) provocatively called "reading the world as well as reading the word," as fundamental to contemporary literacies in general. Obviously, literacy practices, understood at this level, ought to engage with the distinctive problems, such as widespread poverty, that are endemic to rurality globally. Our book then takes up key problems in educational analysis such as social justice, power, difference, and change, connecting them to cultural and language practices in rural education, broadly understood.

Further, the focus of the book is predicated on the relationship between rural literacies, new understandings and formations of rurality, and what might be called *ecosocial justice*—a concept extending the established notion of social justice to take into account ecological and environment challenges and injustices (Martusewicz and Edmundson 2011; Orr 2004). This is an important and innovative contribution to the existing literature, and to the field more generally.

It is appropriate at this point to make some preliminary observations about rurality, rural studies, and rural education, as an established field of study. This is the third key conceptual strand that informs and infuses the book. Rurality itself is a contested and problematic concept that is caught up in what might be called an oppressive biopolitics. In contemporary societies, rurality has come to represent a category of alterity, a collective and complex identity position that can be either assigned or embraced. It is this very complexity, and the diversity of human and physical geographies that the term rural subsumes, that speaks to its enduring importance. In countries like Australia, Canada, Finland, and the United States, there are massive tracts of rural land that have been acquired forcefully, in most cases from Indigenous people. Today, these lands contain some of the most valuable resource deposits on the globe, and ironically, some of the most economically disadvantaged people. It must also be said that many of these people are disadvantaged principally by their deep connections to place (Berry 1977; Theobald 1997) and by their inability or unwillingness to become mobile, detached, and "educated," in the Western sense of learning to live comfortably disengaged from land and sea. It is becoming increasingly clear that historic patterns of colonial/capitalist exploitation and degradation of these lands and the "ruralized" people who are consigned to them is a situation that is both unsustainable and unconscionable.

Given the problematic nature of our key concepts, rural and literacy, many of our contributors were from the outset rather resistant to the whole idea of the rural as a frame of reference, as well as an object of concern. Even so, we believe that thinking of "rurality" remains important and productive, notwithstanding the conceptual and definitional difficulties associated with the term. In this regard, we agree with Donehower, Hogg, and Schell (2011, p. 10) that "the rural" must be understood "not only demographically and geographically but culturally as well"—all the more important, given the postmodern turn and the emergence of new formulations and problematics such as "post-rurality."

The question of *(dis)advantage* is crucial here. Thinking through the relations between space and equity, education and poverty, literacy and social justice, is clearly a matter of some urgency. Addressing the rural in these terms is crucial. At issue is the structural disadvantage experienced in and by rural communities, socially and educationally. More generally, though, the challenge of widespread rural poverty is linked with environmental degradation and racism. In America, a recent report (*Rural Policy Matters*, August 2009; see also Johnson and Strange 2005) identifies 900 rural schools districts (representing 10 percent of the total) as having the highest percentage of student poverty. No doubt similar cartographies could be produced for other countries. In Canada as well, income and unemployment are unevenly distributed, with some rural areas such as Atlantic Canada, northern Saskatchewan, and Manitoba, for instance, suffering greater stress (Canadian Rural Secretariat 2012). In the case of Australia, mapping rural poverty and associated forms of disadvantage is something still to be done. There is no doubt, however, that rural poverty is a significant issue. Taking account of social and educational disadvantage with specific regard to rural (especially inland) Australia remains important, notwithstanding understandable concerns about stigmatization and deficit rhetorics. As Australian rural sociologist Geoffrey Lawrence (1997, p. 32) writes,

> [I]n the context of increasing economic polarisation in the countryside and widespread and continued poverty among isolated rural (but especially Aboriginal) populations it could be argued, with some force, that a

return to studies of the causes and consequences of rural social disadvantage is long overdue.

Like more urbanized spaces, rural locales are deeply networked and connected. Today, in a more thoroughly globalized world, the opportunities that present themselves for transnational, collaborative rural education and literacies research are considerable.

Becoming REAL

An immediate context for the book is the establishment of the Rural Education and Literacies Research Network—called, in short, REAL. A concept originally proposed in the mid-1990s, by Bill Green and Jo-Anne Reid, REAL is a transnational network of literacy scholars and rural education researchers who work for the most part in specific national contexts. To initiate the network, we (i.e., Green and Corbett) made a successful application for preliminary funding from the Social Sciences and Humanities Research Council of Canada (SSHRCC) in its International Opportunities Fund. This enabled us to call for expressions of interest, out of which formed a group that first met in New Orleans, in early 2011, to workshop the preliminary accounts of "rural literacies," which subsequently became the chapters here.

We firmly believe that bringing together rural education scholars and literacy researchers in this way contributes to informed understandings of rural social space and provides fresh understandings of key problems of rural economic and social development—problems that are increasingly global in scope. Further, and more specifically, questions of rural-regional sustainability are also questions of how rural populations and rural educators understand and manage emerging literacies and textualities, within a globalized and increasingly networked world.

A recurring theme internationally is the variability of educational performance of rural students, particularly relative to those living in the larger centers. For instance, until recently in Australia, this was a constant feature of mainly anecdotal understanding, namely that children and young people from inland rural Australia were educationally disadvantaged relative to their metropolitan counterparts. That has now been confirmed by recent formal evidence, including that arising from the OECD Programme for International Student Assessment (PISA) and other international assessment programs (Welch, Helme, and Lamb 2007). Quite a few Canadian studies have come to similar conclusions (Canadian Council on Learning 2006; Wallin 2009). But it is what is actually being measured and accounted for that is most relevant here. Educational performance and achievement scores are theoretically broader in their reference than just literacy and numeracy, but in practice it would seem that all too often they are effectively reduced to these kinds of reductionist formulations. This is a particular problem in thinking through the relationship between literacy studies and rural education in Australia—although it also pertains to other countries and jurisdictions, in varying degrees. This is to take due account of what has been called, following Bell (2006), "the 'transnational rural' or the way the rural can be imagined globally" (Gorman-Murray, Darian-Smith, and Gibson 2008, p. 41). REAL may well be an appropriate forum to investigate such issues and anxieties, nationally and globally.

However, these questions should not limit the mandate of REAL. Indeed, as we indicate in this book, that mandate extends well beyond the sometimes limited and limiting (albeit still powerful) version of literacy that predominates in policy and schooling, to embrace more open-ended, expansive, inclusive versions, in which "literacy" becomes seemingly more metaphorical. A Deleuzian view of literacy as multiplicity might well be appropriate here, thereby allowing for a more generous and generative understanding of what the project of rural literacies might entail, as a field of possibility.

This book is, hopefully, just a beginning. Already it has occasioned a series of gatherings at meetings and conferences of the American Educational Research Association (AERA), the Canadian Society for the Study of Education (CSSE), and the Australian Association for Research in Education (AARE). We hope that REAL continues to evolve, and gather momentum, with this book being just the first in a series of projects addressed to the articulation of literacy studies and rural education. We see it as a platform for ongoing and expanding transnational dialogue and rich research collaborations that enhance and consolidate literacies work in our national contexts.

A Brief Tour of the Book

The book is organized thematically into four sections: Conceptualizing Rural Literacies, Literacy/Pedagogies, Place and Sustainability, and Mobilities and Futures. From the beginning of the project, the authors have debated the problematic histories and uses of our two central concepts: "literacy" and "rural." Both, it seemed to many of us, grew out of binary conceptions that have done more to marginalize, discipline, and restrict than they have to open educational, social, cultural, and economic possibilities. Thus, we began our work from a place of deep discomfort, a discomfort that runs through each of the chapters, most of which speak to substantive literacy work in rural contexts. In an important sense, this is a book in which a group of literacy scholars, working in multiple contexts, trouble their own readings of the rural, with the explicit intention of moving forward by troubling the fixities that are embedded in the common images of both literacy and rurality.

Bill Green's conceptual overview links issues and concerns in rural education with extensive contemporary developments in literacy scholarship and particularly with the sociological/ethnographic turn in literacy studies represented by the NLS. Green sets out several key tensions that are taken up in the chapters that follow. He demonstrates, using spatial theory, how rurality and literacy are both concepts that can be understood only relationally. There is no essential rural, for instance, and the idea of rurality makes sense only when it is placed within a semiotic matrix in a relationship of difference from other concepts (e.g., urban, modern, developed, etc.). Phil Cormack also takes up relationality as he draws upon poststructuralist theory to offer a complex, interconnected, understanding of both rurality and literacy/literacies.

Green further addresses the tension between conceptions of literacy that emanate from neoliberal educational discourses and those alternative situated literacies of emplacement. This tension runs through virtually all of the chapters, as authors grapple with the always-difficult relationship between standardization of curriculum, standardized assessment, and literacy practices and those alternative situated practices that reflect an embodied sense of place. This tension has played out in different but complementary ways in literacies scholarship and in rural education scholarship, respectively, and one key contribution of this book is to explicitly bring these discourses into conversation with one another. For Green, literacies are simultaneously multidimensional cultural-critical practices and operational skillsets, and many of the chapters address literacies as culturally located and diverse rather than singular. This is in part a question of scale, a point made by Green, Margaret Somerville, and also Pauliina Rautio and Maija Lanas, in this volume. Indeed, as Kathryn Hibbert suggests, literacy and standardized (child, youth, and adult) literacy assessment is often mobilized as a way of defining an educational hierarchy of places, with rurality as deficient and left-behind on the time/space margins. Conceptions of literacy range in scale from the international comparative down to conceptions of literacy as a practice of living in place, and by scaling up or down, governance, disciplinary, and surveillance arguments and policy are made in the neoliberal state.

In this book, literacies are also conceived as implicated in environmental and sustainability practices that, in rural areas, represent commitments to subsistence and cultural activity (including mathematical reasoning, as Craig Howley shows) as well as to emotional and spiritual connections between people, animals, and the nonhuman world. To use the language of Actor Network Theory, the land, the farm, the village, place, or indeed "Country" (as Margaret Somerville characterizes it) are "actants" with which human agents correlate. This is also illustrated in Lyn Kerkham and Barbara Comber's analysis of how stewardship, eco-social justice, and affinity with the land problematize classic boundaries and binaries that separate people and place and integrate literacies pedagogy with solidarity, struggle, activism, and environmentalism. Similarly, Ursula Kelly shows how the land itself can be brought to life as a powerful textual agent/persuader. Green speaks to the established but still emerging framework of place-based or place-sensitive education that has (both through the lens of the NLS and that of rural education scholarship) kept alive the importance of the local. Both movements have been criticized for truncating analysis and practice at the level of the immediate locale, and we hope this book sufficiently problematizes the idea that rurality is associated only with the small and insular place.

These chapters illustrate how small rural places are not insular and disconnected from modernity, and powerful literacies are fluid personal negotiations. Kim Donehower offers a substantive look into the lives of rural "hyperliterates," juxtaposing what might be called unschooled literacies of desire with literacies of compulsion, as found in formal educational contexts. Donehower's work presages a number of later chapters by challenging the way that literacy has been co-opted by efforts to create a mobile, flexible, neoliberal subject, in investigating the placed conditions that have actually supported rural people who engage enthusiastically and deeply with (print) literacy. Kate Cairns' analysis of a personal development simulation game in a Canadian rural middle school is a good example of the tension between literacy pedagogies that deliberately inculcate neoliberal sensibilities and students' own literate engagements with their home places and how they enact resistances to the way they are framed pedagogically. Pauliina Rautio and Maija Lanas also take up the theme of literacies of desire in their analysis of Finnish Laplanders' conceptions of beauty as a way of relating to the symbolic and the imaginary landscapes they inhabit. These are literacies in the rural, indeed in the very bodies of people living in places they consider "good enough," aesthetically satisfying, and beautiful. Michael Corbett and Ann Vibert also find a *jouissance* as Atlantic Canadian middle school students improvise with video cameras, exhibiting powerful literacies that represent their own desires and fantasies. At the same time, though, these students and their teachers and parents also worry about the restricted and conventional literacies that seem to really count in the world of the neoliberal school, where they are expected to constitute themselves as disciplined (global) subjects. Lyn Kerkham and Barbara Comber also address the challenges of competing commitments and complex identity negotiations of environmentally sensitive rural literacy educators who both live and teach in rural communities as they enact a rich yet always problematic and tension-filled pedagogy of place.

Ursula Kelly's haunting chapter on a Newfoundland media tourism promotion that is ubiquitous throughout Canada develops a complex argument about how the campaign invokes natural imagery aligned with emotionally laden depictions of rural lifeways to create texts that, perhaps ironically, invite the viewer/tourist to "find yourself here." Kelly argues that simply seeing these texts as a commodification of the rural undervalues the complex psychoemotional work that the texts accomplish. These texts invite connections both for the tourist and for the resident, connections that point to the relational nature of both literate and rural phenomena. Neither rurality nor literacy can then be understood as stand-alone concepts, causing Kelly to wonder: "what is the role of rurality within modernity?" For Jo-Anne Reid, literacies represent an opportunity for a fundamental renegotiation of relationships, a powerful point she makes looking at how her own son and other young males negotiated a complex, multilayered masculinity in a rural space, participating in a nationally broadcast filmmaking project about youth and violence—like Corbett and Vibert, she is concerned with moving image production as a ("new") literacy practice. Hibbert's take on virtual literacies, and the way that rural places can be brought together and represented in online spaces outside the constrained boundaries of formal educational sites, imagines that the Internet ironically creates opportunity for place-based educational practices. The problem of renegotiation is also taken up in Margaret Somerville's chapter, which opens with an explicit rejection of the concept of the rural because of the way it is formed in fundamentally colonial, oppressive, and marginalizing binaries. Somerville enacts her research on Australian Aboriginal lands in concert with her research participants, using a concept she calls "thinking through Country" as both a methodology and a perspective.

Somerville also explicitly problematizes the complexity of relationships in the research act, highlighting the centrality of reflexive awareness. The relationality of literacy practices is also illustrated in Karen

Eppley's account of a county Fair. At one level, the Fair is a celebration of traditional farming practices and lifeways, but at another level, Eppley shows how most aspects of the Fair are inflected by complicated intersections of family farming practices and values, agrarian traditions, corporate agriculture, presentational literacies (such as the formal essay delivered by Fair Queen candidates), and commodification. Eppley demonstrates how the Fair is ultimately a postmodern "mess" of multiple tensions, practices, and literacies. Eppley's account, like that of several others in the collection, balances the analytical lens of the scholar with the self-reflective analysis of a lived practice. Also, in the analyses of Corbett and Vibert, Kerkham and Comber, Cairns, and Hibbert, and even more explicitly in Kelly, there is a powerful association between rurality and loss—perhaps the most familiar single trope in rural education scholarship.

But, importantly, loss and the work of mourning that Kelly invokes are aimed at moving forward into new spaces of possibility. Indeed, most of the chapters are pedagogical accounts of a substantive and generative rural education practice. Phil Cormack's analysis of the work of a group of rural teachers in Newfoundland, on Canada's Atlantic coast, argues that there is nothing in contemporary neoliberal curriculum that necessarily precludes the development of place-based educational practice—a point made by Kerkham and Comber as well. This reminds us again that the separation of educational questions into sterile binaries (place-based versus standards-based, for instance) obscures potential for emergent, perhaps "tactical," forms of educational practice that straddle boundaries and categories. Some of these boundaries are spatial, but others are disciplinary. Craig Howley adopts the image of the "stranger," another common trope in rural literature, to engage a reading of rurality and mathematics education. Just as reading and writing practices have been distilled to a generic and often disciplinary notion of literacy, so too have mathematical practices been reduced to "numeracy." It is the very abstraction of mathematics that gives it what Howley calls its "formatting power." In neoliberal discourses of educational change, standardized measurement, and placeless curriculum, literacy and numeracy have been anointed, abstracted, and elevated as a decontextualized, purely objective set of readily testable quantifiable skills.

Rural literacies then represent for us a confluence of theorizations and practices about place and pedagogy, text and reading practices, and place and space. To use Yi-Fu Tuan's (1977) imagery, place is a stopping point in the multiple flows that space represents. We can imagine place, accordingly, as a plant in a littoral zone washed by the incessant advance and retreat of the tide. The plant remains for a time, but it is continually changed by what flows through, in, and around it. Rural literacies are multiple, mutable, and mobile, and ever relational. They inevitably float in a global sea.

References

Bell, D., 2006, "Variations on the Rural Idyll," in P. Cloke, T. Marsden, and P. Mooney (eds.), *Handbook of Rural Studies*, Sage, London, pp. 149–60.

Berry, W., 1977, *The Unsettling of America: Culture and Agriculture*, Avon, New York.

Canadian Council on Learning, 2006, *The Rural-Urban Gap in Education*, http://www.ccl-cca.ca/pdfs/LessonsInLearning/10–03_01_06E.pdf.

Canadian Rural Secretariat, 2012, *Community Information Data Base*, http://www.cid-bdc.ca/home.

Comber, B., H. Nixon, and J-A. Reid, 2007, *Literacies in Place: Teaching Environmental Communications*, Primary English Teachers Association (PETA), Sydney.

Davis, M., 2004, "Planet of Slums: Urban Involution and the Informal Proletariat," *New Left Review*, vol. 26: 5–34.

Donehower, K., C. Hogg, and E. E. Schell, 2007, *Rural Literacies*, Southern Illinois University Press, Carbondale.

——— (eds.), 2011, *Reclaiming the Rural: Essays on Literacy, Rhetoric, and Pedagogy*, Southern Illinois University Press, Carbondale.

Edmondson, J., 2003, *Prairie Town: Redefining Rural Life in the Age of Globalization*, Rowman, Lanham, MD.

Freire, P. and D. Macedo, 1987, *Literacy: Reading the Word & the World*, Bergin & Garvey, New York.

Gorman-Murray, A., K. Darian-Smith, and C. Gibson, 2008, "Scaling the Rural: Reflections on Rural Cultural Studies," *Australian Humanities Review*, vol. 45: 37–52.

Gruenewald, D. A. and G. A. Smith (eds.), 2008, *Place-Based Education in the Global Age: Local Diversity*, Lawrence Erlbaum Associates, New York and London.

Johnson, J. and M. Strange, 2005, *Why Rural Matters 2005: The Facts about Rural Education in 50 States*, Report of the Rural School and Community Trust Policy Program, Arlington.

Lawrence, G., 1997, "Rural Sociology—Does It Have a Future in Australian Universities?" *Rural Society*, vol. 7, no. 1: 29–36.

Martusewicz, R. and J. Edmundson, 2011, *EcoJustice Education: Toward Diverse, Democratic, and Sustainable Communities*, Routledge, New York.

Orr, D., 2004, *Earth in Mind: On Education, Environment, and the Human Prospect*, Island Press, Washington.

Rural Policy Matters, August 2009, *High-Poverty Rural, Small Town Districts Concentrated in Distinct Regions*, http://www.ruraledu.org/articles.php?id=2279.

Schafft, K. A. and A. Youngblood Jackson, 2010, "Introduction: Rural Education for the Twenty-First Century," in K. A. Schafft and A. Youngblood Jackson (eds.), *Rural Education for the Twenty-First Century: Literacy, Place and Community in a Globalizing World*, The Pennsylvania State University Press, University Park, pp. 1–13.

Theobald, P., 1997, *Teaching the Commons: Pride, Place and the Renewal of Community*, Westview Press, Boulder, CO.

Thomson, P., 2006, "Miners, Diggers, Ferals and Show-Men: School-Community Projects that Affirm and Unsettle Identities and Place," *British Journal of Sociology of Education*, vol. 2, no. 1:.81–96.

Tuan, Y-F., 1977, *Space and Place: The Perspective of Experience*, University of Minnesota Press, Minneapolis.

Wallin, D., 2009, *Rural Education: A Review of Provincial and Territorial Initiatives 2009*, Government of Manitob, Winnipeg, MB.

Welch, A., S. Helme, and S. Lamb, 2007, "Rurality and Inequality in Education: The Australian Experience," in R. Teese, S. Lamb, and M. Duru-Bellat (eds.), *International, Studies in Educational Inequality: Theory and Policy, Vol 2: Inequality in Educational Systems*, Springer, The Netherlands, pp. 271–293.

Woods, M., 2007, "Engaging the Global Countryside: Globalization, Hybridity and the Reconstitution of Rural Place," *Progress in Human Geography*, vol. 3, no. 4: 485–507.

PART I

Conceptualizing Rural Literacies

CHAPTER 1

Literacy, Rurality, Education: A Partial Mapping

Bill Green

Introduction: Rural Literacies?

How might we go about understanding and researching rural literacies? Is it indeed appropriate to speak of "*rural* literacies"? Is it possible or even meaningful to refer to *rural* literacies, with the adjective in this case being a genuine modifier? What does the adjective "rural" do? How does it add value to either literacy studies or rural education, as scholarly fields? What relationship exists between literacy studies and rural schooling, and between literacy studies and rural education more generally? This chapter seeks to engage and explore questions such as these, in order to open up discussion and debate in this undervalued and misrecognized area.

Donehower and her colleagues, as originators of the term, confirm that properly understanding rural literacy is indeed an issue: "As we tried to define rural literacies for the purposes of [our] book, it was telling that we couldn't find a specific definition that we could work within or against in the field of literacy studies" (Donehower, Hogg, and Schell 2007, p. 4). Their proposal is that it refers, in brief, to "the uses of literacy in rural contexts": "Rural literacies... refers to the particular kinds of literate skills needed to achieve the goals of sustaining life in rural areas"—that is, "pursu[ing] the opportunities and creat[ing] the public policies and economic opportunities needed to sustain rural communities" (p. 4). Further, they argue for "a notion of rural literacy based on a concept of sustainability" (p. 12). They explicitly connect such work with a larger agenda, linked to notions of global citizenship, and involving a view of "rural literacies that are multiple and that encourage identification among rural, urban and suburban citizens" (p. 193). The latter is particularly important: it allows the project of rural literacies to be associated with a distinctly ethical commitment, working toward global ecosocial sustainability. They clearly want this concept and its accompanying program to function as advocacy for rural people and rural communities. "Rural communities have been ill-served in the past by both a lack of research on rural literacy and by research and education initiatives that mischaracterize rural literacy" (p. 27).

This provides a useful platform to work from here. It is important to note that Donehower and her colleagues make no claim to a definitive account of the territory, clearly seeing their work as needing to be extended and supplemented. Nonetheless, that work constitutes an important reference point for research and scholarship addressed to literacy studies and rural education—as is both confirmed and extended in their most recent publication (Donehower, Hogg, and Schell 2011).

In my (Australian) context, very little work exists on rural literacy, and there is little sense of how a rural literacies research program might be qualitatively different and distinct from literacy research per se. A recent preliminary survey of the Australian literature revealed just a handful of papers and reports, and a single national study specifically focused on literacy and rurality (Muspratt, Freebody, and Luke 2001). Rural locations and circumstances do feature in articles on Indigenous education and literacy studies, but without marking rurality as a significant category. More recently, there have been several papers addressed to results of standardized testing programs that reveal disparities relating to rural and Indigenous populations. By and large, however, little attention has been given, to date, to the notion that there may well be distinctive features of literacy in the rural context, or that literacy and rurality can be brought together differently, outside of a hegemonic schooling logic. This indicates that research is urgently needed in this respect, focusing specifically on literacy, rurality, and education—on rural literacies in Australia.

There is more work being done in this area outside Australia (e.g., Brooke 2003; Edmondson 2003; Kelly 2009), even though it is at best a small (sub)field. Also, much literacy research and scholarship effectively still overlooks the rural, and thereby marginalizing it. As Donehower and colleagues observed, "literacy research in our field is skewed toward urban sites and subjects" (2007, p.12). Hence we are much more likely to find work on topics such as "city literacies" (Gregory and Williams 2000), "English in urban classrooms" (Kress et al. 2005) or "urban literacies" (Kinloch 2011)—work for which the reference point is the modern(ist) city, producing, in effect, whether acknowledged or not, a form of metro-normativity. Understanding literacy as "translocal" and "situated," and linking to critical-cultural work on space(s) and place(s), is, therefore, an important avenue for developing a research program addressed to rural literacies, or the relationship between literacy studies and rural education.

Space, Literacy, and Rural (Teacher) Education

Politico-administrative jurisdictions like states or provinces, or nations, bring together populations *and* territories, as objects of sociopolitical management. One way of understanding contemporary developments with the public use of data is as a heightened form of spatial governance (Jackson 2004). Governing space is a distinctive form of social power. Governing the spatial field involves practices of normalization. Furthermore, policy—organized as it is by the logic and politics of population—is usefully seen as addressed to the relationship between space and power. This includes education policy. And yet policy would seem curiously "space-blind" (Green and Letts 2007, p. 63; Green 2008). This is notwithstanding the observation that "[e]ducational phenomena are distributed in space" (Marsden 1977, p. 21), a formulation described as "a key defining element, however naturalized, in the practice and institution of education" (Green and Letts 2007, p. 59). The particular relevance and importance of this for rural education is clear.

As Cloke (2006, p. 18) has observed, "[t]he idea of rurality seems to be firmly entrenched in popular discourse about space, place and society in the Western world." Indeed, the concept of rurality itself is "inherently spatial" (Halfacree 2006, p. 44). Building on this idea, Green and Letts (2007, p. 63) argued that what is needed is "a critical socio-spatial framework, a social-dynamic theory of space and spatiality whereby there is a dialectical relationship between space and society, practice and representation, and an emphasis on the social production of space"—more specifically, a way of "thinking *differently* about issues of space, equity and rural education" (p. 58; emphasis added). Moreover, this needs to be appropriately complex and sophisticated, and in this regard, it is useful to think of the rural as *real-and-imaginary*, following Soja (1996), or of rurality as pertaining to real-and-imaginary spaces and places. This allows due consideration of desire, fantasy, and anxiety, and the power and pleasures of the Symbolic, and provides a basis for drawing in psychoanalytic work as a further resource for rural education research *and* rural literacy. In our case, we were able to think of inland NSW and specifically the Far West ("out there") as an object of "racially-charged fantasies and anxieties" (p. 71). This is particularly resonant given the significant proportion of Aboriginal people living in these areas and the ongoing challenge of Aboriginal education in NSW, and indeed in Australia more generally, with literacy remaining a key and crucial area within which Indigenous disadvantage is realized.

A matter of particular interest arising from this work is what such an argument opens up in terms of a critical account of (rural) educational space. Taking a historical perspective, Green and Letts (p. 61) note "the view, deeply entrenched in the Australian system, that location is of no consequence to the delivery of education, that distance can be effectively annulled, and that space simply doesn't matter." Such a view appears to be even more supported and substantiated by contemporary arguments that introducing new digital technology into schooling overcomes many of the difficulties and disadvantages of rural education. The logic is remarkably consistent. Despite strong assertions that place matters, and a historical commitment to equity, this logic produces a particular form of governmental, normalizing space, making it hard to sustain place-based initiatives or to develop more effective equity programs.

This problem is noted by Jan Nespor and others, including exponents (and their critics) of what has been called *place-conscious education* (Gruenewald and Smith 2008), itself increasingly being drawn into new rural educational research and scholarship. Also, gradually more and more official maps and profiles are being produced, based on quantifiable, statistical data, operating at a range of scales. For Nespor (2004, p. 320), there are "powerful forces at work to produce totalizing maps that allow distant students and teachers to be plotted with respect to one another." Referring specifically to the United States, but more generally indicating the pervasive rhetoric of "standards" in education policy and practice, he writes:

> Buttressed by recent legislation, the standards portray schooling as a smooth, homogenous system, and the tests presuppose a static population in long-term engagement with neighbourhood schools. (p. 320)

In his account of "educational scale-making," Nespor presents a number of scenarios, "scalar stories" in effect, introducing a set of characters (Zena, Jerry, Chester) and tracing their various trajectories and relationships in space-time. Here, "children are defined by the way they reflect off the standards and tests, that is, accordingly to whether or not they pass."

Their situational specificity is obscured; where they and their families "live or work or how often they have moved is masked" (pp. 320–321). Moreover, "student learning takes a form that can be scaled at the level of the state, making all students within that political sphere comparable and summable, according to a standard metric" (p. 321). Place *and* specificity disappear. While Nespor's focus is predominantly on the city, and on "imagin[ing] different ways for teachers to know cities, regions and communities" (p. 323), there are clear implications here for rural education, and for engaging with issues of space and equity for rural schools and communities.

There are implications too for researching rural literacies. In NSW, for instance, there is a considerable history of standardized literacy testing, now subsumed within the new National Assessment Program for Literacy and Numeracy (NAPLAN). While there is still little public analysis of how students in inland NSW fare as a distinct grouping within the total population, Indigenous students are consistently marked out as falling below state averages—especially in more remote locations—along with others from lower socioeconomic backgrounds. This is consistent with research drawing on available PISA and National Benchmark data demonstrating "the underachievement of rural and remote students in the area of literacy when compared to the performance of students in metropolitan areas of Australia" (Pegg and Panizzon 2007, p. 188; Welch, Helme, and Lamb 2007). Despite more enlightened forms of policy related to literacy pedagogy emerging in Australia, and widespread endorsement of "critical literacy," a gap still exists between theoretical and practical ideologies.

Nonetheless, along with continuing work on disadvantage and poverty, and ongoing concerns with social justice, new interest has developed in notions of place and community—more specifically, place-based community (Nixon and Comber 2009; McInerney, Smyth, and Down 2011). These concepts and proposals have increasingly been drawn into rural educational research (White and Reid 2008; Reid et al. 2010) and, relatedly, work on literacy education and environmental change (Comber, Nixon, and Reid 2007; Cormack, Green, and Reid 2008). Yet, how this has connected with state and national policy agendas heavily invested in standardized testing, committed to accountability, and in practice still oriented to print (Tan and McWilliam 2009) remains uncertain. Do place-referenced pedagogies contribute to enhanced scores in literacy tests? At this stage it is impossible to know. However, there is a case for claiming that accountability regimes such as these constrain the possibilities for place-sensitive work. This is particularly so if they encourage a tighter nexus between teaching and testing, or teaching to the test (Mills 2008). The challenge is to develop a research program that combines critique and creativity, or innovation, and engages with the potential of socially critical and responsible initiatives with regard to literacy, place, sustainability, and rural education.

Making such connections enables a direct link to the work of the Lancaster group on "local literacies" (Barton and Hamilton 2008) and "situated literacies" (Barton, Hamilton, and Ivaniic 2000). The project of situated literacies is especially generative, however, and immediately relevant. Indeed, there is a potentially useful resonance between notions of situated literacies and place-conscious education, in ways that (to my knowledge) haven't been recognized or capitalized on to date. At the same time, mindful of the critique that such work has attracted (e.g., Brandt and Clinton 2002) and wanting to move beyond its primarily ethnographic orientation, I want to put a somewhat different spin on the term. Following Soja (1996), literacies are to be understood as *socially*, *historically*, and *spatially* situated. Although Soja certainly sees these as profoundly interrelated, within what he calls a "trialectic," it is the spatial that I focus on here, very briefly. Understanding literacy as spatially situated compels attention to how literacy is realized in space, whether that is the spatial field of the nation or the district, or whatever, and within which are inescapably socio-spatial hierarchies. Hence literacy becomes thinkable in terms of the social difference-dynamics of space, place and scale, and associated trajectories: for instance, what flows from where to where, with what effect. Hence, what has been described as "spatial justice" (Soja 2010) emerges as a focus concern. Introducing time as well as movement into consideration further enriches the picture. What such a revised view of situated literacies enables, then, is a larger field of reference and a broader research repertoire, bringing in explicitly sociological (and sociocultural), historical *and* geographical perspectives, and opening up inquiry accordingly.

Researching (School) Literacy: The New Literacy Studies and Beyond

Within literacies research, much has been made in recent times of the significance and value of the New Literacy Studies (NLS). This is regarded, rightly, as a matter of informed consensus referring to a burgeoning body of work that takes due account of literacy as sociocultural practice, of culture and history, of multimodality and digital technologies, and above all else of power (Baynham and Prinsloo 2009; Janks 2010). This work is openly and avowedly "ideological," following Brian Street's (1984) pioneering ethnographic studies of literacy, and subsequently, important arguments from literacy scholars such as Colin Lankshear, Allan Luke, Glenda Hull, and others. It is also "worldly" as a matter of principle, oriented to social life and social organization, as well as social justice. Recently, there has been an important "practice turn" in literacy studies, which seems likely to be extremely generative.

What remains striking, however, is the sharp and enduring disjunction between this scholarly consensus and the educational mainstream—specifically, the everyday worlds of policy and classrooms. This disjunction is not only apparent in work seeking to engage with the challenge and opportunity of the new technologies—the so-called digital revolution—where much is heard of a marked discrepancy between policy and research (Tan and McWilliam 2009; Luke and Woods 2009). It is also apparent with regard to politics, and what may be called the socially critical imagination. Whereas It is commonplace to acknowledge the relationship between literacy and power as an organizing frame (Janks 2010), taking up a more generalized educational and social praxis can sometimes seem more gestural than real, or perhaps simply hopeful, and ever-aspirational. Reducing the world's manifest inequalities and effecting global social change accordingly remains a distant goal. Growing interest in the notion of the "translocal" is a welcome development (Brandt and Clinton 2002), as is a global focus on literacy and poverty, although emphasis on locality, on *place*, continues to be important, and enormously productive, as a body of invaluable critique emerges, increasingly displaying a rich theoretical and political sophistication.

Even so, connecting (back) to schools and classrooms, and to teacher education, to formal schooling and professional development, constitutes a major challenge. Much of the early NLS work was indeed outward-referenced, deliberately, even programmatically so; it was addressed primarily to *non*school literacy, to textual practice *outside* or *beyond* the schools. The task was seen as one of bringing the outside in, somehow, and certainly of effecting policy and changing classrooms, but at some future moment. Although there are increasing signs of reengagement with formal education, as Street (2012) outlines in his recent review, a gap exists between rhetoric and reality in this regard, between advocacy for a new and expanded understanding of literacy practice and what continues to happen, in the general run of classrooms and schools.

In that context, it is appropriate and timely to recall an important essay by Jenny Cook-Gumperz, from 1986, in which she points to an increasingly complicated relationship between literacy and schooling. In tracing the emergence of a singular, official literacy, she describes a shift

> from the eighteenth century onwards... not from total illiteracy to literacy, but from a hard-to-estimate multiplicity of literacies, a *pluralistic* idea about literacy as a composite of different skills related to reading and writing for many different purposes and sections of a society's population, to a twentieth-century notion of a single, standardised *schooled literacy*. (Italics in the original)

She continues thus:

> The breaking up of the pluralistic concept of literacy led indirectly to the establishment, even by the end of the nineteenth century, of a stratified and potentially standardisable notion of literacy that came to be tied to systematic schooling. (p. 30)

It is worth emphasizing, first, the irony of a widely recognized opening-up of literacy to difference and the world in the present-day, and hence the return to "multiplicity," and, second, the link that Cook-Gumperz makes between "school(ed) literacy" and what she calls "the test paradigm" (p. 37). Literacy and assessment are brought together, as it were organically. To articulate this more bluntly, literacy is what gets assessed. What counts as literacy is what gets tested, or is testable, and measurable, and this becomes a major constraining, shaping force with regard to literacy pedagogy. This is the literacy that *really* counts, at least in schooling and in policy. Literacy defined thus, or constructed in these terms, becomes normative, hegemonic.

It is this particular version of literacy that must be examined as a crucial object of concern here, as a counterpoint. That is certainly not to preclude other foci—far from it. Rather, it is to seek to keep this arguably dominant version firmly and clearly on the research and scholarly agenda. This version of (school) literacy has too often been accepted as more or less monumental, such that it needs to be worked with and around, rather than tackled directly. I'm not at all sure that is the case. This is particularly relevant, it seems to me, in thinking about rural education and rural literacies—both in Australia, given the now entrenched NAPLAN, but also with regard to programs such as No Child Left Behind (NCLB) in the United States, and perhaps also globally, given the increasing significance of the OECD Programme for International Student Assessment (PISA) and other such initiatives (Comber 2011).

As already indicated, an important reference point for contemporary literacies research remains the NLS. Baynham and Prinsloo (2008, 2009) have provided useful summary accounts of the field. They write: "It is now some twenty-five years since Literary Studies took a new direction, turning away from questions of pedagogy and the psycholinguistic processes of the individual reader-writer and looking outside the classroom to study literacy in its social context" (2009, p. 1). This emergence has involved a shift from "psychology" to "sociology" as a disciplinary metaframe, and a new emphasis on "ideological" as opposed to "autonomous" models of literacy (Street 1984). While somewhat problematical in their "from . . . to" logic, such accounts appropriately point to a decisive change of focus in literacies research, and a growing emphasis on matters of contextualization and contestation, complexity and contradiction. A richer picture has emerged of literacy as a social practice, of literacy pedagogy and literacy education, including policy, and of the opportunities and challenges for research and scholarship.

There has also been considerable development within the NLS, as might be expected. Baynham and Prinsloo (2009, p. 1) refer to this as three distinguishable "generations." "First-generation Literacy Studies" focused on local and contextual literacy events and practices, and was largely ethnographic in orientation, "studied in particular contexts" (2008, p. 2). In this perspective, "literacy practices are thus studied as variable, contexted practices which link people, linguistic resources, media objects, and strategies for meaning-making in contextualised ways" (p. 6). "[S]econd generation" literacy studies place growing emphasis on power and difference. Retaining an "emphasis on the complexity of communicative action," these forms of NLS "are also concerned to apply fresh analyses on how particular acts or events of communication and literacy connect up with wider social categories, cultural understandings, and forms of social organization" (p. 8).

Finally, and most recently, "third-generation" research as they see it continues such sociocultural emphases and orientations, including a consistent concern for the empirical. But focus shifts "from the local to the translocal, from print based literacies to electronic and multimedia literacies[,] and from the verbal to the multimodal" (Baynham and Prinsloo 2009, p. 2). These recent summary accounts of the field highlight a turn to "practice" (see also Collins and Blot 2005), thus pointing to what has been described as *practice theory and philosophy* (Green 2009) as a new reference point, conceptually and methodologically. It is this that they present as "the future of literacy studies." However, there are some notable absences or "blindspots" in this agenda, to which I now turn.

Placing Literacy

Prinsloo (2005) usefully points to what he calls the "placed" nature of (new) literacies research in the NLS tradition, suggesting that it is referenced to particular places or locations, and indeed unevenly distributed across the globe. He is concerned with literacy work in the context of "the globalised periphery" (Prinsloo and Rowsell 2012), especially that associated with information and communications technologies (ICT). While there has been some attention in the literature to "place-as-context" and "place-as-inequality" (Green 2012b), this has been limited, with little attention to date given to questions of location, or geography. This includes any specific reference to rurality, notwithstanding the fact that much pioneering work done in the NLS was clearly located in rural settings—in Heath's early work, for instance, or indeed Freire's work with peasant communities. Even Prinsloo's work in South Africa (e.g., Prinsloo and Breier 1996) lacks any explicit reference to the rural, even though at the turn of the millennium "more than 41% of the population [was] in rural areas" out of a total of 44.8 million (Ministry of Education 2005, p. 6).

Rurality appears to be something of a blindspot, then. That further supports the view that literacy research, along with educational enquiry more generally, tends to be metro-centric, and organized by a metro-urban normativity. This can be understood as a matter consistent with the development of modernity, with its twin axes of industrialization and urbanization, and the historically specific articulation of state and nation. Yet clearly there are populations and territories outside and beyond the metropolis, and in most countries. Are these simply part of the whole, to be subsumed within it? Or is there, rather, a significant form of difference in play here, and correspondingly, a complex geo-identity, locally, regionally, nationally, and globally? This suggests another way of thinking about literacy, with literacies to be (re)conceived in terms of multiplicity, traced and mapped in their spatial distribution and referenced to different places, always relative to a socio-spatial hierarchy. Such a move reintroduces considerations of power, specifically in relation to difference, and compels a reassessment of the matter of "context" in literacy research. Here I am particularly concerned with *geographical* dimensions of context—that is, with geography as a significant contextual consideration.

Geography here is to be understood as explicitly involving matters of space, place, and scale in ecosocial life, including literacy and education. As Crang and Thrift (2000, p. 3) observe, "no social process exists without geographical extension and historical duration." Similarly, Prinsloo (2005) calls for a revised, expanded view of context in literacy studies, one that moves beyond a fixation on the "local" (and a restricted notion of "place"), and is extended in space and time (Prinsloo and Rowsell 2012, p. 272), and which (it can be added) works with a fully relational, scalar sense of local-global dynamics. Geographical phenomena such as "space," "place," "scale," and "region" are inextricably and irrevocably social in nature, that is, a matter of social relations (Allen, Massey, and Cochrane 1998, p. 65).

Place is clearly a key concept here, and has been increasingly mobilized in literacy research. But it is also (still) a problematical notion, as various commentators have observed (Nespor 2008; Ruitenberg 2005). The range of constructions in circulation include "place-as-inequality" and "place-as-transformation" (Comber 2012), place understood as "(relative) location," and as "place-as-event"—the latter drawing expressly on Massey's (2005) view of place in terms of "social relations and practices, . . . socio-spatial dynamics, movement, becoming" (Green 2012b, p. 378). In pointing to place as *relative* location, I want to emphasize that location is always relative to other locations, or other places, and these in turn are to be related to other contexts, other spaces, and even other scales of reference. Places differ, moreover, not simply literally or physically (i.e., scientifically) but also culturally and historically. Moreover, they can also differ politically, and must always be understood in terms of power and privilege. This is also to evoke notions of "center" and "periphery," in their dynamic multiplicity. Spatial fields are themselves differentiated. They constitute a socio-spatial hierarchy. Places relate to and differ from other places; and some places are more powerful than others. An immediate relevance here is that rural places are defined, in part, in their distinction from metro-urban places, from the metropolis, or the city. Massey (2005, p. 160) notes that it is "the persistent focus on cities as the sites which most provoke disturbance in us," and asks whether this is "perhaps part of what has tamed (indeed is dependent upon the taming of) our vision of the rural." Such propositions are further support for the notion of metro-urban normativity, since cities are clearly significant "other" places in this regard, with various effects on their external environs, their hinterlands.

Hence it is useful to take up, briefly, Prinsloo's argument about the "placed" nature of literacy research to suggest that what we call rural literacies here should be understood as positioned and produced within national *and* global peripheries. They are, therefore, meaningful both in themselves and in their relation to other, arguably more powerful sites with regard to literacy practices and formations. These "other" sites are more likely than not to be cities—in Australia, the major capital cities, all located on the coastal rim. Rurality itself needs to be understood as context for literacy praxis and inquiry, or at least a crucial aspect of it. Here it becomes appropriate, too, to consider work specifically on the notion of "rurality as context" (Balfour, Mitchell, and Moletsane 2008, p. 98). That account usefully seeks to articulate "a dynamic and generative theory of rurality" (p. 97), with rurality expressly understood with regard to globalization, modernity, power, (dis)advantage, and agency. At the same time, the profound challenges associated with rural life (in this case, in South Africa) are clearly acknowledged. There is much here, I suggest, with a direct bearing on literacy studies and literacy pedagogy, and rural education.

Practicing Rural Literacy

As already noted, an important development in literacy studies has been the emergence of an explicit focus on *practice* as a distinctive organizing concept. This links with renewed interest in practice theory and philosophy (Schatzki, Knorr Cetina, and van Sauvigny 2001), and in particular with Bourdieu's work on practice and habitus (Grenfell et al. 2012). Ivanič (2009) has suggested that the field would benefit from being more precise in its use of the term "practice," distinguishing three common usages, and preferring ultimately to focus on "small-scale 'micro' practices'" in literacy. But it is the other two uses that I focus on here, namely, literacy practice as "what is being done with written texts," and "any social practice which is textually mediated" (p. 100).

These latter formulations are immediately apposite for thinking about rural literacies because they emphasize, first, on the role and significance of "reading" and "writing," and "texts," in the construction of rurality. This links with poststructuralist arguments that discourse constitutes its objects, and suggests a conceptual relationship between "discourse(s)" and "practice(s)" well worth further thought. But it also, importantly, directs attention to the manner in which the discourses and practices associated with literacy are active in producing rurality as an object of interest and concern. This ranges from the literacy work of rural schools to the everyday manifestations of textuality and academic forms of research and scholarship, "performing rurality and practicing rural geography" (Woods 2010). From a research perspective, it can be asked: What is being done with texts by students and others in rural settings? What are rural readers and writers, in and out of school, using texts for? How are rural students (and others) using texts, and how well are they doing this? With what effects?

Relatedly, this view of literacy practice provides a basis for conceptualizing rurality itself as a social and discursive practice, an interplay of the real and the representational, material and semiotic, (re)produced as much in our actions and interactions as in our words and texts. Rural literacy in such a view becomes a matter of attending to text(s) *and* context(s). This is further enhanced in and by accounts of "post-rurality" in which emphasis is placed on "[t]hinking affectively about rurality" and attending to "what it is like to be 'in' the rural, to take the rural's own forces seriously—to go from viewing the rural to being-in-the-rural" (e.g., Halfacree 2009, p. 453). This is work scarcely begun in (rural) literacy pedagogy, but is potentially very promising.

Another way of thinking about the project of rural literacies is to work from a sociocultural model of literacy pedagogy that presents literacy as a matter of three integrated, simultaneous aspects, or "dimensions": the *operational*, the *cultural,* and the critical, all working together in a single instance of literate activity (Green and Beavis 2012—see Cormack, Chapter 7, this volume). Briefly, the *operational* dimension involves a focus on the forms of language and communication (and their associated technologies) at work in literate practice, in what might be called its technical and compositional aspects. The *cultural* dimension refers to the meaning systems that are relevant and appropriate in the particular literacy activity, bringing together matters of culture, discourse, and knowledge. In the *critical* dimension, recently elaborated as the "critical-reflexive" dimension (Green 2012a), consideration is more directly given to social power, and the kinds of reflexivity that are important in both praxis and inquiry. Conceptually, these dimensions are cross-referenced and interrelated, integrated, and work simultaneously, with none having any necessary priority, other than either analytically or strategically.

This model presents a useful lens on rural literacies. It provides, first, a way of restricting, constraining, what counts as literacy—an often unacknowledged problem in literacy research. Seeing literacy as drawing on the material-semiotic resources of language and communication, it enables an inclusive view of contemporary literacy as "integrat[ing] written, oral, and audiovisual modalities of interactive human communication with screen-based and networked electronic systems" (Baynham and Prinsloo 2009, p. 14). While such matters can be explicitly taught, to some degree, the outcome can only be limited, especially if done in isolation, or decontextualized. What Prinsloo (2005) has observed regarding the so-called new literacies (and indeed the new technologies) applies here; that is, it is all too easy to focus merely on what is tangible, or objective, realized in curriculum as assessable "skills" or "competencies." The result is the encouragement of "restricted forms of practice, on the assumption of [these skills'] general applicability across all contexts" (p. 89). An informed agreement about what is encompassed by those forms of technologically enabled language and communication, brought together (and assessed) as literacy—a "grammar," in effect—would assist in moving toward more comprehensive, meaningful practice. However, this requires us to think beyond limited views of curriculum and literacy. It means thinking the operational dimension *together with* the cultural dimension, in line with the notion that learning language is learning culture, and vice versa. Context matters, both situationally and culturally.

It is in this regard that we can look at the cultural-discursive dimension of rural literacy for its distinctiveness. The question to be asked is: To what extent is the textwork produced in rural settings representative of what might be called rural culture? With regard to rural school literacy, this is likely to be limited, especially where there is high-stakes standardized testing, *unless* there is also some informed engagement with place-conscious pedagogies—some sense of working from and with "place" as curriculum. Such approaches take rural culture and its associated forms of knowledge seriously, along the lines, for example, of Corbett's (2008) account of the distinctive knowledges, values, and capabilities of the coastal community he studied. As he writes, "members of fishing families do not talk about fishing in Standard English, but rather in a nuanced language specific to fishing but also to the particular bioregion in which the practice of fishing is carried out" (p. 122). The implications for (school) literacy practice and pedagogy are very clear, especially given the complex historical relationships between spoken and written language, Standard English and the politics of literacy.

The critical-reflexive dimension remains crucial, moreover, and not simply with regard to rural literacies. This dimension relates to the capacity to recognize the workings of power in textual practice—structural *and* productive—at whatever scale of realization. Even so, it can be argued that being aware of this dimension of literacy is vital if the logic of disadvantage associated with rurality (as it were, structurally) is to be resisted and indeed overturned. Rural literacy cannot be dissociated from the larger politics of language and technology, culture and history, and the global transformations of (rural) industries, environments, and populations.

References

Allen, J., D. Massey, and A. Cochrane, 1998, *Rethinking the Region*, Routledge, London and New York.

Balfour, R. J., C. Mitchell, and R. Moletsane, 2008, "Troubling Contexts: Toward a Generative Theory of Rurality as Education Research," *Journal of Rural and Community Development*, vol. 3, no. 3: pp. 95–107.

Barton, D. and M. Hamilton, 2008, *Local Literacies: Reading and Writing in One Community*, Routledge, London.

Barton, D., M. Hamilton, and R. Ivanic (eds.), 2000, *Situated Literacies: Reading and Writing in Context*, Routledge, London and New York.

Baynham, M. and M. Prinsloo, 2009, "Introduction: The Future of Literacy Studies," in M. Baynham and M. Prinsloo (eds.), *The Future of Literacy Studies*, Palgrave Macmillan, Houndmill, UK, and New York, pp. 1–20.

Brandt, D. and K. Clinton, 2002, "Limits of the Local: Expanding Perspectives on Literacy as a Social Practice," *Journal of Literacy Research*, vol. 34, no. 3: 337–356.

Brooke, R. (ed.), 2003, *Rural Voices: Place-Conscious Education and the Teaching of Writing*, Teachers College Press, New York.

Cloke, P. 2006, "Conceptualizing Rurality," in P. Cloke, T. Marsden, and P. Mooney (eds.), *Handbook of Rural Studies*, Sage, London, pp. 18–28.

Collins, J. and R. K. Blot, 2003, *Literacy and Literacies: Texts, Power and Identity*, Cambridge University Press, Cambridge.

Comber, B. 2011, "Making Space for Place-Making Pedagogies: Stretching Normative Mandated Literacy Curriculum," *Contemporary Issues in Early Childhood*, vol. 12, no. 4: 343–348.

———, 2012, "Mandated Literacy Assessment and the Reorganisation of Teachers' Work: Federal Policy, Local Effects," *Critical Issues in Education*, vol. 53, no. 2: 119–136.

Comber, B., H. Nixon, and J-A. Reid, 2007, *Literacies in Place: Teaching Environmental Communications*, Primary English Teachers Association (PETA), Sydney.

Cook-Gumperz, J. 1986, "Literacy and Schooling: An Unchanging Equation?," in J. Cook-Gumperz (ed.), *The Social Construction of Literacy*, Cambridge University Press, Cambridge, pp. 16–44.

Corbett, M. 2008, "Wharf Talk, Home Talk, and School Talk: The Politics of Language in a Coastal Community," in K. A. Schafft and A. Youngblood Jackson (eds.), *Rural Education for the Twenty-First Century: Identity, Place and Community in a Globalizing World*, Pennsylvania State University Press, University Park, Pennsylvania, pp. 114–131.

Cormack, P., B. Green, and J-A. Reid, 2008, "Writing Place: Discursive Constructions of the Environment in Children's Writing and Artwork about the Murray-Darling Basin," in F. Vanclay, J. Malpas, M. Higgins, and A. Blackshaw (eds.), *Making Sense of Place: Exploring Concepts and Expressions of Place through Different Senses and Lenses*, National Museum of Australia, Canberra, pp. 57–75.

Crang, M. and N. Thrift, 2000, "Introduction," in M. Crang and N. Thrift (eds.), *Thinking Space*, Routledge, London and New York.

Donehower, K., C. Hogg, and E. E. Schell, 2007, *Rural Literacies*, Southern Illinois University Press, Carbondale.

———, 2011, *Reclaiming the Rural: Essays on Literacy, Rhetoric, and Pedagogy*, Southern Illinois University Press, Carbondale.

Edmondson, J. 2003, *Prairie Town: Redefining Rural Life in the Age of Globalization*, Rowman, Lanham, MD.

Green, B. (ed.), 2008, *Spaces and Places: The NSW Teacher (Education) Project*, Centre for Information Studies, Wagga Wagga, NSW.

———. 2009. "The Primacy of Practice and the Problem of Representation," in B. Green (ed.), *Understanding and Researching Professional Practice*, Sense, Rotterdam, pp. 39–54.

———, 2012a, "Into the Fourth Dimension? Literacy, Pedagogy and the Future," in B. Green and C. Beavis (eds.), *Literacy in 3D: An Integrated Perspective in Theory and Practice*, Australian Council for Educational Research (ACER), Camberwell, Victoria, pp. 175–188.

———, 2012b, "Literacy, Place and the Digital World," *Language and Education*, vol. 26, no. 4: 377–382.

Green, B. and C. Beavis (eds.), 2012, *Literacy in 3D: An Integrated Perspective in Theory and Practice*, Australian Council for Educational Research (ACER), Camberwell, Victoria.

Green, B. and W. Letts, 2007, "Space, Equity and Rural Education: A 'Trialectical' Account," in K. N. Gulson and C. Symes (eds.), *Spatial Theories of Education: Policy and Geography Matters*, Routledge, London and New York, pp. 57–76.

Green, B., P. Cormack, and H. Nixon, 2007, "Introduction: Literacy, Place, Environment," *Australian Journal of Language and Literacy*, vol. 30, no. 2: 77–81 [Special Issue].

Gregory, E. and A. Williams, 2000, *City Literacies: Learning to Read across Generations and Cultures*, Routledge, London and New York.

Grenfell, M., D. Bloome, C. Hardy, K. Pahl, J. Rowsell, and B. Street, 2012, *Language, Ethnography and Education: Bridging New Literacy Studies and Bourdieu*, Routledge, New York and London, pp. 27–49.

Gruenewald, D. A. and G. A. Smith (eds.), 2008, *Place-Based Education in the Global Age: Local Diversity*, Lawrence Erlbaum Associates, New York and London.

Halfacree, K. 2006, "Rural Space: Constructing a Three-Fold Architecture," in P. Cloke, T. Marsden, and P. Mooney (eds.), *Handbook of Rural Studies*, Sage, London, pp. 44–62.

———, 2009, "Rurality and Post-Rurality," in R. Kitchin and N. Thrift (eds.), *International Encyclopedia of Human Geography*, vol. 9, Elsevier, Oxford, pp. 449–56.

Ivanic, R. 2009, "Bringing Literacy Studies into Research on Learning across the Curriculum," in M. Bayhnam and M. Prinsloo (eds.), *The Future of Literacy Studies*, Palgrave Macmillan, Houndmills, UK, and New York, pp. 100–122.

Jackson, M., 2004, "Pedagogy's Topographies of Power," *ACCESS: Critical Perspectives on Communication, Cultural and Policy Studies*, vol. 23, no. 2: 13–20.

Janks, H., 2010, *Literacy and Power*, Routledge, New York and London.

Kelly, U. A., 2009, *Migration and Education in a Multicultural World*, Palgrave Macmillan, New York and Houndmills, UK.

Kinloch, V. (ed.), 2011, *Urban Literacies: Critical Perspectives on Language, Learning and Community*, Teachers College Press, New York.

Kress, G., C. Jewitt, J. Bourne, A. Franks, J. Hardcastle, K. Jones, and E. Reid, 2005, *English in Urban Classrooms: A Multimodal Perspective on Teaching and Learning*, Routledge, London and New York.

Luke, A. and A. Woods, 2009, "Policy and Adolescent Literacy," in L. Christenbury, R. Bomer, and P. Smagorinsky (eds.), *Handbook of Adolescent Literacy*, Guildford Press, New York.

Marsden, W. E., 1977, "Historical Geography and the History of Education," *History of Education*, vol. 6, no. 1: 21–42.

Massey, D., 2005, *For Space*, Sage, London.

McInerney, P., J. Smyth, and B. Down, 2011, "'Coming to a *Place* Near You': The Politics and Possibilities of a Critical Pedagogy of Place-Based Education," *Asia-Pacific Journal of Teacher Education*, vol. 39, no. 1: 3–16.

Mills, K. A. 2008, "Will Large-Scale Assessments Raise Literacy Standards in Australian Schools?," *Australian Journal of Language and Literacy*, vol. 31, no. 3: 211–225.

Ministry of Education, 2005, *Education for Rural People (EPR)—South Africa*, Working paper prepared for the Ministerial Seminar on Education for Rural People in Africa: Policy Lessons, Options and Priorities, Addis Ababa, Ethiopia, September 7–9.

Muspratt, S., P. Freebody, and A. Luke, 2001, "Technologies of Inclusion, Geographies of Exclusion: Schooling and Literacy in Small Rural Communities," in P. Freebody, S. Muspratt, and B. Dwyer (eds.), *Difference, Silence, and Textual Practice: Studies in Critical Literacies*, Hampton Press, Cresskill, NJ, pp. 153–188.

Nespor, J., 2004, "Educational Scale-Making," *Pedagogy, Culture and Society*, vol. 12, no. 3: 309–326.

———., 2008, "Education and Place: A Review Essay," *Educational Theory*, vol. 58, no. 4: 475–489.

Nixon, H. and B. Comber, 2009, "Literacy, Landscape and Learning in a Primary Classroom," in M. Somerville, K. Power, and P. de Carteret (eds.), *Landscapes and Learning: Place Studies for a Global World*, Sense, Rotterdam, pp. 119–138.

Pegg, J. and D. Panizzon, 2007, "Inequities in Student Achievement for Literacy: Metropolitan versus Rural Comparisons," *Australian Journal of Language and Literacy*, vol. 30, no. 3: 177–190.

Prinsloo, M., 2005, "The New Literacies as Placed Resources," *Perspectives in Education*, vol. 23, no. 4: 87–98.

Prinsloo, M. and M. Baynham, 2008, "Renewing Literacy Studies," in M. Prinsloo and M. Baynham (eds.), *Literacies: Local and Global*, John Benjamins, Amsterdam, pp. 1–16 [preprint manuscript].

Prinsloo, M. and M. Breier (eds.), 1996, *The Social Uses of Literacy: Theory and Practice in South Africa*, John Benjamins, Amsterdam.

Prinsloo, M. and J. Rowsell, 2012, "Digital Literacies as Placed Resources in the Globalised Periphery," *Language and Education*, vol. 26, no. 4: 271–277.

Reid, J-A., B. Green, M. Cooper, W. Hastings, G. Lock, and S. White, 2010, "Regenerating Rural Social Space? Teacher Education for Rural-Regional Sustainability," *Australian Journal of Education*, vol. 54, no. 3: 262–276.

Ruitenberg, C. 2005, "Deconstructing the Experience of the Local: Toward a Radical Pedagogy of Place," in K. R. Howe (ed.), *Philosophy of Education 2005*, Urbana, IL: Philosophy of Education Society, pp. 212–220.

Schatzki, T. R., K. Knorr Cetina, and E. van Sauvigny (eds.), 2001, *The Practice Turn in Contemporary Theory*, Routledge, New York and London.

Soja, E. W., 1996, *Thirdspace: Journeys to Los Angeles and Real-and-Imagined Places*, Blackwell, Oxford.

———, 2010, *Seeking Spatial Justice*, University of Minnesota Press, Minneapolis and London.

Street, B., 1984, *Literacy in Theory and Practice*, Cambridge University Press, Cambridge.

———, 2012, "The New Literacy Studies," in M. Grenfell, D. Bloome, C. Hardy, K. Pahl, J. Rowsell, and B. Street (eds.), *Language, Ethnography and Education: Bridging New Literacy Studies and Bourdieu*, Routledge, New York and London, pp. 27–49.

Tan, J. P-L. and E. McWilliam, 2009, "From Literacy to Multiliteracies: Diverse Learners and Pedagogical Practice," *Pedagogies*, vol. 4, no. 3: 213–225.

Welch, A., S. Helme, and S. Lamb, 2007, "Rurality and Inequality in Education: The Australian Experience," in R. Teese, S. Lamb, and M. Duru-Bellat (eds.), *International, Studies in Educational Inequality: Theory and Policy. Vol. 2: Inequality in Educational System*, Springer, Dordrecht, pp. 271–293.

White, S. and J-A. Reid, 2008, "Placing Teachers? Sustaining Rural Schooling through Place-Consciousness in Teacher Education," *Journal of Research in Rural Education*, vol. 23, no. 7: 1–11.

Woods, M 2010, "Performing Rurality and Practising Rural Geography," *Progress in Human Geography*, vol. 34, no. 6: 835–846.

CHAPTER 2

Why Not at School? Rural Literacies and the Continual Choice to Stay

Kim Donehower

The title of this chapter refers to a curious fact that I, and other,[1] literacy researchers have noted while interviewing "hyperliterates"—people who read and/or write extensively as adults, when those activities are not required by a job or pursuit of a formal educational degree. Even though some of these individuals fondly remember a certain teacher, when asked how much credit schools should get for their lifelong avocational literacy, the answers ranged from "not much" to "not at all."

This chapter explores possible reasons for these responses to better understand the ways that schools could support the kind of lifelong reading and writing activities that play a useful role in rural sustainability. Much discussion of the role of literacy in rural sustainability, particularly at the level of educational and governmental policy, centers on the reading, writing, and digital literacies that support economic development. In 2012, the United States' educational reform paradigm identified the purpose of schooling as making students "college- and career-ready" (National Governors Association 2010). One dominant phrase, circulating among policy makers and academics, to describe the problems facing rural communities was "brain drain," the condition in which the more educated members of a rural community leave, taking their literate skills with them, to enrich the economies of cities or suburbs.[2] US secretary of education Arne Duncan (2011) links the two phrases when he explains his presence on the White House Rural Council solely in terms of the ways education helps "provide local business with skilled employees," citing a rural employer who told him that "[roughly] half of the recent high school graduates who apply for jobs...lack the literacy and math skills needed for employment." Internationally, UNESCO (2006) describes the link between literacy and sustainability as "work[ing] under the assumption that literacy is necessary for greater participation in economic, social, and political life" (p. 3). In such formulations—which are, at least, broader than the United States' focus solely on economics— "economic" is nonetheless typically the first item in the list.

Economic factors are critical in rural communities' survival; but I am interested in exploring the ways noneconomically directed literacy activities serve to enhance and sustain rural life. To investigate this, I've been interviewing residents of Hammond,[3] North Dakota, a town of about 500 in the east-central part of the state, roughly equidistant from North Dakota's four urban centers. Hammond boasts a strikingly high percentage of hyperliterates, engaged in book clubs, religious study groups, local history writing groups, and other such avocational literacy activities. Hammond also does notably better than many surrounding communities in keeping its population stable, employed, and culturally and civically active. In fact, Hammond's economic development director suggests that limited housing stock is the only reason why Hammond's population has not increased while those of surrounding towns and villages have declined.

It is impossible to know how much school actually did shape these hyperliterates' lifelong relationships with reading and writing. Instead, we must consider why these informants might not wish to credit school for their active literate lives. None of those cited in this chapter reported hating the overall school experience or having the archetypal demon English teacher with the red pen who forever damaged their literate self-esteem. There did not seem to be any extreme, or particularly strong, emotions attached to school for the people in the Hammond study. In *Captain Beefheart's Piano: Confessions of an Unrepentant Illiterate*, Michael Corbett describes how his musical literacy "allows me to detach from the community of practice that is my musical surround" (2008, p. 149). Similarly, there is a kind of detachment from schooling, from the "literate surround," that these hyperliterates feel, even as the surround, including the school, inevitably affects their relationships with literacy.

It is also impossible to argue causation between the presence of hyperliterates in Hammond and its sustainability success. Instead, I see Hammond as a valuable site to explore the nature of literate activities in a successful rural town. In this chapter, I focus on one particular threat to rural sustainability—outmigration—and the relationship that avocational literacy activities might have to this issue. Finally, I consider the role that rural schools might play in enhancing literacies that allow rural people to make the choice to stay in their communities.

Before I offer my analysis, I would like to define the other key terms in my title. First is the phrase "rural literacies." In our book of that name, Charlotte Hogg, Eileen Schell, and I (2007) define "rural literacies" as "literate skills needed to achieve the goals of sustaining life in rural areas" (p. 4). The word "literacy" has seen its usage broadened to the point that in popular discourse, it means little more than "some kind of knowledge base about something." My interest, however, is in the specific practices of using written texts—reading, writing, and discussing them, whether in print or digital forms, to sustain rural life.

I use the phrase "the continual choice to stay" to describe the counterpoint to outmigration. I want to emphasize that one's relationship to one's rural community is ongoing, continually being managed, shaped, and redefined. I also choose this phrase to explicitly challenge the portrayal of "stayers" in *Hollowing Out the Middle: The Rural Brain Drain and What It Means for America*. Written by sociologists Patrick Carr and Maria Kefalas (2010) and based on a study sponsored by the MacArthur Foundation, this book-length treatment of rural outmigration is written to appeal to academics, policymakers, and the general public and will likely have wide influence. It is unfortunate, then, that the book is subject to so many typical urban- and class-based biases,[4] particularly in its portrayal of rural "stayers" and "returners."

In brief, Carr and Kefalas (2010) represent the "choice" to stay as a largely emotional, unreflective, unexamined process. Early in the book, Carr and Kefalas generalize that "simply put, leaving is something that young people must be pushed, prodded, and cultivated to do, whereas staying just sort of happens" (p. 9). Stayers "value work over education"; Carr and Kefalas chalk this up to "the immediate gratification of having one's own money against the vaguer possibilities of what a degree and a career might mean for the future" (p. 62). Fear and anxiety are repeatedly asserted as typical of small-town dwellers[5] and as the forces that motivate Stayers to stay and Returners to return. About Returners, Carr and Kefalas claim that "being surrounded by strangers and leading a fast-paced life" was "unwelcoming and disorienting, and, given the choice, [returners] prioritize the familiar over the possibility of something else" (p. 23).

This notion of "the familiar," and that small towns are homogenous, static, isolated places, is a theme throughout the book. For Carr and Kefalas, learning to find nuance and diversity within small-town life, and managing to live in a rural community and yet feel a connection and relationship to people and communities in other places, is not an option.[6] Diversity must be imported; one of their major recommendations is that rural communities should encourage immigrants to settle there. In terms of rural isolation, the authors go out of their way to enforce this image in overblown terms: "hundreds of miles away from the nearest city, the world surrounding Ellis orbits around this speck on the map at dizzying speed" (p. 56). For Carr and Kefalas, the place boundaries between the rural and the urban/suburban are firm. They assume that rural people will have no knowledge of a band such as The Pixies, making little mention of the technologies—print, digital, radio, television, and so on—or of the relationships—with friends and family members who have left the community but maintain close contact with those still there—that make the rural and urban/suburban boundary much more permeable.

In this chapter, I argue that rural stayers and returners do not necessarily live in their communities primarily as a result of fear and anxiety about the outside world, or as a result of poor impulse control and the need for "immediate gratification," but rather from a conscious choice that is continually made and remade. This choice requires both emotional and intellectual work, and as such, literacy activities—reading and writing texts—have a particular role they can play in locating rural people and places within a web of human relationships across rural, urban, and suburban boundaries, and in creating nuance and enjoyment in rural life.[7]

Relationship Capital: Spanning the Boundaries of "Here" and "Away"

Carr and Kefalas's work is striking in the ways its discussion of "human capital" largely leaves out the notion of human relationships. Unsurprisingly, given the nature of the term, "human capital" in *Hollowing Out the Middle* refers primarily to the ability of people to create economic opportunity, for which Carr and Kefalas see a college degree as a prerequisite. The choice to stay is also represented as an economic one, about "the immediate gratification of having one's own money" (p. 67) rather than the long-term gratifications of maintaining close family relationships or one's relationship with a specific geography or community. While economics are surely a factor in any person's life choices, relationships have a powerful sway over individuals' decisions about where to live and how to feel about that choice.

The literacy activities that I observed, participated in, and had described to me in Hammond emphasized a continual negotiation of relationships both within and outside the community. In interviews with informants, early positive associations with literacy were almost always scenes of relationship and human connection—being read to by parents, grandparents, or siblings, reading to siblings or others, writing and performing skits with siblings and friends. Even examples of solitary literacy—hiding with a book, avoiding chores—were about managing relationships, including the need to set boundaries, maintain distances, and fashion an individual identity in counterdistinction to the rest of the group, while still retaining group membership.

In terms of group membership, literacy was often practiced as a communal activity in which individuals brought different meanings to texts, distinguishing their readings from and connecting them to the readings of their community peers and, sometimes, to the imagined readers the text addressed. Two local histories offer a basic example. Both the centennial history of Hammond, written and compiled by the local historical society, and a self-published history of nearby Blomgren, by a local farmer, combine mini-essays written by different people with no editorial effort to smooth out the differences in style, tone, or persona. Idiosyncratic voices and ways of sharing history are tolerated, and the effect emphasizes both the communal nature of the enterprise and individuals' various ways of describing and explaining history.

A meeting of a youth Bible study group displayed both the communal/idiosyncratic balancing act and the negotiation of a reader's relationship to a text with a setting and implied audience very different from the context and lives of the readers themselves. Cosponsored by the local Evangelical Free Church and Lutheran Brethren Church, the two most conservative Protestant denominations in town, this youth Bible study group might seem to have conformist goals of standardizing teens' reading of the scriptural text. However, the method this group used, borrowed from evangelist Anne Graham Lotz's book: *I Saw the Lord: A Wake-Up Call for Your Heart*, emphasized the importance of individualized reading in combination with collaborative interpretive consensus about the scriptural text. The group leaders had prepared an interpretive chart in four columns. Its first step was to "read God's word," in this case, Mark 9:2–8. Step two, "What does God's Word say?" instructed readers to "list the facts." Step three, "What does God's Word mean?" directed readers to "learn the lessons." Step four, "What does God's word mean to me?" was subtitled "listen to His voice." Step five, written in the bottom-right corner of the page, asked "How will I respond to God's Word?" and directed "live it out!"

The sequence moves through conformist objectives in step two, with its emphasis on "facts," or one right answer, to the apparently more important work of coming to a personal experience of the text, steps four "what does God's word mean to me," and five, "how will I respond to God's word." The intervening step, between "facts" and personal interpretation, was a communal discussion activity. The facilitators wrote the teenagers' individual summaries from steps one and two on chart paper for the group to consider and elaborate on, prodded with questions by the two leaders. After much time spent in this collective effort, participants were directed to write individually and then describe which of the "lessons" connected to their individual lives to the extent that they could be acted on concretely. The teens were encouraged not to copy one another's answers, but to articulate their own personal relationships to the passage. The facilitators' takeaway message was that any part of the Bible, no matter how distant from present-day life in the setting or situations it described, could be made to "speak personally" to a reader if the right reading methods were used. Literacy, then, was an act of managing both one's relationship with a text—a text constructed within a context far from the time and place in which it was being read—and distinguishing how one's reading could differ, albeit in subtle ways, from one's local peers, while still operating within communal standards of acceptability about the "facts" of the reading.

This sort of negotiation, among oneself, one's local peers, imagined others, and the imagined author and audience the text suggests, is aptly captured by Deborah Brandt's description of "literacy as involvement" in her book of the same name. Brandt (1990, p. 103) asserts that reading and writing are largely about "sustain[ing] the processes of intersubjective life":

> Readers [...must keep] track of the complicated perspectives that are often laid side by side in a text with only the subtlest indications of change. [...] Textual relationships are less logical than they are social: they arise out of recognizing what is mine, yours, ours, his, hers, theirs, its. But especially what is ours—because reference in written discourse is always *in reference to* the participants, writer and reader, and to their joint business at hand. (p. 91)

This recognition of "what is mine, yours, ours [...b]ut especially what is ours," and the idea of the "joint business at hand" between local reader and potentially far-away writer, was on display during a women's book club discussion that I attended, held in a defunct café in a neighboring village. The group discussed comedian Steve Harvey's *Act Like a Lady, Think Like a Man*, an advice book for single mothers on how to secure marriage. During the nearly two-hour discussion of the text, each woman's personal background was brought to bear to explore what this book, with its very different target audience of urban, African American women in their twenties and thirties, might have to say to us, including whether we might give the book to our daughters or granddaughters to read. The event focused on discovering what "joint business at hand" we had with the distant, urban author, as well as a sorting out of "mine, yours, ours, his, hers, theirs, its" as we examined how our individual relationship histories gave us certain perspectives on Harvey's take on gender relations.[8] While we were certainly "hundreds of miles away" from the urban dating scene Harvey described, this world was not "orbit[ing us]" at dizzying speed" (Carr and Kefalas 2010, p. 56), rendering it incomprehensible or frighteningly unfamiliar. To the contrary, the entire discussion centered on both connecting to, and distinguishing ourselves from, the scenarios Harvey described.

In her influential essay in *A Global Sense of Place*, geographer Doreen Massey (1994, p. 146) notes that the sort of unsettling "time-space compression" Carr and Kefalas describe "is . . . now frequently found in a wide range of books and journals." Massey is reluctant, however, to embrace the notion that globalization necessarily disrupts and destroys a sense of place, or puts those with a strong sense of local place on the defensive. She asks, "how, in the face of all this movement and intermixing, can we retain any sense of a local place and its particularity?" (p. 146). She wonders, "is it not possible for a sense of place to be progressive; not self-enclosing and defensive, but outward-looking? A sense of place which is adequate to this era of time-space compression" (p. 147). Massey suggests we consider the following:

> [T]he specificity of place which derives from the fact that each place is the focus of a distinct *mixture* of wider and more local social relations. There is the fact that this very mixture together in one place may produce effects which would not have happened otherwise. And finally, all these relations interact with and take a further element of specificity from the accumulated history of a place, with that history itself imagined as the product of layer upon layer of different sets of linkages, both local and to the wider world. (p. 156)

While it is a stretch to say that this particular book-group discussion directly addressed all these layers of history and social relations, it is possible to see how the discussion located each of the participants as a product of a "distinct mixture of wider and more local social relations" (p. 156). The continual sorting out of "mine, yours, ours, his, hers, theirs, its" (Brandt 1990, p. 91) practiced in the book club seems vital in remaining comfortable with one's identification as rural amidst the tremendous cultural, political, and economic forces at work, driving people toward suburban and urban lives as the "normal" or "default" positions. In concluding *Rural Literacies,* Hogg, Schell, and I advocated for rural literacies that "encourage mutual identification among rural, urban, and suburban citizens" (p. 193). In her chapter of the book, Schell (2007, p. 98) argues that "mutual identification" should replace the "rhetoric of sympathetic identification" that infuses so many depictions of the US farm crisis. Mere sympathy for the plight of family farmers is not enough, she argues: urban and suburban consumers must come to see the ways their lives are interdependent with the rural farmers who feed them.

Mutual identification is important for the rural individual as well. Aside from the necessity for rural people in agricultural and tourist economies to connect to suburban and urban markets, the idea of a sophisticated mutual identification, one that explores the nuances of connections, differences, and distinctions among rural, suburban, and urban life, seems a vital component in the continual choice to stay.

Autotelic Literacies: Finding Nuance and Enjoyment in Rural Life

Much talk about the role of literacy in rural sustainability is locked in an instrumentalist mode—literacy as a means toward economic or cultural development, communal bonding, civic participation. Even literacy theorists have had difficulty speaking of literacy outside the idea that literacy has purposes beyond itself. Sylvia Scribner (1984) documents the classic metaphors that circulate in both academia and popular media of "literacy as adaptation" (to meet one's basic, usually economic, needs), "literacy as power," usually of the political variety, and "literacy as state of grace," to develop spiritual or moral character. As both Scribner and Harvey Graff (1991) note, there is generally little evidence for causal relationships between literacy and these other things, and in the case of literacy for political power, there is as much if not more evidence that the causal relationship works the other way round. Stanley Fish (2008) has argued that no credible instrumentalist argument can be made for the value of the humanities in general, that they are, simply, goods in themselves. This is not a productive rhetorical gambit, however, when trying to justify public funding for literacy.

This, perhaps, is why Brandt's *Literacy as Involvement* had limited impact on the educational establishment. The book describes a non-instrumentalist, or at the least, less instrumentalist, vision of literacy. Brandt (1990, p. 39) argues that "written texts do not only have the archival function. They also have a here-and-now role in helping people sustain the work of writing and reading" (p. 39). In other words, literacy can be both exotelic and autotelic. It can be both a means to another end, such as preserving data or ideas, *and* an end in itself, in which the goals of reading and writing are to get oneself to keep reading and writing.

This is similar to one of Mihalyi Csikszentmihalyi's conditions for individuals to reach a "flow state" or have an "optimal experience" (Csikszentmihalyi 1991).[9] The gratifications of such experiences, Csikszentmihalyi writes, are not pleasure, but rather enjoyment, which is a more active, involving experience than pleasure (p. 46). Csikszentmihalyi asserts that for an experience to be a "flow" experience, the key factor is that it must be predominantly autotelic (p. 67). Of the nature of the autotelic experience, he writes:

> The autotelic experience of life, or flow, lifts the course of life to a different level. Alienation gives way to involvement, enjoyment replaces boredom, helplessness turns into a feeling of control, and psychic energy works to reinforce the sense of self, instead of being lost in the service of external goals. When experience is intrinsically rewarding life is justified in the present, instead of being held hostage to a hypothetical future gain. (p. 69)

Hyperliterates' descriptions of reading and writing often echo Csikszentmihalyi's description of flow. They report experiences beyond mere "pleasure," sometimes staying up late to read and paying the consequences the next day—losing track of time is one marker of flow. Writing is rarely described in pleasurable terms, but rather as a sort of compulsion. James Rundberg, the author of the Blomgren history, which is 146 pages long and written mostly by him, explicitly stated during our interview that he was "not a writer," even as his text lay on the table between us. He explained that he had never done particularly well in English in school. Nonetheless, the project was "something he wanted to do," a need that overrode his reluctance to think of himself as someone who enjoyed or was good at writing. Brandt (1990, p. 68) argues that writing "is excruciatingly involving because it requires so much of a human being's attention. Part of the normal reluctance to write is that reluctance to get so involved." That level of involvement, Csikszentmihalyi suggests, can be psychologically gratifying, if not experienced as pleasure.

Rachael Waller (2011), in her dissertation study of elementary reading instruction in a North Dakota town, probes the psychological gratifications of reading for rural people concerned about sustaining their community. In her interviews with teachers, observations of classrooms, and structured reading activities she led with children, Waller identifies a theme she calls "becoming one." She argues that "children become one with literature both through escaping and by developing connections to real-life events" (p. 112). Waller sees the experience of becoming one with a written text as a partial antidote for what one of her informants called being "stretched out." Stretched out refers to the stress induced by the sorts of economic, cultural, and demographic pressures that drive outmigration and contribute to rural collapse (p. 134).

The becoming one process of existing simultaneously in the world of the text and in one's own present-day circumstances echoes Brandt's notions of "involvement" and balancing in a text "what is mine, yours, ours, his, hers, theirs, its." The relational aspects of reading and writing described in the previous section seem to have an important role in creating "involving" literacy activities in which participants might experience flow. A different, but related view of becoming one is detailed in Pauliina Rautio and Maija Lanas's chapter in this volume (chapter 11), in which aesthetic literacy—the ability to make aesthetic judgments of an experience—requires the same kind of undivided attention in-the-moment, "of exploring one's relation and conceptions of the world, translating this relation into an aesthetic claim and opening it up for negotiation and reiteration" (p. 231).

So, Why Not at School?

Others[10] have written about the ways in which schooling is not structured to encourage flow experiences with literacy, and it is not difficult to imagine how school literacy, particularly beyond the elementary grades, might strip away aspects of human relationship from the processes of reading and writing. The case of Sarah Lance offers some clues as to why hyperliterates in Hammond might discredit school in the formation of their lifelong relationship with reading and writing. Sarah moved to Hammond with her family in the sixth grade. In her twenties at the time of the interview, she was married and lived in Bismarck, the state capital. Her whole family (mother, stepfather, and siblings) were avid readers, and as all of the children had moved away from Hammond, they maintained their family relationship via selecting a book and passing it among them. At the point of our interview, their most recent text had been Gregory Maguire's *Wicked*. Each family member had read the book, mailed it to the next person, and then they had all gone to New York to see the musical version together. It was unclear how much they had actually discussed the book; the point was to use their reading of the common text to maintain a family bond.

Strikingly, Sarah told me during our interview that while she had always been an avid reader—like many hyperliterates, she couldn't remember ever not being able to read—she had read less than usual while she was in high school. The reason, she said, was because she had to do so much reading "for school." "School reading," then, was not *reading* for Sarah; in fact, it interfered with the kind of reading that made her, in her mind, an avid reader.

The issue here is not simply one of pleasure in reading self-selected books compared to assigned texts. Brandt (1990) notes David Olson's objection to the language of school textbooks:

> [P]articularly in school textbooks, the social relationship of writer to reader and the relationship of writer to message are irrelevant to the making of meaning...Textbook language is virtually bereft of illocutionary markers.

Olson points out:

> The language carries few indicators of social relationships and human intentions; rather [...] the language of textbooks appears as a series of disembodied assertions, impersonal and authoritative. (p. 21)

Much of the "assigned reading" in school, particularly outside English classes, and even in the directive material in English textbooks themselves, are written in ways that deemphasize the fact that an actual person or people wrote the text and that an actual person is reading it. Brandt (1990, p. 5) argues that "learning to read is learning that you are being written to, and learning to write is learning that your words are being read," but if this is the case, many school textbooks are written in ways that obscure this notion.

Sarah explicitly credited no teachers with fostering her lifelong relationship with reading—and Sarah began her career as a teacher, herself. She does say that the school librarian "probably helped a little bit," because "she was really good at recommending books," echoing the way that Sarah and her mother pass along to each other books that they like, and highlighting that the librarian got to know Sarah as an individual so she could recommend books that would appeal to her. Otherwise, Sarah did not experience reading and writing in school as embedded in personal relationships.

In addition to enhancing their relationships with people through literacy, hyperliterates also continually renew their relationships with literacy itself. Perhaps one reason hyperliterates are so quick to discredit school's effects on their lifelong reading and/or writing habits is because school, especially in the current era, often represents reading and writing solely in exotelic terms. Aside from the practice of Sustained Silent Reading or other forms of free voluntary reading,[11] which can suggest that the goal of reading is to get yourself to keep reading, most classroom practices emphasize exotelic arguments for doing reading and writing and exotelic criteria for assessing them. It is possible that hyperliterates might find this as an exploitation or commodification of what they experience as an autotelic relationship. When the goals of reading and writing are to get a job or pass a test to help a school maintain its funding stream, a relationship that many hyperliterates describe in terms of "love" or "compulsion" or as part of their "nature" becomes devalued.[12]

The idea that a major goal of reading and writing is to sustain the process of reading and writing also runs counter to the ways current US educational structures prize efficiency. As Mike Rose (2011) notes, the drive in the United States to view and assess public education by the criteria of "scientific management" as practiced in the business sphere has a long history. Paul Nachtigal (1982) describes how "efficiency" has long been a hallmark of rural school reform efforts (pp. 15–16). In its current incarnation, we see the value of efficiency in high-stakes assessments. No standardized writing test that I know of examines how long students can sustain the act of writing; instead, most value how much comprehensible text can be produced in a short period of time. Even the rare "untimed" writing assessment places no value on the writer's level of engagement with the activity. Standardized reading assessments, such as the ACT test that many US universities require as part of the college admissions process, allow students less than a minute per question, which includes the time it takes to read the selections. This is barely time enough to extract the "facts" from the text, let alone engage with the reading as a distinct human being.

The goal of reading and writing in these instances is to get it over with, not to keep it going. Engagement becomes a handicap. Brandt (1990, pp. 89–90) argues that "expert readers know how to transform a text into an episode in which they are centrally involved"; in these testing scenarios, such a tactic would likely lead to a failing grade. Similarly, the sheer size of curricula, most still operating under a coverage model, and of textbooks, set a "get it over with" agenda and make it clear to teachers that pushing efficiency, not involvement, is the only way to successfully do one's job. Involvement or engagement take time to cultivate, and, if successful in Csikszentmihalyi's sense of flow or Brandt's involvement, take time to play out. A drive for efficiency prohibits hyperliterates from being able to fully involve themselves in their reading or writing. Hence Sarah describes how school reading meant she could spend less time really *reading*.

As I consider the definition of rural literacies that Hogg, Schell, and I asserted in *Rural Literacies*—"literate skills needed to achieve the goals of sustaining life in rural areas" (p. 4)—I am struck by how exotelic it is, with the instrumentalist terms "skills" and "goals" seeming very prominent to me. We went on to use language from Deborah Brandt's description in *Literacy in American Lives* (2001) of the way literacy is generally represented as a resource, to further describe these "skills" as those that would allow rural people "to pursue the opportunities and create the public policies and economic opportunities to sustain rural communities" (Donehower, Hogg, and Schell 2007, p. 4). I don't disagree with this depiction of what is needed to sustain rural life, but it seems to me this exotelic language omits the necessity, in fact, the instrumentality, of noninstrumentalist or autotelic literacies in sustaining rural life.

In addition, language that always defers the merits and uses of literacy to some future time doesn't serve to motivate students well. The United States has embarked on a massive experiment adopting the Common Core Standards for K-12 education, all of which are couched in the verbiage of creating "college- and career-ready" students. This rhetoric plays well to adults who are invested in forever bemoaning, and profiting from, the perceived inadequacies of public education. But the vision of K-12 education as a 13-year slog toward college or career is unlikely to inspire or engage the students who are the targets of the packaged literacy programs and standardized testing systems that Common Core will spawn.

In this context, how are rural schools to promote autotelic literacies, or the sorts of "slow literacies" that permit losing track of time and fully involving oneself in a text? As Jacqueline Edmondson and Thomas Butler (2012, p. 226) note,

> The threat to rural education comes from outside experts who seek to standardize school knowledge through mandated curriculum and tests

[. . .]. But the threat also comes from the inside as teachers accept dominant discourses of public education that have become pervasive and largely unquestioned.

Perhaps teacher training and continuing education programs are a place to address the disjuncture between many teachers' own autotelic enjoyment of "personal" reading and writing and the kinds of exotelic literacies they enforce in their classrooms. How do rural teachers themselves experience literacy? How does it help sustain them in their continual choice to stay? Rural teachers sometimes have more freedom than their urban and suburban counterparts to experiment in their classroom spaces—to resist, at least occasionally, the drive for efficient, get-it-done, text-centered, context-free reading and writing. If they can mutually identify with their students, considering the ways their teaching affects students' literate lives beyond school walls and testing forms, perhaps they can come to articulate and advocate for the exotelic role of autotelic, involving, relational literacies in sustaining rural communities.

Notes

1. Deborah Brandt, personal conversation.
2. Despite the pervasive rhetoric of "brain drain," some research suggests a rural "brain gain" of educated adults in their thirties and forties, with their young children, is countering the outmigration of recent high school and college graduates in some rural areas. See "Continuing the Trend: The Brain Gain of the Newcomers," by Ben Winchester (2012), a research report of the University of Minnesota Extension Center for Community Vitality.
3. All place and personal names are pseudonyms.
4. For more nuanced analyses of the factors that spark rural outmigration of talented young people, see Michael Corbett's *Learning to Leave* and Paul Theobald and Kathy Wood's *Learning to Be Rural*.
5. One of the fundamental methodological problems of *Hollowing Out the Middle* is the way that Carr and Kefalas claim to offer readers "the *real* story of small town America" (italics in the original) based on their study of a single community, whose site selection stemmed from the fact that it was the only small Heartland community to which the researchers had a local connection.
6. For a contrary view of the diversity of rural communities, see Michael Corbett and Ann Vibert's chapter in this volume (chapter 13).
7. This vision of literacy echoes Louise Rosenblatt's assertion in *Literature as Exploration* (1995) that the reading and discussion of literature offer particularly fertile ground for students to learn how to reason in the presence of strong emotion. Similarly, Martha Nussbaum (1997) argues in *Poetic Justice*

that the reading and contemplation of literature connects private emotions with reasoned public actions. My stance is that literacy itself, whether to consume and produce "Literature" or other types of texts, has the potential to integrate emotion and reason in the thinking of the reader or writer.

8. For a more extensive discussion of the ways literacy-as-involvement played out in this book club meeting, see my forthcoming *Connecting Literacy to Sustainability: Revisiting Literacy as Involvement*.

9. See Maija Lanas and Pauliina Rautio's chapter in this volume (chapter 11) for a more nuanced way of understanding "optimal experience" in rural life.

10. See Michael Smith and Jeffrey Wilhelm's *Reading Don't Fix No Chevys* (2002).

11. See Stephen Krashen's *Free Voluntary Reading* (2011, Heinemann), and *The Power of Reading: Insights from the Research* (2004). Also, Kelly Gallagher's *Readicide: How Schools Are Killing Reading and What You Can Do about It* (2009) documents the decline of SSR time in the United States as a result of high-stakes reading tests geared toward the quick assimilation of "main ideas" from short pieces of disconnected text.

12. Pauliina Rautio (2012, personal communication) suggests that the relationship between a love of literacy and the choice to stay in a rural community might be reciprocal, that perhaps "non-instrumental reading practices sustain staying but also that staying sustains non-instrumental reading practices." This is an intriguing notion deserving of further research; rural "returners" in Ben Winchester's research on rural Minnesota cite a "slower pace of life" as one reason for their return. Such a slower pace could be conducive to the sorts of "slow literacies" referred to in the conclusion of this chapter.

References

Brandt, D., 1990, *Literacy as Involvement: The Acts of Readers, Writers, and Texts*, Southern Illinois University Press, Carbondale.

———, 2001, *Literacy in American Lives*, Cambridge University Press, Cambridge.

Carr, P. and M. Kefalas, 2010, *Hollowing Out the Middle: The Rural Brain Drain and What It Means for America*, Beacon Press, Boston, MA.

Corbett, M., 2007, *Learning to Leave: The Irony of Schooling in a Coastal Community*, Fernwood, Halifax, NS.

———, 2008, "Captain Beefheart's Piano: Confessions of an Unrepentant Illiterate," *International Journal of Critical Pedagogy*, vol. 1, no. 2: 148–159.

Csikszentmihalyi, M., 1991, *Flow: The Psychology of Optimal Experience*, Harper Perennial, New York.

Donehower, K., 2014, "Connecting Literacy to Sustainability: Revisiting Literacy as Involvement," in J. Duffy, J. N. Christoph, E. Goldblatt, N. Graff, R. S. Nowacek, and B. Trabold (eds.), *Literacy, Economy, and Power: New Directions in Literacy Research*, Southern Illinois University Press, Carbondale.

Donehower, K., C. Hogg, and E. E. Schell, 2007, *Rural Literacies*, Southern Illinois University Press, Carbondale.

Duncan, A., 2011, "White House Rural Roundtable Meeting in Tennessee," *Homeroom: The Official Blog of the U.S. Department of Education,* http://www.ed.gov/blog/2011/08/white-house-rural-roundtable-meeting-in-tennessee/.

Edmondston, J. and T. Butler, 2012, "Sustaining a Rural Pennsylvania Community: Negotiating Rural Literacies and Sustainability," in K. Donehower, C. Hogg, and E. E. Schell (eds.), *Reclaiming the Rural: Essays on Literacy, Rhetoric, and Pedagogy,* Southern Illinois University Press, Carbondale.

Fish, S., 2008, "Will the Humanities Save Us," *New York Times,* January 6, http://opinionator.blogs.nytimes.com/2008/01/06/will-the-humanities-save-us/.

Gallagher, K., 2009, *Readicide: How Schools Are Killing Reading and What You Can Do about It,* Stenhouse, Portland, ME.

Graff, H., 1991, *The Legacies of Literacy: Continuities and Contradictions in Western Culture and Society,* Indiana University Press, Bloomington, IN.

Graham Lotz, A., 2006, *I Saw the Lord: A Wake-Up Call for Your Heart,* Alive Communications, Colorado Springs, CO.

Harvey, S., 2009, *Act Like a Lady, Think Like a Man: What Men Really Think about Love, Relationships, Intimacy, and Commitment,* HarperCollins, New York.

Krashen, S., 2004, *The Power of Reading: Insights from the Research,* Libraries Unlimited, Santa Barbara, CA.

———, 2011, *Free Voluntary Reading,* Libraries Unlimited, Santa Barbara, CA.

Massey, D., 1994, "A Global Sense of Place," in D. Massey (ed.), *Space, Place, and Gender,* University of Minnesota Press, Minneapolis.

Nachtigal, P., 1982, "Rural School Improvement Efforts: An Interpretive History," in P. Nachtigal (ed.), *Rural Education: In Search of a Better Way,* Westview Press, Boulder, CO.

National Governors Association Center for Best Practices, Council of Chief State School Officers 2010, *Common Core State Standards,* http://www.corestandards.org/.

Nussbaum, M., 1997, *Poetic Justice: The Literary Imagination and Public Life,* Beacon Press, Boston, MA.

Rautio, P. and M. Lanas, 2013, "The Making of 'Good Enough' Everyday Lives: Literacy Lessons from the Rural North of Finland," in B. Green and M. Corbett (eds.), *Rethinking Rural Literacies: Transnational Perspectives,* Palgrave Macmillan, New York.

Rose, M., 2011, "Déjà vu All Over Again: A Lesson from the History of School Reform," *Washington Post,* March 21, http://www.washingtonpost.com/blogs/answer-sheet/post/deja-vu-all-over-again-a-lesson-from-the-history-of-school-reform/2011/03/27/AFE26rlB_blog.html.

Rosenblatt, L., 1995, *Literature as Exploration,* 5th ed., Modern Language Association, New York.

Scribner, S., 1984, "Literacy in Three Metaphors," *American Journal of Education,* vol. 93: 6–21.

Smith, M. and J. Wilhelm, 2002, *Reading Don't Fix No Chevys: Literacy in the Lives of Young Men,* Heinemann, Portsmouth, NH.

Theobald, P. and K. Wood, 2010, "Learning to Be Rural: Identity Lessons from History, Schooling, and the U.S. Corporate Media," in K. Schafft and A. Y. Jackson (eds.), *Rural Education for the Twenty-First Century: Identity, Place, and Community in a Globalizing World*, Penn State Press, University Park, PA.

UNESCO, 2006, February–May, "Gaining Literacy, Gaining a Voice," *Education Today*, no. 16: 3, http://unesdoc.unesco.org/images/0014/001444/144403e.pdf.

Waller, R., 2011, *Finding Your Home in a Book: Sociocultural Influences on Literacy Learning in a Rural School*, Unpublished doctoral dissertation, University of North Dakota, Grand Forks, ND.

Winchester, B., 2012, *Continuing the Trend: The Brain Gain of the Newcomers*, University of Minnesota Extension Center for Community Vitality, http://www.extension.umn.edu/communitybrain-gain/docs/continuing-the-trend.pdf.

CHAPTER 3

Find Yourself in Newfoundland and Labrador: Reading Rurality as Reparation

Ursula Kelly

This chapter is one part in an ongoing series of readings of cultural texts that render complex relations of place, people, and culture. My central purpose is to rethink the representational dynamics, cultural politics, and educational possibilities of these texts (Kelly 2009). Here, I examine the texts of the widely circulated and highly regarded *Find Yourself Here* advertising campaign of Tourism Newfoundland and Labrador (2011), so as to analyze the psychosocial characteristics of these texts. My focus is on the reinvention, through these texts, of notions of rurality and place and the economic, sociocultural, and psychic processes of which they are a constitutive part. I argue that such texts offer opportunities for multilayered readings, utilizing various codes that attend to dimensions of rurality important to a reconceptualization of rural education and literacies.

"Uncommon Potential"

In recent years, despite a worldwide economic recession and downward movement in the tourism sector, visitors to the province reached unprecedented numbers due, in large part, to the overwhelming success of marketing initiatives of Tourism Newfoundland and Labrador that include the *Find Yourself Here* multimedia advertising campaign begun in 2006. The campaign is part of a near US$20 million marketing budget for a tourism industry that recorded a 15 percent increase in visitors to the province from 2003 to 2007. Tourism currently directly adds close to US$400 million annually to provincial revenues. The campaign has won numerous "industry best" awards at national and regional levels. By industry standards, the campaign is a huge success on which the province plans to build, with a goal to double annual tourism revenue by the end of this decade. This vision is outlined in the strategic plan for Newfoundland and Labrador Tourism entitled *Uncommon Potential: A Vision for Newfoundland and Labrador* (2009, p.10).

The *Find Yourself Here* campaign is a series of advertisements composed largely, although not exclusively, of rural scenes. The television advertisements are constructed using a multimedia semiotics consistent with the history and culture of the province. They are composed of striking natural and cultural images that are accompanied by a score that combines composed music, containing original mnemonics, and natural sounds (lines of clothes flapping in the wind, a crackling fire and whistling kettle, waves crashing against shoreline). The advertisements end with a short punch line followed by the appearance of the provincial logo. These advertisements consistently present idealized versions of a pristine, powerful, and compelling landscape, inhabited but unharmed, and scenes of everyday and night life that evoke comfort, camaraderie, and security, outside modernity. As someone with an affinity to these images and for whom they bear at least some resemblance to (or a reassembly of) a cultural life once had, once lived, these texts stir a powerful emotional turn to a "once (upon a) time." But, like memory itself, sometimes, these images are intensified, oversaturated, misrecognized. For example, the images and relations recalled in *Top 40* (http://www.youtube.com/watch?v=BPu6cAvkGC4) feel utterly inside me, in ways both real and fanciful. But their power is tinged with the bittersweet, for their recall is positioned within both discontent and loss. What is depicted both was and was not "quite like that" and both is and is no longer.

But there is an appeal to these images that exceeds such affinity and any proximity of place, and which cannot be explained (or dismissed) on the basis of what some might call nostalgia. Though nostalgia is a significant and complex contemporary emotive force (Hutcheon 1998; Gopinath 2003; Matt 2007), it does not fully explain the appeal of these texts. Marketers count on advertising campaigns to strike an emotional chord with market (and marketing) savvy consumers, many of whom are aware of being emotionally manipulated as they succumb blissfully to its effects. Critical literacy has provided only limited means for understanding such contradictions of "emotion and intellect," perhaps because its analytic repertoire is designed to "read" surfaces more so than psyches, effect more so than affect. Such readings may render a satisfying account of ideology and social relations, but an unsatisfying account of the emotional and psychic relationships tapped and triggered by textual encounters. Such a literacy stops short of the kind of readings that would convey the complexity of everyday meaning and the desires and bedevilment that are its impetus (Kelly 1997). There is no good reason why this theoretical and pedagogical gap should persist. As Lemke reminded us, "literacies are legion" and, he argued, literacy itself cannot, perhaps, be any more precisely defined than as "a set of cultural competencies for making socially recognizable meanings by the use of particular material technologies" (1998, p. 283). Ways of reading are taught within sociocultural and affective contexts; cultural competencies are developed. In the context of late modernity, competencies in a variety of interpretive codes, including those that articulate the complex workings of desire, are essential to any notion of critical literacies for these times.

As studies in Canada (Jasen 1995; McKay 1994; McKay and Bates 2010; Overton 1996) and elsewhere (Gaffey 2004; Wright 1985; Storey 2006) have shown, tourism is a sophisticated and carefully regulated industry of ideological image production and cultural representation. It is also a carefully orchestrated and emotionally manipulative platform of mythmaking and identifying (re)invention and (re)formation. The *Find Yourself Here* campaign is not only about attracting tourists; it is also about province (re)making, a reconstitution of Newfoundland and Labrador for residents and others who may have a real or phantastical relationship to the place. The images of *Find Yourself Here* sell well this particular and beloved place, one that is, still, despite its own roar toward urbanity, a "rural place." But these images also mobilize nationalist sentiment and cultural redefinition. It is important to investigate this complexity and to inquire into these workings, for in the questions and the considerations they bring forth may reside insights into how rurality is entangled in the nature of our desires and dreams, our devastations and demons, and in who and what we are—our identities.

Such understandings of the entanglement of texts, places, histories, and identities may also offer something to the emerging field of *rural literacies*. To address this point, in this chapter I pose the following questions: what specific relationships of culture, people, and rurality do the advertisements of the *Find Yourself Here* campaign (re)invent or suggest? What do these texts suggest about the role of rurality within modernity? In addition, what does their success suggest about the (changing) role of Newfoundland and Labrador within a wider cultural sphere?

Tourism in Newfoundland and Labrador

During my childhood in the 1950s and 1960s, a white wooden rectangular sign hung in the front sun porch window of our home in Gambo, Newfoundland, announcing in bold black letters framed by a black border, the words "Tourist Rooms." Ours was a "Tourist Home," one of a small number in outport Newfoundland in those days selected to accommodate visitors to the province and other "boarders." I understood little of the meaning and politics of a nascent tourism industry. For me, the sign elicited mixed feelings. I felt a certain pride about our home and my mother's skills and grace as a host and homemaker and my father's wit and charm as a conversationalist and storyteller. But, for a shy child, living in a tourist home also meant having to cope with strangers and to share with them the family dinner table—always the formal dining room table when we had guests—and the one household washroom. It explains, I think, the amount of time I spent in my bedroom, a retreat to reading and music, avoiding the awkwardness of making conversation with people I did not know but who insisted on commenting on the color and curl of my hair and my politeness. These awkward presences, over which I had little control, help explain my still lingering difficulty with visitors in my home space. In retrospect, those tourist visitors did provide rare access to worlds and ways that brought difference to my life. To them, I surely represented something more closely aligned with the meaning of those red-haired, freckled faced children who now look out at me from my television or computer screen: an iconic innocent of the folk of the place.

Contemporary efforts around tourism in Newfoundland and Labrador build on many aspects and concerns of these early post-Confederation with Canada days. The government of that time acknowledged the potential of a tourist industry, while it worried that the province was not ready to receive the visitors who would come as a result of public relations efforts (Overton 1996). In the current context of successes and planned expansion, this concern remains. Commenting on the need to improve services for visitors in rural areas, then minister of tourism Terry French observed, "Although many [visitors] come to the city, many of them want to go to rural Newfoundland and Labrador...They want to see what we offer in our ads, and that's outside our major centres" (McLeod 2011, p. A3).

Nor has the current industry veered greatly from its historical raison d'etre as a redress for the economic difficulties of the rural, the impetus of which, now, is the catastrophic collapse and closure of the 500-year-old fishery in 1992, an event that decimated rural and outport communities and forced irrevocable change on the inhabitants whose livelihoods depended on it. The subsequent outward migration within Canada and elsewhere has been stemmed only recently, though not before the overall population of the province had been cut by 12 percent. The internal provincial trend of urbanization, from rural areas to the capital city of St. John's and its surrounding areas, in response to industry-related growth and opportunities in oil, gas, and other resource-based sectors, further exacerbated this decline, leaving rural communities with fewer people, eroding infrastructure, limited industries, and high unemployment. Tourism continues to be seen as a viable response. In *Uncommon Potential: A Vision for Newfoundland and Labrador* (Vision 2020), it is stated:

> Our industry has a vital role to play in addressing the challenges of urbanization. Rural communities are the heart and soul of our province, and the foundation of travel experiences. By investing in our tourism industry, we are investing in rural Newfoundland and Labrador, and keeping our communities alive and vibrant. (p. 17)

Rurality may be the heart, soul, and *psyche* of the province, for what is less explicit, although powerfully implied in and targeted through the *Find Yourself Here* campaign, is the promise of psychic redress or reparation within modernity: the rural as "a therapeutic tourist space" (Overton 1996, p. 32) for the target audience of "alienated, affluent moderns" (p. 36). The nature of this mutually beneficial arrangement—economic for psychic health and well-being, in which the rural is packaged and commodified to meet the needs of alienated moderns—is not a new construction, and this particular version has an established lineage, in the history of tourism in Newfoundland and Labrador and elsewhere (Averill 2007; Overton 1996; Wright 1985). But, as Kenelm Averill asks in another context—a question central to complex critical literacy—"just how does societal change affect the emotions in such a way as to lead us toward idealization of the countryside?" (2007, p. 168).

The developers of the *Find Yourself Here* campaign seem to understand well the answers to this question. Within it, this target market remains, still: "well-educated and literate" with "higher than average household incomes" who are interested in "discovering and experiencing the unspoiled natural environment" and "unexpected and intriguing experiences" (*Marketing Activities and Partnership Opportunities* 2006, p. 10). It is not hard to decipher the subtext: urban, intellectual, affluent, overworked, stressed, and unhappy, a New Times pedigree of displaced cosmopolitan elites for whom the psychic theme may be found in the lyrics of Joni Mitchell, "we've got to get ourselves back to the garden" (or, as Newfoundland-born singer Kim Stockwood croons, "back to the water"). But why Newfoundland and Labrador? In the campaign literature, this question is both asked and answered:

> Why would anyone want to visit Newfoundland and Labrador? It's far away. There isn't a single mega-theme park. Strangers often talk to you. Well, these are exactly the kinds of reasons why you should come. (p. 8)

And in experiencing "the realness of Newfoundland and Labrador" (p. 8) and "the uncomplicated and somewhat spiritual feeling you get" (p. 9) when you are here, you just might discover something inside yourself, too. Thus, the clever double entendre: Find yourself here.

In so many of these ways, the present campaign may be viewed more as a continuation of past efforts (Overton 1996), fuelled by a conflation of unprecedented forces: the power and ubiquity of newer technologies; the realignment and compression of time/space; and the intensification of fractured and fragmented subjects within modernity. The extent to which the rurality imagined and mobilized in these advertisements and for these times preserves, as iconic only, a rurality *for* tourists remains a critical question. For this conflation of forces creates other needs, too, the expression and realization of which have mobilized rural commodification, gentrification, and repopulation. Tourism as rural economic salvation may be a Trojan horse, carrying other interests and realignments, which though increasingly felt, have not been fully scrutinized. From this perspective, the exchange—economic for psychic well-being—may not be balanced or desirable. If the rurality that is psychically needed is mythologized and historically and socially selective in ways that can exacerbate or maintain oppressive relations and undermine sustainability, its implications are unsettling. Are there ways to read these advertisements and their contexts to gain insight into such a problematic nexus? Also, what might such readings reveal about how a psychic need for the rural may be tapped for more progressive purposes both within rural places and elsewhere?

Rural Phantasies

In his analysis of rural imagery and English culture, Kenelm Averill (2007) draws on Kleinian psychoanalysis to link the idealization of rural landscape to the pathologies and anxieties of late modernity. He argues that the social conditions of late modernity—time/space compression, fast-paced change, intensification of work, fragmentation of family and community life—interfere with interpersonal and psychic life. The rural becomes an idyllic haven from stresses, chaos, and insecurities. In this sense, Averill begins with the well-established use of the rural as a therapeutic space for affluent cosmopolitans. But, importantly, Averill does not beg the question of how dramatic change creates emotional conditions that lead to rural idealization. Through an analysis of the characteristics of the rural and its representational character, he presents a convincing account of the role of rural phantasy in contemporary (psychic) life (Averill 2007, p. 166). Positioned as "an endlessly giving and wholly good object" (p. 166), he argues that the rural is constructed as a place of release, reassurance, respite, and repair, and thereby restores psychic balance and rebuilds psychic resilience. Likewise, what does the *Find Yourself Here* campaign suggest about the nature of these rural phantasies and the ruptures and dissonance to which they speak?

Find Yourself Here

The *Find Yourself Here* campaign is built on a platform of (natural) "creativity" containing three pillars—people, culture, and the natural environment—and a "brand personality" that is "natural and uncomplicated, warm and unpretentious, spontaneous and inventive, with an effortless wit and engaging sense of humour" (*Marketing Activities and Partnership Opportunities* 2006, p. 8). *Clothesline*, an advertisement produced early in the campaign, exemplifies the platform and brand. Colorful clotheslines reminiscent of day-to-day cultural life, run through scenes of rural landscape and domesticity. Tended by women and children, they speak to the axiom that "around here, not every work of art hangs on a wall" (http://www.youtube.com/watch?v=c3GAKBJ9riA). A more recent advertisement, *Counting,* positions the rural as a theater and features visitors driving along coastline, pointing to numerous whales and icebergs as if in a wonderland of sea and wild life–a natural theme park where "they pass by here every year, by the thousands—of course, show times may vary" (http://www.youtube.com/watch?v=fQeV_alOLsg). This natural creativity plays against institutionalized urban galleries and museums and the structured lives of which they are a part.

The role of emotion to the *Find Yourself Here* campaign is explicitly framed. The advertising thrust is not "about" products.

> The creative strategy is to elicit an emotional response–a "feeling" about this unique place we call home... [P]eople don't buy "products"; they buy benefits. The real benefit is several layers below the tangible tourism "product"—in the emotion of the brand, and the feelings it evokes. (*Marketing Activities and Partnership Opportunities* pp. 8 and 6)

What are these beneficial emotions? What do they tell us about how, and for what, the rural is positioned as a beneficial emotional space? The priority target market for these advertisements is the nonresident "touring and explorer market," people who "have money, time, and a keen interest to explore destinations that are off the beaten track, unusual and unspoiled places where few have gone before" (p. 5). The campaign is designed

> to reflect the uncomplicated and somewhat spiritual feeling you get when you're in Newfoundland and Labrador... [and] to persuade consumers that a visit here is a chance to discover a wonderful, naturally exotic, and unexpectedly different place, off the beaten track. Perhaps more importantly, a visit to Newfoundland and Labrador is an opportunity for visitors to discover something inside themselves. (p. 9)

Yet, there is nothing at all "uncomplicated" about this appeal. The depth with which landscape can speak to us, enter, and move us, is a compelling and meaning-rich dynamic. How can it be understood? Read?

Averill's (2007) research offers one way to consider the resounding success of this campaign through an analysis of its emotional appeal. Here, too, the emotional pleasures of a place are associated with distinct qualities somewhat different from those identified by Averill in the United Kingdom. Here, I analyze four broad and interrelated representational themes emerging from the *Find Yourself Here* campaign and discuss their appeal within late modernity. These representational themes are: *environment*—vast, abundant, untouched; *ethos*—ancient, mystical, spiritual; *relationships*—secure, resilient, enduring; and *culture*—creative, spontaneous, harmonious.

Find Yourself Here, in a Place That Is

Vast, Untouched, Abundant
Within Kleinian psychoanalysis, love and hate are the emotional underpinnings of psychic life, from childhood, when the child struggles with its feelings in relation to its first love (usually the mother) and her partial

satisfaction of its needs, into adulthood where these struggles can be reignited through other encounters. In her psychoanalytic account of love and reparation, Melanie Klein discusses the process of displacing love, through which the child learns to extend the first feelings of love onto other symbolic objects, a process considered central to the development of personality and relationships, and of culture more generally. The child must separate from its mother's love and part of this process is to lessen the intensity of this love by displacing it onto others and other things. This displaced love is reinstated onto objects and loving experiences with friends, work, companion animals, country, and so on, and keeps in check the haunting effects of initial separation.

In her discussion of displacement, Klein explicitly discussed the psychic instincts of the explorer as one way the child reinstates the lost mother. Klein argued that, in exploration, "the escape from her and the original attachment to her find full expression" (1937/1975, p. 334). The beautiful land that lures the explorer becomes a symbol of the lost object to whom it is possible, through phantasy, not only to return, but also to repair and to improve on those initial relations: to restore the lost mother. Such restoration serves as a reminder of goodness and a stabilizing factor in psychic life, where, to maintain healthy relations, love and hate must be kept in balance, a balance always threatened by disruption and change. According to Klein, when disruption occurs, the importance of symbolic objects to the restoration of psychic health is crucial. In this psychic scenario, the appeal of the representations of vast and untouched abundance is an opportunity for psychic reparation and the building and maintaining of psychic resilience. Herein, it is possible to see a need for the rural in ways that are relevant to but are not generally considered or tapped in debates about sustainability and care and their reparative possibilities.

The *Find Yourself Here* campaign presents the rural as "love object" in complex and beguiling ways. There are images of lush, sensuous sea, sky, and landscapes, brimming with passion captured on a palette drawn from natural, physical, and social environments rich in color and contrast. It is a vibrant, highly textured and lyrical space. It is a space in which struggle and danger are at bay, and where one is embraced by its warmth, seduced by its charms, and reassured by its safety. It offers emotional pleasure and spiritual renewal. It is an idyllic setting, a symbolic ideal of a mother's love, featuring women and children aplenty. Several of the advertisements imply a notion of motherland. Women are more often pictured close to or in the home, while other advertisements explicitly articulate the themes of mother and child, as a way to imagine nature: "Every mother has a favourite. Even Mother Nature: 16 feet of fresh powder every year" (http://www.newfoundlandlabrador.com/#). In this way, following Massey (2000), the alignment of mother and nature also reproduces problematic notions of mother and gender.

Likewise, a full-page newspaper advertisement that features a picture of the mountains and waterways of Torngat Mountains National Park in Labrador is grounded explicitly in this kind of psychic appeal. The photo bears the caption, "Some places are simply too big to fit into modern life" (*Globe and Mail*, March 5, 2011, p. T12). In a bubble just above the province's name and logo, it states:

> There's nothing modest about 300,000 square kilometres of pristine, ancient beauty. Imprinted with stoic mountains, bottomless fjords, and some of the last glaciers in North America. But the journey within, nothing short of epic, is even greater. Which may be, as it turns out, the biggest reason of all to find yourself here. (p. T12)

That this journey is a life journey is central to the impact of the advertisements. In the video advertisement entitled *Gros Morne*, the viewer is told, when "on your journey through life, make sure your biography has at least one extraordinary chapter" (http://www.youtube.com/watch?v= oHmsHU1zuoc&feature=related). Such appeals tap into the explorer's need for a blank slate against which to rediscover and recover, to find oneself, once more and after all, *here*.

Ancient, Mystical, Spiritual
Such images of vastness—of land, sea, and sky—populate most of the advertisements, often accompanied by powerful images and sounds that conjure ancient, mysterious, and spiritual dimensions of Newfoundland and Labrador. Combining image, sound, and symbol to evoke ancient and mysterious ways, still vibrant in the present, sets the stage for the spiritual encounter that is a promise to "find yourself here." For example, in *Edge*, an ancient mariner-type figure walks across a vast landscape of ancient rock and forest to the edge of towering cliffs and the expansive waters of the North Atlantic at Brimstone Head, Fogo Island. The male narrator proclaims: "The people of the Flat Earth Society believe this place is one of the four corners of the world, the very edge of the earth." As the camera closes in and he turns to face it, with a sly grin and a twinkle in his eye, sounds resembling ancient voices can be heard as the narrator concludes, "Well, that's just foolishness, isn't it?" (http://www.youtube.com/

watch?v=RMkM5Yja9u8&NR=1). Likewise, in *Vikings*, children trek to the reconstructed ruins of the Viking settlements of L'anse aux Meadows, where they peer with trepidation through the fenced enclosure. The male narrator says, "And so they came, five centuries before Columbus, fearless warriors out to discover a new world. The Vikings. While they left behind their mark, they have long since gone." A door to one of the houses blows open, the children run in fright, and he adds, "As far as we can tell" (http://www.youtube.com/watch?v=7BZWtthl25U&feature= related). Like the children, the curious are invited to come and find out for themselves.

Ancient Land, a rare two-minute advertisement, is one of the most powerful and complex in the campaign. Set in the Torngat Mountains of Labrador, it features a young Inuit girl child, tracing a white line—as if a lineage of people who are *of* and in relation to the land—in the stone of the mountains, themselves pictures as deep, veined, and mystical structures. Symbols of aboriginal spirituality appear: the caribou, Inuktitut poetry, and the Inuit throat singing of Lucy Idlout. The landscape is complex and, in ways, dark and incomprehensible, as if a symbol of the psyche itself. The ancient and aboriginal are aligned. "Throughout this land, for thousands of years, it's been said that everything has a spirit. Not surprisingly it's where you might find your own" (http://www.youtube. com/watch?v=QHNFsN7rqSY&feature=related). It is difficult to view this text apart from the ravages of racism and colonial abuse. Yet, herein, there seems to be a space for another level of recognition, one that moves beyond a cynical reading of commodified inclusion. David Greenwood (2009, p. 3) writes:

> It is not uncommon to speak of colonization and cultural violence... but the objects of violence in these contexts are usually the 'subaltern others' who stand in binary opposition to the White, privileged, or educated class of 'mobile modernity'. It is more difficult to acknowledge... that all of us carry a psychic or soul-wounding inherited by the colonial mindset, which is the foundation of our educational systems. White people need to acknowledge this wound in order for it to be healed in themselves as well as in space and time.

Greenwood does not probe the psychic dimensions of this wound and he is quick to acknowledge that he is not equating positions of injury—those of Aboriginals and whites. Rather, he is seeking to stoke remembrance, using a metaphor of native survival, "of a deeper and wider narrative of living and learning in connection with others and the land" (p. 5). Is a text such as *Ancient Land* one through which to begin to imagine and to repair what Wendy Brown calls "wounded attachments" (Brown 1993, p. 391)? Such questions allow for a dovetailing of the concerns and goals of psychoanalysis and spirituality, distinct areas that arguably share the common goal of a pursuit of wisdom and self-knowledge. Both constitute inner journeys; both deal with the intangible, the immaterial. The impetus of both psychoanalysis and spirituality, it can be argued, is to increase goodness in the world, to inspire through an enriched inner life, the extension of loving goodness onto others, often as reparation. The spiritual quest on offer in these texts is the quest for self-knowing and self-discovery: to find your (spiritual) self here and to reap the reparative rewards it brings.

Secure, Resilient, Enduring

Carefree children, solitary but content women of the home and wise men of the land and sea, (heterosexual) couples, young and old, and intergenerational groups such as those at a "time" (or a party) populate the advertisements. Children are usually running, curious, and carefree, in a vast yet unthreatening outdoors. The world pictured is one in which relationships last, families maintain close ties, and children grow untethered from confinement and fear. It is a picture in which harmony and security abound and everyone knows their place. *Place Names* aligns the longevity of communities with enduring relationships, to love and solace: Heart's Desire, Paradise, L'Anse Amour, Conception Harbour. This place has stood the test of time and its resilient character will help restore one's own relationships. In an age of simulacra, it offers a substantial alternative to a contemporary and dominant notion of family vacation: "Where exactly is this place? It's as far from Disneyland as you can possibly get" (http://www.youtube.com/watch?v=aXJNYi4ByXc&NR=1). Yet, some may argue that the restoration of "relic" communities from a vanished (largely fishing) history—a common practice to build tourism attractions in struggling outport communities—is a "Disneyfication" of culture and memory: A highly selective and sanitized fabrication that nonetheless functions as a register of loss, sublimation, and the necessity of mourning.

The children, who roam throughout the advertisements, have a key role in this mourning (see, in particular, *Counting, Place Names, Top 40, Clothesline, Half-Hour,* and *Architecture*). These iconic children tie us to the past often moving with backs turned to the viewer (as if to lead us into the past). They are melancholic beckonings to the lost (loved) objects of a past time: ghosts of children past. But children also tie us to the future and promise something "not yet"—the rebirth that comes by moving through melancholia to mourning. So few children now live in rural Newfoundland and Labrador because prior generations left in the tens of thousands two decades ago when the northern cod fishery closed and the oil sands of Alberta offered economic refuge. While many are now returning to retire, they raise the ratio of old to young and their monied impact realizes both the benefits and problems of rural gentrification (Scott and Gkartzios 2010). The intergenerational family, so commonly pictured in the advertisements, is deeply fragmented, each family now a microcosm of a worldwide Newfoundland and Labrador diaspora. Yet, these images offer to assuage these pains of contemporary life and provide some solace from the devastations that have created them, as they may also feed disavowal and its deleterious effects.

Creative, Inventive, Harmonious
The images in the advertisements suggest that in Newfoundland and Labrador, joy underscores life, finding its expression in spontaneous eruptions of creative force. *Architecture* suggests it is a place that looks like no other, its color, design, and cultural quirkiness manifested in land, people, places, and things—an architecture of the soul. It reaffirms that "in a world oddly bent on conformity, there is something strangely encouraging about a place that is anything but" (http://www.youtube. com/watch?v=gE3OORLTAzM). It is a place where relationships, work, and play are in harmony. In many of these advertisements, creativity and procreation conflate as newly weds and young parents burst with the energy of new life. The tempo of life exists outside—or in opposition to—the demands of modernity. Life moves at its own speed, in its own time (zone). In *Half-Hour* (http://www.youtube.com/watch?v=Be4ufvmpPRw), the province's unique time zone is used to capture what is framed as a unique and uniquely paced life: "When you are always a half-hour ahead, you never feel the need to catch up." This tempo of life is exaggerated, as the movement of everything—the sea, land, and sky and caribou, sheep, icebergs, whales, and children—slows, and movement lulls and sedates, like a mother's lullaby. Even the capital city of St. John's has its own tempo. The soundtrack of *500 Years* uses a snare drum to emulate the timbre of a military march so as to underscore a long and captivating history, a city at once old and modern, slow and bustling, cosmopolitan and natural, urban and small. A large village, really, that offers the best of both worlds and where one can imagine wanting to stay, for "a place that's been captured by the Dutch,

the French, and the English is no stranger to holding people captive" (http://www.youtube.com/watch?v=mthuKmagC_e&feature=related). This captivating sense is evidenced in the high numbers of nonresident home sales and in the stories of those who, having seen the advertisements, come to visit and stay. Thus, these images are tied to increasing worldwide trends toward counterurbanization (Scott and Gkartzios 2010) and, arguably, the psychic dynamics discussed herein.

Here, in the Real World: Reading Rurality as Reparation

To find or to recover one's self, one must, in some way, be lost, broken, or absent. Yet, while so much is lost, the *Find Yourself Here* campaign suggests that *all* is not lost, and *you* are not lost, if you find yourself here. Can the psychic needs and emotional power, tapped by the campaign, be directed toward a rejuvenated will to care and to repair the symbolic object—the rural? As Averill (2007) notes, such representations and their effects are far from trivial both because of their nationalist overtones (which can mobilize people in regressive and exclusionary, as well as productive, ways) and more pointedly because "rural idealization answers to the need for unconscious defence; hence, demand for [rural idealization] is demand for the security that phantasies of an untainted countryside offer" (p. 171). They have political potency beyond rural places, for "ideological commitments cannot be arbitrarily divorced from daily emotional strivings and struggles" (p. 171).

But what of the real people who daily inhabit the places on which this rural dream world is based? The *Find Yourself Here* campaign mines stories, memories, and spaces of real people struggling to make sense of real struggles, and to grieve real losses to build a tourism industry. From the inside, these representations can tap an overwhelming melancholia, a negation of loss and change, as they also overwhelm and shroud much of "what was." But mourning what is lost is not possible without melancholia. Might the representations recall the value of what is gone and what remains, as it builds the psychic resilience of the subject to move through melancholia and, with mourning, to form attachments to new, more productive and wiser ways of being? The "remains" in these texts—which are so devoid of references to the messiness of a past of fishing, a present of oil drilling and resource mining, continued widespread indifference to the Aboriginals, or the ill-effects of loss and change on communities and families—could also be considered a list of cultural priorities. For, what *do* require stewardship *are* the interconnected pillars: the bounty of land and sea, the blessings of relationships, the centrality of a spirited and spiritual life. The very things advertised *are* the very things threatened or lost.

Vision 2020 positions the people of the province as one of its main tourist attractions, using words such as authentic, hospitable, and warm to describe us. Yet, also noted is the importance of "growing our people" (*Uncommon Potential* 2009, p. 41) in relation to tourism, and, specifically, "to instil a sense of pride" (p. 43) *in an industry*, through education and development, so as "to deliver on our 'creativity' brand experience" (p. 43). The domestication and commodification of identity and experience are part of the fulfillment of these tourism goals and the subsequent economic revitalization through tourism is an antidote to the physical resettlement program of early Confederation. While rural residents may not be legislated out of their places, *this time*, it might be argued that a "resettlement of the mind" (Dalton 1989, p. 41) is in progress (pardon the pun) and with it a reinvention of history, memory, identity, and place.

The *Find Yourself Here* campaign is not only a beckoning toward but also an active cultural mobilization of "the dawn of a new day" so evocatively captured in the rebranding of the province. This process, begun in 2004 and completed in 2006, corresponded with and complemented the *Find Yourself Here* campaign. In the promotional video for the launch of the new provincial brand, the brand concept is introduced. It evokes the pillars of the provincial brand—creative, resilient, inventive—in minimalist music and lyrics and with key historic and contemporary symbols rendered in water color, crayon-like caricatures within a fast-paced and "moving" account. This new brand is meant to reassure, to assuage anxieties as well as to reinstate a wounded pride—to repair a damaged psyche: "From the sea, from the waves, comes a will, comes a way. Across this land, across this place, comes a new life, a new day. Comes the dawn of a new day" (http://www.youtube.com/watch?v =D2yO_fZr13U&feature=related). It is a campaign designed to move residents through melancholia—a continued preoccupation with the past through a hope for its return—to mourning—to new attachments and hopes in the dawn of a new day.

Beyond this province, reparative inclinations are also evident. Within Canadian Confederation, Newfoundland and Labrador has been unjustly positioned as a poor, "primitive" cousin, a national burden and embarrassment. The Newfoundland and Labrador emerging in the twenty-first century strategically rebuts these misrepresentations and the politics of place and nation that maintained them (Kelly 1993) and is now being *re*discovered. The positive attention toward the province is, in part, the result of many now seeing it as if for the first time, and, as part of this renewed gaze, building restorative relations so as to repair and atone for past destructive ones. The *Find Yourself Here* campaign can claim some credit here as can former premier Danny Williams, under whose leadership the campaign was initiated. Such reparation is part of the strategic, if unstated, objectives of the campaign, for part of the psychic return is not only to find oneself but also to find in others, as part of finding oneself, that which was previously neglected or injured—the redemptive second chance, the chance "to get it right this time," to learn to live better within the relations from which one has been estranged or separated.

Literacies of Transience, Loss, and Place

Within current configurations, rural literacies are often bulwarks against decay and death, part of what it means to defend, to survive, to reimagine, and to thrive—to sustain—within rurality *despite* the challenges of changing times. These goals of rural literacies are important as well as problematic. In any context or place, we read and write, view and represent, think and speak, so as to make sense of our lives, to suture what is torn, to repair what is broken, to heal so as to dream anew. The melancholy of literacy—wherein representation is a monument to loss—can be productive in this important way, as both a record and an acknowledgment of what is lost. It is not possible to mourn without melancholia—the refusal of loss until one (or a culture) is able to bear acceptance of loss. In whatever scripts, using whatever languages and codes, this melancholic project is a key part of late modernity and the realization of loss that is a part of these times: to find new representations, new meanings, new attachments. In this regard, literacy, like education, will have to be rethought as something different, something more and, even, something less, so as to engage such complex sociocultural, ecological, and emotional times. An analysis of what is happening in Newfoundland and Labrador, and the representational machinery that is part of its mobilization, suggests some of what must be considered and their important implications for discussions of rurality, place, and literacies. The nature of the psychic struggles on which the *Find Yourself Here* campaign derives its power and appeal suggests additional and potent possibilities for rural literacies as conceptualized by Donehower, Hogg, and Schell (2007), for sustainability and sustainable practices offer one direction through which to learn to love and to protect the good object and to offer a healing response to the dissonance of contemporary life everywhere.

To grasp more clearly and profoundly how rural places should or might matter in these times, it is necessary to understand better how they already matter, that is, the manner in which they already figure in our everyday lives, as real and phantastical, as places in which we live or as places for which we desire. As researchers and scholars within rural literacies, our own work may be indicative of how rural places matter to us and to those communities about which we care and for which we advocate. This work may also suggest how rural places have been and remain essential to our own lives and to how we manage and reconcile our losses: research as reparation. This investment is both a blessing and curse, for it impassions research and writing, but it can also often limit what it is possible to see in—and to ask of—places. To argue that rural places matter is to subvert or to beg other questions, too: Do *all* places matter? How do places matter? Why should places matter? Who decides if and how they do matter? Using what criteria? As Doreen Massey (2004, p. 21) suggests, "not all places are 'victims' and ... not all of them, in their present form, are worth defending." Nor can places only or primarily matter because they are "what remains" of something long gone. But oftentimes it is argued that they do, for this reason alone, and this way of mattering may not build the kind of resilience now needed for subjects nor places, or for very long. Such educational conversations are difficult but necessary.

The project of rural literacies cannot succeed well without encouraging, as part of its educational repertoire, a more critical subject. But it must also encourage a psychically resilient subject, one that can more creatively engage in the challenges offered by the ebbs and flows of these times that mark all people and places: a subject for whom transience (and its associated change and loss) is tolerable and beneficial. A lack of such resilience may explain some of the phenomena that characterize rurality in terms of who leaves and who stays (Corbett 2007), who returns and who cannot or will not, and the nature of their experiences of staying and leaving. When rural youth express symptoms of deep dismay and unease, upon staying or leaving, it is important to understand the emotional toll of each and both. Bell Hooks (2009) considers some of these complex dynamics in her account of leaving Kentucky. There are so many aspects of the dynamic of place attachment and so many questions to which we do not yet have compelling answers. For example, to what extent might a refusal to leave be linked to unmanageable anxieties?

Or, how might a resistance to ecological citizenship link with unresolved aggressions? Greater insight is needed into the nature of the psychic role of the rural for those who inhabit it. Then, educators might respond more carefully and caringly to such insights beyond the imperatives and demands of current prevailing assumptions about rurality, rural people, and their educational needs.

Rural people and their stories are part of the fabric of the *Find Yourself Here* campaign largely through their absence. Their mythologized presence is part of a re-creation of Newfoundland and Labrador for tourism, using the "renewal resources" of land, culture, and people (*Uncommon Potential* 2009, p. 45), and, through tourism, the re-creation of rural identities and histories. The implications of such a reinvention for communities in the long term are unclear. As earlier noted, Vision 2020 clearly states that tourism has a key part in addressing the challenges of urbanization. Yet, standing still in time-space so that others may move psychically forward stunts and immobilizes those caught in the mime of preservation. Part of the strategic action plan for Vision 2020 includes building visible leadership in environmental sustainability and developing, through education and incentive, "an environmental code of conduct to guide all elements of tourism development" (p. 35). Recent debates about snowmobile use within Terra Nova National Park by residents of Charlottetown, a small community in the Park, suggest a stubborn tension between the preservation of the environment and rural culture. A wide-ranging debate about the tradition of gravel pit camping in the province demonstrates the tensions between the aesthetic of the new tourism and rural culture. Increasingly strict regulations around woodcutting for fuel, cabin building, boating, hunting, and fishing likewise suggest government efforts to legislate and realign rural practices. Rural residents are keenly aware of the cultural impact of these changes, and of the fundamental losses they entail. The gains remain less clear.

If part of a project of rural literacies is to reshape the relationship to place toward an ecological agenda, the realization of what Cormack, Green, and Reid (2007, p. 74) call "active ecological citizenship," for many rural citizens, it is "learning to love again" (Brown et al. 2006) or learning to love anew, beyond melancholia and other strictures of attachment to no longer tenable notions of place and rurality. The focus offered here, on the psychic nature of attachments and longing, is important for its precise preoccupation with this analysis and renewal of love. Despite its commercial bent, this, too, is part of the aim of the *Find Yourself Here* campaign. It offers both a turning toward—part of the "dawn of a new day" and a turning away from what is lost, the end of a day, an era, and a time/space.

A literacy that promotes productive readings of these myriad forces can contribute meaningfully to the development of a citizenry that can reshape—as well as read against the grain of—such forces. The *Find Yourself Here* campaign is a provocative text, one that lends itself well to the consideration of complex questions about culture, place, and identity, the meanings of rurality, and the role of representational texts and politics within a reimagined project of literacy, education, and place. In literate spaces, such as public school classrooms, these texts might be used to extend and to deepen dialogue about the matter(ing) of things rural, across space-time-places, and the reparative initiatives that might respect and inspire the agency and creativity of all of us for whom rurality matters. But a large part of this discussion must focus on the thorny issues of loss and its monuments—those commemorative representational texts—and how, in these textual places, we might learn to read so as to see loss as it intersects with hope, a site from which to build places anew.

References

Averill, K., 2007, "Englishness, the Country, and Psychoanalysis," *Psychoanalysis, Culture & Society*, vol. 12: 165–179.

Brown, W., 1993, "Wounded Attachments," *Political Theory*, vol. 21, no. 3: 390–410.

Brown, W., C. Colegate, J. Dalton, T. Rayner, and C. Thill, 2006, "Learning to Love Again: An Interview with Wendy Brown," *Contretemps*, vol. 6: 25–42.

Corbett, M., 2007, *Learning to Leave: The Irony of Schooling in a Coastal Community*, Fernwood Books, Halifax.

Cormack, P., B. Green, and J. Reid, 2007, "Children's Understanding of Place: Discursive Constructions of the Environment in Children's Writing and Artwork about the Murray-Darling Basin," in F. Vanclay, M. Higgins, and A. Blackshaw (eds.), *Senses of Place: Exploring Concepts and Expressions of Place through Different Senses and Lenses*, National Museum of Australia Press, Canberra, pp. 57–75.

Dalton, M., 1989, *The Time of Icicles*, Breakwater Books, St. John's, NL.

Donehower, K., C. Hogg, and E. E. Schell, 2007, *Rural Literacies*, Southern Illinois University Press, Carbondale.

Gaffey, S., 2004, *Signifying Place: The Semiotic Realisation of Place in Irish Product Marketing*, Ashgate, Surrey, UK.

Gopinath, G., 2003, "Nostalgia, Desire, Diaspora: South Asian Sexualities in Motion," in J. E. Braziel and A. Mannue (eds.), *Theorizing Diaspora*, Blackwell, Oxford.

Government of Newfoundland and Labrador, 2006, *Creative, Resilient and Inventive: New Brand Embodies Essence of Newfoundland and Labrador*, http://www.youtube.com/watch?v=5aevrkSXsBc.

Greenwood, D. A., 2009, "Place, Survivance, and White Remembrance: A Decolonizing Challenge to Rural Education in Mobile Modernity," *Journal of Research in Rural Education*, vol. 24, no. 10, http://jrre.psu.edu/articles/24-10.pdf.

Hooks, B., 2009, *Belonging: A Culture of Place*, Routledge, New York.

Hutcheon, L., 1998, *Irony, Nostalgia, and the Postmodern*, http://www.library.utoronto.ca/utel/criticism/hutchinp.html.

Jasen, J., 1995, *Wild Things: Nature, Culture and Tourism in Ontario 1790–1914*, University of Toronto Press, Toronto.

Kelly, U. A., 1993, *Marketing Place: Cultural Politics, Regionalism, and Reading*, Fernwood Books, Halifax.

———, 1997, *Schooling Desire: Literacy, Cultural Politics, and Pedagogy*, Routledge, New York.

———, 2009, *Migration and Education in a Multicultural World: Culture, Loss, and Identity*, Palgrave Macmillan, New York.

Klein, M., 1937/1975, *Love, Guilt and Reparation and Other Works 1921–1945*, Hogarth Press, London.

Lemke, J. L., 1998, "Metamedia Literacy: Transforming Meanings and Media," in D. Reinking, L. Labbo, M. McKenna, and R. Kiefer (eds.), *Handbook of Literacy and Technology: Transformations in a Post-typographic World*, Lawrence Erlbaum, Hillsdale, NJ.

Massey, D., 2000, "Travelling Thoughts," in P. Gilroy, L. Grossberg, and A. McRobbie (eds.), *Without Guarantees: In Honour of Stuart Hall*, Verso, London.

———, 2004, "Geographies of Responsibility," *Geografiska Annaler: Series B, Human Geography*, vol. 86, no. 1: 5–18.

Matt, S. J. 2007, "You Can't Go Home Again: Homesicknes and Nostalgia in U.S. History," *Journal of American History*, vol. 94, no. 2: 469–497.

McKay, I., 1994, *The Quest of the Folk: Antimodernism and Cultural Selection in Twentieth Century Nova Scotia*, McGill-Queens University Press, Montreal.

McKay, I. and R. Bates, 2010, *In the Province of History: The Making of the Public Past in Twentieth Century Nova Scotia*, McGill-Queens University Press, Montreal.

McLeod, J., 2011, "Everyone Loves Those Tourism Ads," *Telegram*, A3, February 29.

Overton, J., 1996, *Making a World of Difference: Essays on Tourism, Culture and Development in Newfoundland*, ISER Books, St. John's, NL.

Scott, M. and M. Gkartzios, 2010, "Rural Gentrification in Ireland: Supply-Side and Demand-Side Explanations," paper presented at the 22nd International Housing Research Conference: *Urban Dynamics and Housing Change—Crossing into the 2nd Decade of the 3rd Millennium*, Istanbul, July 4–7.

Storey, D., 2006, "Images of Rurality: Commodification and Place Promotion," *The Rural Citizen: Governance, Culture and Well-Being in the 21st Century*, University of Plymouth, Plymouth, http://eprints.worc.ac.uk/120/1/Storey.pdf.

Tourism, Culture, and Recreation, Government of Newfoundland Labrador, 2006, *Marketing Activities and Partnership Opportunities*, http://www.tcr.gov.nl.ca/tcr/publications/2006/marketingplan2006.pdf.

————, 2009, *Uncommon Potential: A Vision for Newfoundland and Labrador*, http://www.tcr.gov.nl.ca/tcr/publications/2009/Vision_2020.pdf.

Tourism Newfoundland Labrador, 2011, *Find Yourself Here: Photos and Videos*, http://www.newfoundlandlabrador.com/AboutThisPlace/Videos/2A278340CD74103F.

Wright, P., 1985, *On Living in an Old Country: The National Past in Contemporary Britain*, Verso, London.

CHAPTER 4

My Roots Dip Deep: Literacy Practices as Mirrors of Traditional, Modern, and Postmodern Ruralities

Karen Eppley

Growing up, I spent my summer days at my grandparents' house. A small ceramic bank in the shape of a dog sitting outside his doghouse stood on the dresser In their bedroom. Each night before bed time, my grandfather would empty his pockets of spare change into the bank. He always kept an eye out for wheat pennies. They would go into the bank, but would never be spent. I loved that heavy little bank and would sometimes dump out the coins and marvel at how much money it seemed to hold.

One of my jobs every afternoon was to walk to the post office for the mail. In my town of 300, the post office had gas pumps out front and doubled as the general store. Like most general stores, there was a well-stocked candy counter: Johnny Apple Treats, Double-Bubble, Nerds, and Kit-Kats were my favorites. At some point that summer, I started helping myself to small amounts of change before going to Walter's store for the mail. I never used the stolen change for the higher priced items such as single-serve bags of potato chips or Coke in glass bottles from the cooler. My purchases were from the candy counter, treats that could be eaten and the wrappers disposed of on the walk home. I started with very small amounts easily rationalized in light of the sweet pay-off, and I grew bolder over time.

I still vividly remember the look on my grandmother's face later that summer when I finally got caught. I was instantly scared and ashamed, and she made only one statement: "Your Pap was saving that money for you to take to the Fair." I was stealing money that was planned as a gift for me. Not just any gift, either. My grandparents saved all year so that we could attend. The gradual filling of the bank each night before bed was the equivalent of crossing days off a calendar counting down to a week more anticipated than even Christmas. The Fair was enormously important in our lives. The week spent there in a pull-behind camper was our one and only vacation, and I stayed there every year throughout my elementary and most of my high school years. To this day, I have never missed a Fair and my children enjoy the same tradition.

I tell this story in order to illustrate the importance of this event in my life and to establish my authority to talk about it, but the Fair is equally important to countless other families in our county. Perhaps there is a similar event in your life. The stories I'll tell about the Fair are about the rural people familiar to me and the kinds of things that they value and know. More importantly, the stories are about a place. Over the course of the chapter, I hope to make clear what relevance an inquiry into a county Fair has to a book about rural literacies.

* * *

In 1874, members of the Progress Grange in Centre County, Pennsylvania, organized a picnic. This was to be an exemplary event without the horse racing and alcohol that plagued earlier fairs (Marti 2008). And, 136 years later, the Centre County Grange Fair is an event during which traditionalism, modernism, and postmodernism[1] coexist in a contemporary rural space that mirrors the complexity of contemporary rural life. It may be tempting to associate modernism with the urban and traditionalism (or the "premodern") with "the rural" (Murdoch and Pratt 1993), but modernism and postmodernism are readily identifiable in the rural "lifeworld" (New London Group 1996) of the Fair. Thus, one goal of this chapter is to complicate the conceptualization of contemporary ruralities as "traditional" or, alternatively, as "modern." I intend to identify how both traditional literacies and modern literacies, along with "postmodern" literacies, are useful frames for understanding complex and contemporary rural lives. The goal here is not to better define or reify rurality by theorizing how it is constituted in these three ways, but to explore the ways in which contemporary ruralities (in the plural) are constituted by a hybrid of contradictory and complementary discourses. The hybridity is the point. This is a poststructuralist act in that it suggests alternative ways to understand and problematize contemporary ruralities and literacies. Poststructuralism is useful to deconstruct and critique the taken-for-granted, commonsense understanding of rurality, modernism, postmodernism, and traditionalism. It opens up discourses and practices to questioning (Davies 2000) by providing strategies to interrogate commonsense knowledge and ideas.

In order to problematize rurality and contextualize particular literate behaviors in this setting, I'll frame some of the literacies in operation at the Fair within traditionalism, modernism, and postmodernism. I'll argue in favor of Street's (1984) ideological model of literacy that theorizes literacies in the plural. One way of understanding rural literacies is "the particular kinds of literate skills needed to achieve the goals of sustaining life in rural areas" (Donehower, Hogg, and Schell 2007, p. 4). For example, in *Prairie Town*, Jacqueline Edmondson (2003) tells stories about residents enacting a variety of literacies in a project of community sustenance and development. The sustenance and development of rural life requires a variety of situated, literate behaviors that enable residents to make decisions about growth and change. This requires an ideological model of literacy that is relativist, sociocultural, and situated (Collins and Blot 2003).

Literacies in the Plural

The literacy inquiry described in this chapter is a situated engagement, focusing on practices or "ways" (Heath 1983) with texts that are not limited to print. This is a diversity agenda: "As we recognize the diversity of our world—and even our local communities—we must re-think our privileging of particular literacy practices—usually print literacies—in theory, research, and practice" (O'Brien, Moje, and Stewart 2001, p. 43). Within this view, literacy requires understanding and participation in "social" practices within particular domains (Gee 2007). Understanding literacy as social practice means not only that what "counts" as a literate activity includes reading, writing, listening, and speaking, but also that meaning is situated within a complex web of social interactions (Dudley-Marling 2011). Accordingly, what counts as text is not limited to print and what counts as reading is not limited to decoding print on a page. Ways with texts, particularly in the context of a country fair, are inherently social and thus always situated. The texts of social interactions are produced for particular purposes and used in socially agreed upon ways (Anstey 2008).

Gee (2007, p. 19) describes a "domain" as "an area or set of activities where people think, act, and value in certain ways." Both oral language and texts such as images, symbols, gestures, or artifacts have particular, situated meanings within domains. The Grange Fair is one such domain. An alternative framing comes from the concept of lifeworld, which the New London Group (1996) defines as a space "for community life where local and specific meanings can be made" (p. 70). The (temporary) life-world of the Fair is a local community marked by context-specific mean-ings, language, and discourses, where language, discourse, and register are all relevant markers of difference (ibid.). As with Gee's concept of the domain, in lifeworlds participants can recognize (or "read") and produce (or "write") situated meanings within this specific context. One cannot understand the complexity of the Fair without seeing it as a space for community life.

One might assume that the literate practices associated with the Fair are all traditional literacy practices, and that rural literacies are based only on traditional agrarian ways of knowing. Stereotypical imagery of rurality in popular culture that represent rural people, their literacies, and ways of knowing as grossly deficient and helplessly behind the times (Podber 2008) inform such assumptions. The stories I tell about the Fair challenge this characterization by describing the complexity and nuances of literate practices in a rural context. Rural citizens must (and do) enact literacies compatible with the frames of traditionalism, modernism, *and* postmodernism, both at the Fair and in everyday life. This recasting of the literate practices of rural people operationalizes Street's (1995, p. 134) caution about considerations of the plurality and locality of lit-eracies. Namely, an approach that says "here's a culture; here's a literacy; here's another culture; here's another literacy" leading only to a reified list of multiple cultures and their literacies. The New Literacy Group's characterization of literacies as "situated" contextualizes literacy in a way that resists such reification (Guerra 2004).

Literacy, says Gee (2007), is the mastery of a secondary discourse. Speaking of literacies in the plural, therefore, recognizes the fact that each of us masters many secondary discourses outside the immediate family or socializing group. Discourses are "'ways of recognizing and get-ting recognized' as certain sorts of 'whos' doing certain sorts of 'whats'" (Gee 2011, p. 178). While arguably "Fair participants" itself is a dis-course group, other smaller and more specific discourse groups can be seen at the Fair. In an article about the social nature of leisure involve-ment at the Grange Fair, Kyle and Chick call these "subworlds" or "social worlds" (2002). For example, social groups organized by the particular animals shown at the Fair are distinct subworlds or discourse groups. There is little crossover between these groups. If a child has entered swine in the Fair, the child and her family devotes their time at the Fair to that project. It is unlikely that the same family has entered steer. Thus, these two groups' social experiences of the Fair are not likely to intersect. The carnival ride operators make another more specific group, while tenters and recreational vehicle owners are another larger group. Members of each of these secondary discourse groups mark themselves as members and recognize other members by being certain kinds of "whos" doing certain kinds of "whats" that are valued or devalued within the group.

The Fair is a microcosm of contemporary rural life, in which literacies associated with traditionalism, modernism, and postmodernism are enacted by participants in ways that challenge not only an autonomous view of literacy, but misunderstandings about the exclusivity of traditional, agrarian discourses in rural life. Fair participants fully engage in twenty-first century, modern and postmodern literacy practices, and also enact literacies compatible with more traditional ways of understanding the world. Hybrids of traditionalism, modernism, and postmodernism, usually associated with particular time periods, coexist in the present. The Fair provides an interesting context for illustrating how all three "attitudes" (Peters and Lankshear 1996) are relevant in rural life. Each makes separate literacy demands that are performed and recognized by different groups of participants.

Traditionalism and Modernism at the Fair

In its rural community, the Fair is a big deal: 2,500 families camp in tents or RVs for the duration of the Fair. The green canvas military-style tent sites set on an asphalt slab are contested in divorces and left in wills. An early article in the *New York Times* compared the value of the tents to a rent-controlled apartment in New York City (Dullea 1994). Some families have returned to the same tenting spot for more than 80 years. Each year, local School Boards have fierce debates about whether to delay the opening of school until after Labor Day in order for students and families to be able to participate. When the dates conflict, many families opt to have their children miss the first week of school rather than miss the Fair. The conflict engages interested community members in debates about the assumed value of traditionalism to various groups. Is the Fair an event important enough for families to warrant delaying the first week of school for everyone? Why (or why not) is it important and to whom? The decisions of the four local School Boards in recent years have been divided by each district's relative rural setting. The two more rural districts more often delay the start of school and the two less rural districts elect not to delay the start of school. The Fair families from the nondelaying districts often interpret this decision as a statement about the educational and social value of the event in the lives of the district's rural residents. The debate itself has become a yearly mid-winter ritual in the county.

Along with the rituals surrounding the Fair and its opportunities for rest and socialization, one aspect of what makes the Fair so important to its participants is the opportunity to submit homemade products for judging. The display of homegrown fruits and vegetables, hand-crafted quilts, crocheted blankets, hand-sewn dresses, floral arrangements and handicrafts fills three enormous buildings. The opportunity for 4-H members to show and sell their poultry, rabbits, and livestock is a cumulating event in the 4-H year, and the arena is always filled to capacity. Even the casual observer can see that farming practices and homemaking are central to the Fair.

The literacies associated with these activities are traditional literacies enacted in the domain of and in service to the family or the family farm. The family farm challenges the separation of business and home that Max Weber proposed as the basis of capitalism in the modern economy (Bauman 2002) because decisions around the operation of the farm are not separate from home and family. The family farm breaks from modernism even while using modern technologies and working within the global economy. Still, work and home are one. Yet the connections of the family farm are deeper even than just work and home. Bauman also talks of the interconnectedness of the community into which the "homestead" is "tightly woven" (2002, p. 77). This is apparent at the Fair, too, in part because the barns, tenting, and RV areas *become* individual neighborhoods within the larger community of the Fair, complete with medical facilities, shopping, entertainment, a hair salon, and the "Grange Fair Jail." More importantly, the Fair fosters relationships with neighbors that are developed and extended in ways that ultimately support the sustenance and development of the participants' rural communities and livelihoods.

Agrarian, Gendered Literacies

Deborah Fink defines agrarianism as "the belief in the moral and economic primacy of farming over other industry," an idea foundational to the collective US ideological framework (Fink 1992, p. 11; Schell 2007). Idyllized rural farm life is central to America's national identity (Bell 2006) and is considered the very best way to be American. Within the discourse of agrarianism, farming is morally superior to other more urban pursuits, particularly those associated with the science and technology of modernism (Hogg 2007).

Agrarianism and traditionalism, however, are not synonymous because not all traditional discourses are agrarian. Thus, literacies associated with traditionalism are not necessarily agrarian. Take, for example, the letters that local residents write to the local newspaper about a wide variety of Fair-related controversies and topics. These letters are conversations about local lives. The authors engage in public debate about how they want to live with others in their communities, but the conversations do not necessarily pertain to farming. The Fair is also an important site for local and state political candidates to interact with voters in a way that is traditional by today's modern standards. Candidates personally distribute campaign materials, bid on baked goods, and roam the grounds with free balloons.

Agrarianism is marked by patriarchal ideas in which the role of women is to support the work of men and to maintain the home (Hogg 2007). The form and substance of women's support, however, is often underestimated and misunderstood (Walker and Sharpless 2006). The Fair appears to be a distinctly gendered space, particularly for those who camp or tent. In Kyle and Chick's ethnography about the social nature of the Fair as a leisure event, female participants characterized the task of meal preparations as providing enjoyable and important opportunities for women's social interactions. They also reported associating the cleanliness and aesthetic appearance of their tent with their sense of self (2002). The Fair as a gendered space is also illustrated when one looks at the entries submitted for judging. Women submit "Family Life" items such as canned goods, houseplants, or needlecrafts. Men claim a select few entries in homegrown produce and almost exclusively make up the tractor pull and "monster" truck entries. Youth livestock has more even representation between girls and boys, but is still dominated by boys. The women of the Grange produce a popular cookbook for sale at the Fair each year, operate an on-site library, greet visitors at the main gate, and complete secretarial tasks at "Headquarters." Four out of twelve Grange Fair Committee Officers are women. The women's work typically is supportive, perhaps less physical, and more anonymous when compared to the work of men. The gendering of the Fair reflects Hogg's observation about the uneven recognition given to men and women's contribution to rural community events:

> The texture of rural women's lives and contributions to the social good of
> their communities are often less visible to outsiders because community

work operates on microlevels and because it is unpaid labor—it is "women's work," the work of supporting the lives and actions of others. Yet it is the crucial work of cultural production and should be seen as an integral part of a critical, public pedagogy fostering literacies that connect the local, national, and global for a more synergistic relationship. (Hogg 2007, p. 121)

The culminating event that underscores the enactment of gender at the Fair is the Grange Fair Queen contest. The Fair stages its own beauty pageant to crown an unmarried young woman "Grange Fair Queen." The Grange Fair Queen makes appearances at various Fair events and represents the Grange Fair at the state-level Fair Queen competition. Each contestant is required to write an essay titled "What the Centre County Grange Fair Means to My Community" (Patrick 2008).

The essay is a modern genre, a standardized prompt assigned for the expressed purpose of evaluating the final product (and its author) in relation to others; yet in the case of the Grange Fair Queen contest, the essays foster traditional literacy practices. The essay prompt explicitly requires candidates to enact traditional discourses that reinforce connections between the Fair and the surrounding community. This is not a straightforward task. Many write about the role of the Fair as an important site for enacting traditions. One writer, quoted at length below, suggests that the Fair is an opportunity for the community to be a better version of itself:

It might seem silly the way we around here get such a stir out of cattle shows, classic Sunset ice cream, and country singers, but it's really much more than that. Fair week is time to slow down and enjoy life the way generations before them did. We all have those memories of pap and gram sitting on the tent porch keeping an eye on the kids running loose everywhere and still finding time to grumble about the scorching sun (or the pouring rain). Grange Fair is together time, it's family time. We all live together for one week as a united community just a call down the aisles away. Nobody's too busy to lend a hand shucking corn for supper or to come down and see the kids blow all their money playing darts. All year long, we live together but with our distance and then we reunited to the true huge family we've been for the last one hundred plus years. The Centre County Grange Fair is a celebration of Centre County life past and present. To this community, it means carrying on the legacy of the picnik.

The author's position highlights the hybridity of rural life. She acknowledges the tension between modernism and traditionalism by prefacing her opinions about family and connectedness as "silly." She also points to the distance between community members and suggests that the divide is due not to physical distance alone. Her phrase, "we live together but with our distance," highlights the irony of a modern community. Rather than living together with distance, the writer seems to prefer living as a "united community" the week of the Fair, in ways based on tradition, relationships, and reciprocity, perhaps indicating her nostalgic interpretation of the past.

The Fair Queen contestant also describes the "fragmentariness" of modernity in a rural community. Bauman describes the same characteristic in an urban setting: "Cast into the densely packed urban environment and bound to spend most of his or her life among strangers, the individual finds it difficult, perhaps impossible, to integrate experiences into a meaningful whole" (1992, p. 170). For Bauman, urban life is the embodiment of modernism. However, the Fair Queen contestant understands that modernism and traditionalism cannot be relegated to their respective urban and rural contexts. She understands the complexity of rural life.

Sandra Harding argues that we do not live in a modern world at all, but one that is traditional or premodern. She argues that modernity is an "illusion" (2008, p. 30) because the networks linking aspects of nature, culture, states and nations, and institutions make for "an incommensurable mix of nature, politics, and discourse" (p. 29). Modernity and its sciences represent a world of broken networks and "dismembered hybrids," not the world in which we live (p. 29). She points out that modernity itself was (and is) conceived by powerful Western men, so it follows that "the assignment of the rest of us to pre-modernity" is a prerequisite to the illusion of modernity (p. 45). The relative invisibility and powerlessness of rural citizens, both historically and in contemporary times, suggests that rural citizens, in addition to women and other marginalized groups, belong within the category of "the rest of us." This isn't to say that modernist discourses have no currency in contemporary rural lives. To the contrary, modernist discourses can be identified as easily in contemporary ruralities as postmodern or traditional. The point instead is that modernity's sleight of hand has Otherized rural life and people.

The essay writer also highlights the importance of traditionalism at the Fair. She describes a strong nostalgic connection to the Fair and its role in her family. For her, the Fair is a time to reenact the leisure activities of her previous generations while interacting with her grandparents in the present. This is a decidedly antimodern value. Attributes such as tradition, connectedness, and agrarianism, often associated with rural life and valued within traditional rural discourses, are incompatible with the project of modernism. Thus, rural life and its people are seen as incompatible with modernism. Attributes commonly associated with rural life (custom, tradition, and communal obligations) are those from which modernism seeks to liberate its citizens (Bauman 1992). It privileges all things new over old: innovation and progress are the ideal and turns on an enduring belief in the power of human reason. To resist the project of modernism deems one primitive, ignorant, and in need of conversion to the "gospel of reason" (p. 165). This suggests that the practice of representing rural people as deficient is deeply rooted in historically dominant ideologies of progress.

Modern Literacies

The beginning of modernism is marked by the transition from faith to reason, from God to man, from "being what one was [to] making oneself what one should be" (1992, p. xiii; emphasis in the original). Bauman (1992, p. 12) characterizes modernism as "a perception of the world." He means that modernity transcends its temporal meaning of "being of recent origin" (p. 163). This understanding of modernism as ideological rather than temporal is useful for rethinking contemporary ruralities and rural literacies because it underlines the ubiquitous capacity of modernism. It cannot be transcended or left behind and is a constant challenge to the privileging of traditionalism in rural life.

As much as the Fair is a celebration of community and tradition, it is also about science, technology, and profit. Especially profit. While there are buildings displaying quilts and tomatoes where a blue ribbon brings a payback of US$4, there is also a strong commercial presence at the Fair. There are three tiers of for-profit ventures. One group is entrepreneurial home-based businesses. In a building directly adjacent to the Family Life displays, one can find makeshift stores selling a variety of products for the home such as water purification systems, windows, vitamins, and cosmetics. Most of these are home-based businesses that challenge modernism's separation of home and work. Locally owned small businesses constitute the second tier: construction and landscaping companies, gift shops, and restaurants. Often the owner herself interacts with potential customers. Many of these second-tier type businesses promote themselves by "bidding up" the children's 4-H livestock projects to three or four times their market value, an act that is at once savvy business practice and supportive of the traditional agrarian practices of the county's youth.

While the first two tiers of business have always been present at the Fair, more recently, global corporations have entered its marketplace. On the outskirts of the main fairgrounds, nearer to the livestock barns, in an area still referred to as the "new part" because of its growth between 1991 and 1995, agribusiness dominates. Charismatic salesmen (and they are all men) "man" elaborate commercial displays seeking to take advantage of an unusual opportunity to interact face to face with their target-market demographic. The unusual result resembles a traditional farmers' market operated by multinational corporations. John Deer, Kubota, Chevrolet, AgCo, and New Holland assert a strong corporate presence. Although agribusiness dominates, Walmart, McDonalds, and Pepsico are also well represented. McDonalds sponsored the 2010 Fair's opening day and both Walmart and McDonalds appear on the 2010 sponsor list for the Grange Fair Queen pageant. These globalized corporations are not exclusively modern constructions, however. It is instead the conditions of postmodernism that enabled the companies to take their current form as transnational corporations, yet postmodernism provides the impetus for their critique (Jameson 2003).

Fair participants' interactions with these businesses require functional literacy. Essential to modernism, functional literacy suggests a generalizable set of "practical" literacy skills necessary for economic participation as an employee or consumer (Barton 2007, p. 192). In this sense, functional literacy supports only the ability of citizens to participate in the marketplace to work and spend; a select few will sell. The role of the school in this project is to prepare students to support the economic goals of the nation and success is measured accordingly (Holme 2004).

The literacy activities of Fair participants in 4-H are a second set of literacy practices situated across modernism, traditionalism, and postmodernism. 4-H is a youth organization, administered by the US Department of Agriculture, which uses a standardized curriculum emphasizing community leadership and economic innovation (http://www.4-h.org/about/4-h-history/). Its original purpose, dating back to the late nineteenth century, was to counteract the discouragement that rural agricultural college leaders perceived among rural youth (Marti 2008). The standardized curriculum emphasizing community leadership embraces putatively postmodern ideas about participatory democracy rather than the representational democracy of modernism. This aspect of 4-H, however, is not highlighted at the Fair. The 4-H activities at the Fair explicitly emphasize science and homemaking in accordance with the organizations' original purpose of improving agriculture (Marti 2008).

While one can visit commercial and educational displays to learn about the role of science in agriculture, modern technology is infused in the Fair. The Fair committee uses digital technology to promote the event via a professionally produced YouTube ad (see http://www.youtube.com/watch?v=foJ8pmvPvvs), offers wireless access for Fair visitors, and a "mid-way cam" that beams live streaming video to the web. The tents that start the week as an asphalt slab are soon transformed into modern homes equipped with microwaves, refrigerators, laptop computers, gaming systems, and satellite TV. Is the Fair a rural event?

The urban/rural binary itself is a modernist idea (Murdoch and Pratt 1993). Within poststructural theory, binaries are other devices that rule out multiplicity and difference in favor of order, coherence, and predictability (Davies 1994). The order of the terms is significant. The first term of a binary is the "normal," whereas the second is defined by its difference from the first or what the second term would be if it did not differ from the norm (Davies and Hunt 1994). Granted, the Fair is an unlikely challenge to the urban/rural dichotomy, but its deconstruction opens up possibilities for thinking differently about rural spaces and those who inhabit them (Helfenbein 2011).

Postmodernism

Postmodernism is an attitude of critique toward modern assumptions that what is new is better and that the past is the story of linear and cumulative cultural evolution culminating in Western civilization (Peters and Lankshear 1996). The "post" in postmodernism does not mean past. Instead, like modernism, postmodernism is an "attitude" (Peters and Lankshear 1996). Michael Bell explains that the relationship between the rural and "postrural" as used by Murdoch and Pratt (1993) is much like the relationship between modernism and postmodernism. In order to understand postmodernity as a category, one must first understand modernism as a material obviousness (Bell 2007), as a starting reality, or a position of default. The two are inextricably linked; postmodernism cannot be understood apart from modernism. The very task of postmodernism is to deconstruct modernism's truths: "Its job has been a sort of site-clearing operation," a dismantling of the "modern artifice" (Bauman 1992, p. ix). In education, postmodernism is suspect of definitive theories about teaching and learning made official by a particular kind of science and methodology based on the absolute truths of the modern artifice (O'Brien, Moje, and Stewart 2001). One example of a deconstructed "truth" is a definition of literacy that privileges print and ignores other modalities (ibid.). The diversity, rapidity, and fragmentariness of the postmodern world requires multiple literacies, *many* ways of making and understanding texts in many forms, including digital texts. Along with traditional and modern ways with texts, Fair participants enact a variety of postmodern literacies.

Postmodern Literacies at the Fair

Postmodernity is about innovation and experimentation with "conventional ways of framing experience" (Peters and Lankshear 1996, p. 18). In the context of the Fair, postmodern innovation and experimentation sometimes takes the form of digital texts. Most of the digital texts produced by Fair participants and self-published online appear to share the postmodern emphasis on creation, as opposed to an emphasis on the final product (Lather 1991). The digital texts accumulate to form a multivoiced history of the event because the tellings require neither advanced technological skills nor equipment. The result is a situated history contributed to and authorized by participants with the necessary literacies enabling them to tell their stories. Within postmodernism, the stories can be interpreted only in light of the authors' relationship (ibid.) with the Fair.

The technology used is not for scientific progress as it would be within modernism, but rather as a means of self-expression and critique. For example, one particularly dedicated individual designed a personal website detailing his Fair experience (http://www.personal.psu.edu/sdb12/gftent/). Other digital texts include participant-authored amateur video tours of the Fair, personal photographs posted on public photo-sharing websites (some as slide shows set to popular country music songs), visitors' blogs written both by lifelong Fair participants as well as those visiting the Fair for the first time, participant-authored reviews written on travel websites, and a wikipage. The Fair also has a presence on Facebook. The "official" group has 2,100 members. Participants express their anticipation of the Fair, share Fair memories, and post reviews of food and attractions. Alternately, there is a fledgling Facebook group with 30 members titled: *I Don't Understand the Very Strange Grange Fair and Encampment.* The group's description claims it is "for those confused by the hot, sweaty, traffic filled carny in Centre County" (http://www.facebook.com/group.php?gid=18828927137&v=info, March 27, 2011).

The critique of the Fair can also be seen in the editorial page of the local newspaper. Three issues dominate these letters: traffic, school scheduling, and the behavior of teenagers at the Fair. Residents of the town in which the Fair takes place voice their opinion about the significant traffic congestion. Residents of the four school districts debate whether the Fair is of great enough significance to delay the start of school until after Labor Day. Other writers express concern over the behavior of teenagers at the Fair, particularly those who frequent the two arcades on the grounds. These are traditional literate acts, residents engaging in public debate about how they will live their lives, but simultaneously are postmodern, critical deconstructions of the event.

Finally, the Fair committee itself is a postmodern construction because "regular" people are temporarily repositioned as powerful, high-level "government" officials in the context of the Fair. This is a fitting example of Bakhtin's (1984, p. 257) conceptualization of carnival because it is a space where participants can enjoy "a second life" when the established social order is up-ended. At the Fair, everyday life is disrupted and some citizens hold positions both powerful and prestigious. While the hierarchical structure of everyday government is reproduced at the Fair, the Fair officers have access to a governmental power unavailable to them in everyday life. The site becomes its own city, with Fair officials responsible for drafting and instituting an array of rules, regulations, and procedures. There is even an on-site "jail" to detain suspects. A select few at the top of the organization hold very powerful positions, a fact commonly noted by letter writers in the editorial pages. Although the unique possibilities offered to those in positions of authority at the Fair are a postmodern phenomenon, the Fair committee has a hierarchical structure like that of modern democracy.

Conclusion

Part of what makes the Fair such a rich site for deconstruction is its inherent tension between traditionalism and modernism. The response to the tension is itself postmodern. Is the Fair a "hot, sweaty, traffic filled, carny," or is it an event crucial to the constitution and maintenance of its rural community? Is it both or something else? Even as a lifelong Fair-goer, I cannot answer, but I am acutely aware of the endless contradictions that constitute the event that is so important to my family and to how I understand myself as a rural resident. While I have suggested here that the event is useful and important (as opposed to a traffic-snarling carny), I don't read the Fair as a nostalgic statement about the value of the rural idyll. The Fair is an apt metaphor for rural life and its literacies: contradictory, complex, strange, and familiar.

The Fair exemplifies the struggle in rural communities between modern and traditional, between the jaded and the charmed. One element on modernity's agenda is the substitution of order for local tradition (Bauman 1992) and the Fair only highlights the questions already in play about these positions. One Grange Fair Queen essayist writes, "My roots dip deep into the traditions of the Grange Fair." And another, "And I feel, we *are* the Grange Fair." As a community, are *we* (modernism's unified "we") modern or are *we* traditional? Are we connected or are we separated? Deconstructing the Fair suggests that we are both, and that we use postmodern literacies to critique, promote, and share our points of view.

The literacy story told here is a "counternarrative" about the rural people who take part in the Fair. It is a story that I hope counters the everyday narratives within which rural life and people are represented as either exemplars of a better and simpler American life or as undesirable (and illiterate) relics of a past better off forgotten. Either story manipulates the public into imagining that there exists a set of cultural ideas common to the nation as a whole (Peters and Lankshear 1996). Nonetheless, official narratives about rural people and communities are powerful and pervasive. They often turn on discourses of lack, where rural literacies and literate practices and rural people themselves are parochial and agrarian (Donehower et al. 2007). Longstanding "truths" about rural life and rural people such as these have supported our American nation's identity since its founding (Bell 2006). Ideas about rural life lie at the very center of "our" collective national identity—if there is one.

In contrast to constructions of rural life as deficient, in other stories rural life is an idyll. It is noble, patriotic, and deeply desirable (see Howley, Eppley, and Howley in press). David Bell characterizes the rural idyll as a "receptacle for national identity—a symbolic site for shoring up what it means to be [American]" (Bell 2006, p. 151). It is manufactured for the distinct purpose of producing national identity (ibid.). Traditional literacies that are about connections and simplicity and modern literacies that are about functioning economically, both complement the rural idyll. Postmodern literacies, however, with an emphasis on using literacy as a tool to deconstruct and critique, where literacies help citizens determine how they want to live together, complicate taken-for-granted truths about how we understand rural people and rural life. Not any one kind of literacy is privileged in rural lives.

My counternarrative about the Fair is an example of Lyotard's "little stories," told by individuals and groups who are misrepresented, silenced, ignored, or forgotten in the official narratives. This little story challenges the idea that contemporary rural life is traditional or even modern, but rather is constituted by traditional, modern, *and* postmodern ways of understanding and acting in the world. The postmodern is as relevant as the traditional or modern. The corresponding literate practices of rural citizens at the Fair suggest a model for literacy instruction in rural schools in which the purpose of schooling is not to ensure economic success, to replicate the current structures and relationships of the community, or to deconstruct and reject out of hand either modernism or tradition. Rather, Fair participants demonstrate that traditional literacy practices were never displaced by modernism's ideas about what counts as literacy in rural communities, and postmodern literacy practices enable participants to critique their communities and communicate with others about its offerings and limitations.

Note

1. Used without the hyphen to signal the deconstruction versus the continuation of modernism.

References

Anstey, M., 2008, "Postmodern Picturebook as Artefact: Developing Tools for an Archaeological Dig," in L. Sipe and S. Pantaleo (eds.), *Postmodern Picturebooks: Play, Parody, and Self-referentiality*, Taylor & Francis, New York.

Bakhtin, M., 1984, *Problems of Dostoyevsky's Poetics*, Indiana University Press, Bloomington, IN.

Barton, D., 2007, *Literacy: An Introduction to the Ecology of Written Language*, Blackwell, Malden, MA.

Bauman, Z., 1992, *Intimations of Postmodernity*, Routledge, London.

———, 2002, *Society under Siege*, Polity Books, Cambridge, UK.

Bell, D., 2006, "Variations on the Rural Idyll," in P. Cloke, T. Marsden, and P. Mooney (eds.), *Handbook of Rural Studies*, Sage, London.

Bell, M., 2007, "The Two-ness of Rural Life and the Ends of Rural Scholarship," *Journal of Rural Studies*, vol. 23: 402–415.

Collins, J. and R. Blot, 2003, *Literacy and Literacies: Texts, Power, and Identity*, Cambridge University Press, Cambridge.

Davies, B., 1994, *Poststructural Theory and Classroom Practice*, Deakin University Press, Geelong.

———, 2000, *A Body of Writing: 1990–1999*, Alta Mira Press, Walnut Creek, CA.

Davies, B and R. Hunt, 1994, "Classroom Competencies and Marginal Positionings," *British Journal of Sociology of Education*, vol. 15, no. 3: 389–408.

Donehower, K., 2007, "Rhetorics and Realities: The History and Effect of Stereotypes about Rural Literacies," in K. Donehower, C. Hogg, and E. Schell (eds.), *Rural Literacies*, Southern Illinois University Press, Carbondale.

Donehower, K., C. Hogg, and E. Schell (eds.), 2007, *Rural Literacies,* Southern Illinois University Press, Carbondale.

Dudley-Marling, C., 2011, "The Trouble with 'Struggling Readers,'" *Language Arts,* vol. 23, no. 1: 1–7.

Dullea, G., 1994, "Same Tent, Same Joy, Every Year," *New York Times,* September 1.

Edmondson, J., 2003, *Prairie Town,* Rowman & Littlefield, New York.

Fink, D., 1992, *Agrarian Women: Wives and Mothers in Rural Nebraska, 1880–1940,* University of North Carolina, Chapel Hill.

Gee, J., 2007, *What Video Games Have to Teach Us about Learning and Literacy,* Macmillan, New York.

————, 2011, *How to Do Discourse Analysis: A Toolkit,* Routledge, New York.

The Grange Fair: An American Tradition, 2005, PBS Plus documentary, Penn State Public Broadcasting, http://wpsu.org/grangefair/.

Guerra, J. 2004, "Putting Literacy in Its Place: Nomadic Consciousness and the Practice of Transcultural Repositioning," in C. Gutierrez-Jones (ed.), *Rebellious Reading: The Dynamis of Chicana/o Cultural Literacy,* Center for Chicana/o Studies, University of California at Santa Barbara, Santa Barbara, CA.

Harding, S., 2008, *Sciences from Below: Feminisms, Postcolonialities, and Modernities,* Duke University Press, Durham, NC.

Heath, S., 1983, *Ways with Words: Language, Life, and Work in Communities and Classrooms,* Cambridge University Press, New York.

Helfenbein, R., 2011, "The Urbanization of Everything: Thoughts on Globalization and Education," in S. Tozer, B. Gallegos, A. Henry, M. Greiner, and P. Price (eds.), *Handbook of Research in the Social Foundations of Education,* Routledge, New York.

Hogg, C., 2007, "Beyond Agrarianism: Toward a Critical Pedagogy of Place," in K. Donehower, C. Hogg, and E. Schell (eds.), *Rural Literacies,* Southern Illinois University Press, Carbondale.

Holme, R., 2004, *Literacy: An Introduction,* Edinburgh University Press, Edinburgh.

Howley, A., K. Eppley, and M. Howley, forthcoming, "Restless Settlers Push West: Settled Farmers Face Hardships," in J. Williams (ed.), *(Re)Constructing Memory: School Textbooks, Identity, and the Pedagogies and Politics of Imagining Community,* Sense, Boston.

Jameson, F., 2003, *Postmodernism: Or, the Cultural Logic of Late Capitalism,* Duke University Press, Durham, NC.

Kyle, G. and G. Chick, 2002, "The Social Nature of Leisure Involvement," *Journal of Leisure Research,* vol. 34, no. 4: 426–448.

Lather, P., 1991, *Getting Smart: Feminist Research and Pedagogy with/in the Postmodern,* Routledge, New York.

Marti, D., 2008, "Agricultural Fairs and Expositions," in H. Sheumaker and S. Wajda (eds.), *Material Culture in America: Understanding Everyday Life,* Santa Barbara, ABC-CLIO, CA.

Murdoch, J. and A. Pratt, 1993, "Rural Studies: Modernism, Postmodernism and the 'Post-rural,'" *Journal of Rural Studies,* vol. 9, no. 4: 411–427.

New London Group, 1996, "A Pedagogy of Multiliteracies: Designing Social Future," *Harvard Educational Review,* vol. 66: 60–92.

O'Brien, D., E. Moje, and R. Stewart, 2001, "Exploring the Context of Secondary Literacy: Literacy in People's Everyday School Lives," in E. Moje and D. O'Brien (eds.), *Constructions of Literacy: Studies of Teaching and Learning In and Out of Secondary Schools*, Lawrence Erlbaum, Mahwah, NJ.

Patrick, D., 2008, "Grange Fair Queen to Hand Off Crown," *Centre Daily Times*, August 10.

Peters, M. and C. Lankshear, 1996, "Postmodern Counternarratives," in H. Giroux, C. Lankshear, P. McLaren, and M. Peters (eds.), *Counternarratives: Cultural Studies and Critical Pedagogies in Postmodern Spaces*, Routledge, New York.

Podber, J., 2008, "Television's Arrival in the Appalachian Mountains of the USA: An Oral History," *Media History*, vol. 14, no. 1: 35–52.

Schell, E., 2007, "The Rhetorics of the Farm Crisis: Toward Alternative Agrarian Literacies in a Globalized World," in K. Donehower, C. Hogg, and E. Schell (eds.), *Rural Literacies*, Southern Illinois University Press, Carbondale.

Street, B., 1984, *Literacy in Theory and Practice*, Cambridge University Press, New York.

———, 1995, *Social Literacies: Critical Approaches to Literacy in Development, Ethnography and Education*, Addison Wesley, New York.

Walker, M. and R. Sharpless, 2006, *Work, Family, and Faith: Rural Southern Women in the Twentieth Century*, University of Missouri Press, Columbia, Missouri.

CHAPTER 5

Another Way to Read "The Rural": A *Bricolage* of Maths Education

Craig Howley

I've got some explaining to do, at least to myself, and this venue is my only chance. Here's the provocation: Secondary teachers of "advanced maths" (algebra, geometry, trigonometry, and calculus) *everywhere* have learned the mantra that "math[s] is everywhere" (Google the phrase to retrieve the evidence), but very few of them bring that everywhere-maths into the rural classroom, as we discovered in the process of conducting a recent study (Howley, Showalter, Howley, Howley, Klein, and Johnson 2011). Now, *everywhere* does not interest me much, except for the rural somewhere, which is, however, a lot like the actual and variable somewheres flagged as "everywhere" insofar as *there, too,* teachers of advanced maths seldom make such connections.

It's a conundrum, or a permanent irony, this everywhere that is really nowhere for such teachers, but one far more for me, apparently, than for them. Because of my illusions: for instance, I *would* specifically like to see a form of maths instruction in *rural* schools that cultivated wide and deep engagement with *rural place* (not just the particular place, but also the idea of rural place as against, or as compared to, other places; and, more importantly, *up to something else*).

I stress to readers that these are my illusions, and that such tenuousness requires the extended explanation that follows. Too often in this field we seem to shout: "I'm right! We're right! Here's the research that proves it." The only thing that makes such hubris applicable is the misguided power of the state. I've had enough of it.

My position is unique, and this uniqueness disqualifies it as a general plan—but at the same time it draws the position into a set of variabilities as wide as those that characterize rural places. If this concept is too difficult to understand, that is because education is itself—thank goodness—too difficult to understand fully, ever. Further, I'd suggest that the variabilities of local educational actors, such as those my illusions exhibit, are part of the place basis (or, more aptly, to follow David Gruenewald and Gregory Smith [2008], place *consciousness*) essential to the form of schooling and teaching that honor and sustain rural place. Place is essential, but so is the consciousness of educators. We are not the machines that the state would prefer; we are teachers.

Backfilling

Because many or some readers of this volume may find the presence of a chapter on maths mysterious or confusing, I offer a brief introduction to mathematics as a sort of literacy.

What is maths? Conventionally, mathematics is the science of space and number. The literate mind can glaze over with such a definition: science, space, number; so what? And typically, starting in elementary school, we learn rules and definitions that supposedly apply to this science. Learn the definitions and rules, and, in the United States (Stigler & Hiebert 1999), knowledge of math occurs, presto! Many, many humans find this presentation boring, abstract, and useless. It seems designed to produce ignorance.

Some maths educators, however, attempt a justification with the parallel construct *numeracy*. Such a construct is foolish, in my view, since the wide adaptability of *literacy* already fits easily: *maths literacy*. And this formulation is not what I'm after, fine enough as it might be for its purposes.

A very few maths educators, more sensibly and modestly and dangerously, adopt the Freirean outlook and write about using maths to read the world (Gutstein 2006). Oh? Maths (*especially* school maths) should have a functional and even political purpose? This is an outlook that makes public sense of school maths, at last. In this formulation, maths is a tool for understanding, much *like* reading, but not reading. More critically, it's not a knowledge about something, but a knowledge in use at present and to use in future. It's not something to forget.

In classical terms, my vision of maths instruction (and perhaps Rico Gutstein's too) is more a *knowledge how* and not so much *knowledge what*. This simple distinction, if applied widely, would alter the whole game of school maths.

In rural terms, this *maths-how* would engage issues of rural place for the benefit of rural place. Students would, with math, read their rural world, and come to new understandings of it and perhaps change it to a certain extent—and they would, prospectively, in the end, retain more math as students and as adults. Far fewer people would come away from the experience hating maths. These are prospective and hypothetical claims, not firm assertions, but many accounts of project-based learning (e.g., Howley et al. 2011; Lewicki 2010; Shelton 2005; Sobel 2004) show students making this claim again and again. I'm more convinced by such testimony than I am by the small overall differences in test scores on which the US What Works Clearinghouse initiative makes its judgments (see http://ies.ed.gov/ncee/wwc/).

My faith in imagination suggests that all of maths through calculus, with the entirely familiar "content" on view in current textbooks, could be taught in this way. This sort of instruction would make maths as dangerous to oppression, consumerism, and injustice as critical literacy.[1]

It's often seemed to me, observing school maths instruction and reading about it as conventionally practiced, that the point of the entire enterprise is to produce several hundred brilliant mathematicians; after all, no more than several hundred PhDs are awarded to US citizens each year (Snyder and Dillow 2011). The remaining millions are (in this fantasy) so much detritus.[2] It's an extreme and perhaps unfair characterization, but it nonetheless captures something of the prevailing folly. It explains why so very, very many people actively hate maths. It's not, in this view, an accident.

Perhaps, even if you do hate maths, you can intuit, even on such a slender basis as the forgoing discussion, the fact that math *is* a species of literacy. I hope so. It should be clear, at any rate, that maths is more, and should in schools be more, than a sentence of indefinite confinement to boring and meaningless calculation resulting not only in incompetence but hatred.

One more thing. Readers should *not* regard this chapter as the confession of an insider. I'm a maths outsider, and in particular on account of my rural commitments. I'm not a certified maths teacher or a maths educator, though I have taught maths and maths students in higher education (where certification is not an issue in the United States; the story is too lengthy to repeat). I do appreciate maths, finding it both uncommonly beautiful and uncommonly useful.

My Recent Maths Education

Given this final confession, narrated above, it was quite an irony that the US National Science Foundation should have sanctioned not only my participation in one of their maths education efforts, but my (co) direction of the research work of that effort. The overall effort, which had a key rural focus, also enrolled 3 cohorts of 15 doctoral students in a rural maths education program of our own design. Those 45 students certainly heard the rural story as part of their experience with us, which included three courses devoted entirely to rural issues; and they reported to our evaluators that what they learned about rural community was the most surprising part of their total experience (St. John, Helms, and Smith 2008).

We also operated a research initiative, which is where my primary responsibilities lay, though I did some teaching as well. We invited colleagues to submit manuscripts and proposals for a Working Papers series that adhered to the Center's research commitments as presented in our theoretical framework (ACCLAIM 2002). We also undertook studies by the Center's faculty and students, published an online magazine, and created an Occasional Paper series that drew their substance from events held by the Center (for the fully archived work, see https://sites.google.com/site/acclaimruralmath/). Overall, we published over 100 research-based documents, many in peer-reviewed venues.

Thinking of Math(s) Education and Intellectual Work(s)

So for the past decade I've been watching people who *think math*: our students and our maths educators and university mathematician colleagues from the United States. I've enjoyed the sight. I want to explain the source and meaning of this enjoyment, however.

As mentioned above, perhaps 80 percent of my nonmaths colleagues in academe (nearly all in education) find maths distasteful, even revolting. My maths education colleagues, however, understand this state of affairs as a challenge: one must take such distaste and revulsion—all too common among the wide public—seriously. At a deep level, however, the complaints of the thoughtfully math-averse resemble those voiced recently by Paul Ernest (philosopher of maths education) and Ole Skovsmose (critical maths educator) in Ernest's *Philosophy of Mathematics Education Journal* (Ernest 2010; Skovsmose 2010). Because I'm concerned that people like maths as well as use it, this odd similarity of positions, especially from those I'm disposed to regard as like-minded, troubles me and so I offer a refutation not so much for the critical maths educators, but for educators concerned with literacy in general. My refutation may seem old-fashioned or culturally conservative. So be it.

The Skovsmose Position

In simplistic form, the fundamental argument of Ernest and Skovsmose is that maths (1) is something people do; (2) people do most eagerly what they're paid to do, and, hence, (3) big companies have achieved ugly, momentous, and evil things with math. I agree that these claims should constitute a truth universally acknowledged. But, of course, they're not popularly acknowledged, and they remain instead a truth widely unacknowledged among educators and in the general public.

Skovsmose (2010, pp. 9–10) hazarded a further claim, however, and this is the one that troubles me: "Mathematics has no nature that ensures that applications of mathematics will be for the sake of everybody". Perhaps against all reason, and in the throes of an unqualified and nonrational passion, I resist Skovsmose's claim for ethical, cultural, educational, and even *pedagogical* reasons.

The Refutation

First, observe that the assertion applies equally to *every* intellectual endeavor (or "discipline") and not only to mathematics. But maybe maths is just more important; Skovsmose (1994) has written previously, for instance, about maths' "formatting power," the power to impose rules and structures on modernist reality, formatting the contemporary world as we mistakenly imagine knowing it through the corporatized maths ("intellectual property") prevalent in industrially standardized consumer goods and corporate services, and in professionally disciplined (standardized) ways of doing business (cf. Foucault 1979). But one can object that natural language, via quite brilliant advertising, formats minds even *more* formidably and flexibly than mathematics and with equally objectionable results. It seems, at any rate, that there is more than one baby and more than one devil in this bathwater.

Second, maths is not only something people do, though it is surely that, but something people create in the doing of it (e.g., *mathematical works*), and which *works* their authors bequeath to an interested public (however narrow or wide, and even if kept perversely narrow by schools, corporate secrecy, and other forms of pride, vanity, and greed). The public for mathematical proofs and for the dissertations of heavily schooled mathematicians is admittedly many orders of magnitude more narrow than for the novels of Jane Austen. But such works exist and persist; and they are available more or less permanently to minds that find their way to them. Certainly, one can esteem works beyond reason (fetishizing an

approved canon, for instance). But to dismiss the works as silly adorn-
ments (e.g., Ernest 2010, p. 8) is to drown the babies in the bathwater
before ever throwing it out!

Third, we are nonetheless left to worry about the relationship between
all these works (and not only in mathematics), and the actions and devils
that make (and one might argue) attempt to unmake them, in the sense
of evacuating their evident, apparent, or real value in hubris, vanity, or
greed. Shall we blame Austen's novel *Persuasion* for the advertising pollution of the twentieth and twenty-first centuries (i.e., persuasion = advertising)? Shall we, as Tolstoy did, blame the *Kreutzer Sonata* (Beethoven)
for inflaming unworthy passions? Shall we blame the *General Theory of
Relativity* for nuclear pollution?

I don't think so. If wondrous or miraculous intellectual works harbor
no necessary good, we educators, I'm afraid, need to ask why we bother
with them and their meanings, and we ought to think up some other
good to occupy our time instead; to the barricades, indeed! But perhaps
education is not about such works, such human legacies, at all. Perhaps
reading the world requires that we, and our students, give consideration
mostly to the evils that beset the world. If that's the case, yes, I do want
a different occupation. My injunction to refashion school math as more
useful, therefore, does not mean abandoning Euclid (the beautiful); it
means incorporating more utility *and* more beauty. Bread and roses.

I'm not arguing the canon of any particular authority, either. Let in
all the good and wondrous work of both high and low origin. And let's
not be too quick to repudiate any of them on the basis of such nuanced
objections as Tolstoy's (in the end he himself repudiated *Anna Karenina*).
I'll keep my Euclid and my *Karenina*. Neither of them, nor their work,
knew Monsanto (founded in 1901). But we can and should also look at
the damage that Monsanto is doing to the local groundwater and to the
nature and purposes of agriculture.

Such work and such works seem, and have always seemed to humans,
a real reason to hope for something better in life. The good seems inherent, generative, and even necessary. What I mean by "real reason" is
evidence: something better has a proven habit of emerging even in evil
circumstances, and the wondrous works themselves are part of that evidence, and they engage and challenge the evil variously.[3]

Though I seem to be keeping my humanism as well as human works,
it's not a species of mystical faith *chez moi*. If we subsequently find that
someone or some outfit has put even good works to bad purpose, whose
fault is that? Language? Mathematics? Human essence? It's easy to slide
into a condemnation of human nature and to long for a posthuman world

not plagued by human intellect, human passions, or humans at all. That slide also seems inappropriate for teachers and for the institution of teaching itself. In short, to the same extent as with reading and writing (broadly understood), rural people and their common purposes need maths to enable and sustain their inquiries, actions, and spirits. Conventional and generic approaches to school maths don't work to this end: they mean to do otherwise, entirely. The discussion next considers why.

The Evil in Maths Education: Four Shibboleths

I usually tell my students that thinking is writing (e.g., Barzun, 2001; Mitchell 1973). In general, I want them to think more thoughtfully, and writing, I argue, enables that greater care. Thoughtful action is a good thing too—but it's far more difficult because, unlike a written draft, one cannot actually retract or revise the action (Arendt 1958). To be good, it has to be right the first time, and it often isn't.

But then, with respect to my claim about writing, I wonder about mathematics. Mathematics alters natural language because its project is the elimination or isolation of ambiguity. Its "language" is rarified and the rarified usage helps to manipulate idealized mathematical objects, and with logic freer of fault than any. In the end I conclude that writing is also important to mathematical thinking; proofs (as with Euclid) must be written to exhibit the famed logic; without the writing (as with the Fermat omission), there is no proof.

More ambiguously, though, I'm unclear what the "text" (or subtext) of mathematics might be when one "reads" *it* as part of the world.[4] Because of the great misuses to which mathematics is subject, some observers, of course, suspect the text and subtext alike to be power, mastery, dominion, or possibly hegemony, somewhat as in Walkerdine's fine exposition (1988). This view of the (sub)text of mathematics leads back to the condemnation of an unchangeable and evil human nature that the world is better off without. My ecology isn't so "deep."

So, again, what is mathematics? The short and stupid answer, again, is this: the science of number and space. But it gets even stupider: for school-bound youngsters, *maths* is whatever happens in maths class. They're just "reading" their world and making the obvious—the logical—conclusion. So do we all.

In this case, though, this reality means that what maths teachers typically do is what nearly the entire population concludes must be maths. How strange is that? *School maths* thus differs from the mathematics claimed by mathematicians, just as do the university disciplines associated with all school subjects. History's not "history," science isn't "science," and artfulness too rarely besets "language arts." All of this, too, is a durable irony.

Shibboleths of the Maths Tribe

Relevant to concern for rural place, how does this sad want in *school maths* (and the institution of schooling generally) play out? I propose four shibboleths to characterize such practice in maths education. If you were a university professor in mathematics ("mathematician") or in mathematics education ("maths educator") you would likely (but not certainly) harbor similar assumptions relevant to school math; I call them shibboleths because they identify members of the tribe:

1. Mathematics is basically *the same everywhere* (this part is axiomatic), and corollary to the axiom, the mathematics to be taught is also the same everywhere.
2. Maths instruction is conducted in better and worse ways, but *best practice is basically the same everywhere.*
3. National standards codify best practice *everywhere* in the applicable nation; and all such standards converge (see 1 and 2).
4. One studies maths instruction in rural schools only to help teachers there conform better to *universally best* practice.

The points may overstate a consensus, but the notion that maths is universally true wins wide approval, as does the notion that the maths to be taught is, at base, the same everywhere (for example, Hoffert 2009; Kantner 2008; Krober 1991; Smith 2002; Stanic and Goodson 1987). Best practice is a time-honored formula and quest in "education science" and among conservative, psychologically oriented "education research scientists" (Egan 2002). The shibboleths perhaps also characterize a dominant "platonic" or "formalist" approach to mathematics (see Ernest 1998, for a full discussion).

I'm inclined, however, not to attribute the status quo to a high-minded devotion to Platonism, but to devotion, at this late hour, to long habit, and especially in the United States, want of well-informed critique. The corollaries are suspicious: for instance, those hostile to bilingual education have argued that because "maths is a universal language," students whose native languages are not English ought not to have much trouble learning maths *in English*! Apparently, mathematicians and maths educators can reach such a conclusion through failure to understand that schooling, and teaching itself, operates via natural language. How's that for illogic?[5]

The fourth of these advertised shibboleths, the one that actually uses the word "rural," has a comparatively strong empirical warrant: one of our studies (Howley, Howley, and Huber 2005) used discourse analysis to examine the *prescriptive literature* directed at mathematics instruction in rural schools. That literature characterized rural schools as mathematically deficient and in need of improvement along the lines of the prevailing notions of universally best practice, as specified, for instance, by national US standards (e.g., NCTM 2000). The main challenge, according to most of the works reviewed, was the nature of the rural deficiencies that got in the way of realizing the prevailing standards of best practice.[6] Most disturbing, however, this literature provided almost no empirical basis for *any* of the prescriptions on offer to US rural schools and teachers. I wrote one of the works exhibiting this second failing (Childers and Howley 1994): the dilemma that this chapter considers belongs to me too, and mathematically speaking, I may be at a particular disadvantage when it comes to "seeing the math." A maths acolyte in high school, I later taught "low-level" maths in a college (and much enjoyed the work), and now happily use mathematics in my own (quantitative) research program and related collaborations with students. But I've never had a maths pedagogy course, and my undergraduate degree is in English and Comparative Literature and not in mathematics education.

Shibboleths of the Rural Tribe

An alternative set of shibboleths perhaps identifies another tribe relevant to this discussion: the rural tribe. Here they are: (1) "rural" refers to an ensemble of meanings and commitments related to land ethic (e.g., Leopold 1949); (2) cosmopolitan (or "metropolitan," if you prefer) cultural hegemony opposes rural meanings, and, in fact, undermines land ethic on a planetary scale (Theobald 2009; Williams 1973; but cf. Appiah 2006); (3) rural meanings and commitments are essential to human and planetary survival; and (4) rural sorts of education (and schooling) are, therefore, also essential to human and planetary survival.

Such assumptions would surely constitute an unusual imposition on the maths education one knows well and loves to hate, but perhaps an imposition no more unusual or intolerable than those of critical theory (see, e.g., Gutstein 2006) or ethnomathematics (D'Ambrosio 1990)— both of which outlooks *are* well represented in maths education. An agenda for mathematics education that honored rural assumptions similar to those in these alternative shibboleths would arguably refocus educational purpose off the corporatist version of (standardized) individualism and onto a more communitarian locally attentive purpose.

Conversations with rural people convince me that such a maths education would be less strange to them than an urban-oriented critical pedagogy or a baffling ethnomathematics, and more welcome than the prevailing decontextualized, useless one. It *would* be useful—instead of irrelevant. It *would* help keep kids closer to home—instead of luring them to escape.

Rural Maths Teachers without Ideological Borders

In the United States at any rate, local schools are less local on account of the increasingly centralized political control of schooling by the state's agenda informed so strongly by corporate design. It's no wonder local rural schools don't embrace the local mission—they are kept overbusy, desperately distracted with engaging, and to some extent foiling, the corporate agenda. Teach twenty-first-century skills! Buy computers! Render your accounts! The state distracts rural schools from the mission of sustaining rural communities, and often studiously (see DeYoung 1995, for an example).

Still, one might look on the bright side and imagine *Maths Teachers with Rural Portfolio*. We actually have an example of such a person, though he teaches at an engineering school: Ron Eglash, currently at Rensselaer Polytechnic Institute.

Eglash has been working with indigenous (and largely rural) students and educators across the world to find and develop, as curriculum, local cultural practices that embed mathematical ideas (fractal village plans in Africa, for instance). Currently, he is turning his efforts to developing *high school* curriculum (a much-needed project, as the opening of this chapter asserts).

Some time ago, Ron wrote a paper (*Black Chaos, White Trash* 2004) for one of our research symposia. Attendees were somewhat stunned by the demonstration: stunned into *appreciation*. This sort of activity supplies local content for "advanced math," and such content is desperately needed, one might say, *everywhere*. Indeed, all else equal, such content would predictably operate, if indirectly, to sustain rural community. All is hardly equal, though, under current circumstances. In any case, other instances of local grasp of content (among maths educators—maths education professors) exist.

Marta Civil (2006), for instance, has studied Mexican American families and found lots of maths in evidence around houses and workshops, and she's detailed the maths in a gardening project in a magazine for teachers (Civil and Khan 2001). Marta's work does not focus on "advanced" high school math, but others' does. Rico Gutstein, previously mentioned, works with high school students in Chicago, applying statistics and other maths techniques to social and political issues. His students make presentations of their findings and sometimes influence action. Real-life examples of alternatives to the conventional, corporatist mode are more numerous than one might suspect, in short. Rural examples in mathematics, perhaps not so much.

One has to grasp the transgressions in play to appreciate why such rural work is so very difficult. The shibboleths of the maths tribe, given previously, explain much. But even when rural phenomena are forced into the standard neutral and placeless curriculum, the point of the instruction remains the production of high test scores, and the conscription of foot soldiers for global economic combat. Politicians and corporate leaders take the scores as warranting mathematics skill relevant to global economic competition. And that's the real mission of the standard program. A communitarian instead of a corporatist mission would require something very different from the public and from the education profession: a cultural and political sea change of a magnitude that cannot be planned.

The Justice of Sustaining Rural Communities

The experience of living rurally is, of course, not some romantic idyll disconnected from corporate depredation, race and class struggle, and injustices of all stripes. *It, too, is life.* But in some accounts, a rural communitarian outlook is inherently conservative; for instance, because of its skepticism of progress, internationalism, and—in some accounts—acknowledgment of the role of exclusion in community identity. In the United States, progressive educators—and the "liberal" public generally—regard rural places as swamps of ignorance, backwardness, and exclusion. They throw up their hands and turn their minds elsewhere, logically enough to problems in their own large backyards. Thus, though I read critical theory—and critical pedagogy—and find it useful and meaningful, it's a bad fit, taken literally, in the rural places I know.

My own experience is with white, "impoverished" Appalachian communities, and I thus grasp the difference between (1) a project to sustain rural community and (2) one that first confronts the world's prevalent injustice manifest in huge cities (where I also lived for six years when young). The outlook is inherently less brash and combative, more neighborly, and such an outlook must itself seem foreign to an urbanized world.

Rural existence is indeed life: but few observers outside its own imaginary realm care much about its struggles or the qualities that make those struggles different from urban ones. They don't understand them and they don't want to understand them. I've yet to encounter in my career an urban educator who *already* exhibits an appreciation either of rural reality or of its neglect by an urbanized world. Over and over I've been asked the rhetorical question: "What's so special about rural anyway? Aren't its problems those of poverty, *just like urban ones?*" The interlocutors don't take "no" for an answer: they are convinced that rural is some place to escape. Sustain rural places? *You must be a mad romantic.*

Nonetheless, the rural difference *is* the prior social justice issue if one is rural like me and many of my colleagues and neighbors. Hannah Arendt (1958) took the same position on being Jewish: when they come for you because they think you're Jewish, you'd better recognize the fact. They have been coming for rural people and rural resources for a very long time. Rural people understand this fact and these processes in their bones.

In the peculiar US circumstance, as I have argued, it seems unwise to abandon the libertory possibilities of mathematics (or philosophy, literature, language learning, "fine" art, theology, opera, and jazz) simply over a deeply realized regret for the misuse to which immense corporate power subjects them all worldwide, in the name of making the poor poorer and the rich so very much richer. If we regard intellect itself as corporate property, we're in trouble, and perhaps more so in the rural United States than elsewhere, as I explain next.

The Obscurity of Mathematics in the US Lifeworld

I'd like to see rural places flourish largely on their own terms, and in a far more egalitarian mode than currently prevails in the United States. Although such an aspiration is a bit more than a pipe dream and rather less than a utopian scheme, that aspiration is the apparent locale for "rural maths education." It seems, admittedly, a crazy aspiration given the norms of curriculum and instruction, not to mention those of the anti-intellectual American culture; again, it has something in common with critical theory and critical pedagogy even as its outrage and its presenting issues are fundamentally different from those that preoccupy critical pedagogy: *rural.*[7] Ron Eglash, Rico Gutstein, and Marta Civil are not going to turn this situation around in maths education, however, because they cannot be everywhere and because, could they be everywhere, their being everywhere would displace those already there; 99.9 percent of the work necessarily remains the province of others. It has to. Otherwise, it's not worth doing.

The idea that rural schools have a mission in the defense of rural places is, however, one that many rural teachers and administrators have yet to grasp (Burnell 2003; Carr and Kefalas 2009; Corbett 2007; DeYoung 1995; Theobald 1997). They've been roundly colonized by their professional training.

The root problem is not the tests, nor even the standardization they suggest and embody, but something far worse: a national US regime founded on greed and disregard of intellect, a combination simultaneously hostile to thoughtfulness and to rural locality, as Wendell Berry has noted repeatedly for decades (e.g., Berry 2010, 1990, 1977). Cultivating hostility to *testing* is thus an apposite distraction into which the state might happily lead educators and the public: the hostility misses the point by a margin sufficiently wide and safe for those managing the regime. And it's a good object of hatred (for such purpose): it's harmlessly but passionately distracting. It traps educators coming and going.

In schools with merely average sorts of students, the general consensus among educators is that no time remains for "fun" or "creative teaching" (see Saltman and Gabbard 2003, for a full account of the operative stringencies). We can't cultivate intellect, in other words, because the poor will not become middle class or hope to become rich *unless* they pass the screed of the test (the screed that levels them and all who touch their schooling).

Maths is not simply a proxy for intelligence, but it legitimately does demonstrate and construct a key portion of the human intellect; that is, intellect-the-social-heritage, an informed collective mind, and not intellect-the-private-property-of-an-individual-mind. Not only individuals but also cultures learn and use mathematics, a far more significant usage than the personal one that corporations seek to appropriate as human capital. One of the damning bits of evidence about US culture, then, is the abandon with which it misuses mathematics (again, cf. Ernest 2010; Skovsmose 2010; Walkerdine 1988).

The culturally determined purposes and distribution of such knowledge tell us more about the culture than about mathematics per se. That is, unless one suffers the distracting illusion that mathematics is only *these* misuses and *this* machinery of invidious distribution. The evil purposes and malicious distribution of maths knowledge are telling us very bad things, of course, about the contemporary United States. We're *not listening* in the United States precisely because we *inhabit* a monumentally anti-intellectual culture, one that weighs with special pressure on the poor generally and on the rural poor and their schooling in particular. It's a fearful space indeed.

In my own telling of this confrontation and fearsome inhabitation (Howley, Howley, and Pendarvis 1995), US anti-intellectualism is not a prejudice against intellectuals, but a prejudice against intellect itself. That circumstance means simply that as a people, and in general, Americans are kept predictably against thinking, especially the speculative sort of thinking involved in such projects as mathematics, philosophy, poetry, and theorizing generally (cf. Hofstadter 1963). The difficulty with practicality—and I believe that maths instruction *must* become more practical—is that the standard of practicality is national, corporate, and economic rather than local, communal, and social. There's another term for this sort of inhabitation: *colonization*. It works best when locality is suppressed, as de Tocqueville (1848) realized so long ago. The life-world of US schooling, including mathematics education, then, is necessarily and perhaps surprisingly anti-intellective and (less surprisingly) antirural.

This insight is all the more reason to prize works of intellect in the United States, but I wonder if the UK's Ernest and Denmark's Skovsmose can be in any way positioned to appreciate this odd circumstance in US schooling. I doubt it. In national terms, in the prevailing neoliberal terms worked out politically, all hope does seem lost.

The galling reality, as I would call it, is that the relevant works of intellect are ontologically—that is, by the necessity inherent in their very existence—*still* the heritage of all people, even in the United States. This reality is not to be lost sight of in our appreciation and valuation of the mathematics that does exist here in everyday life—so-called street mathematics. What seems needed are forms and cultural workers in schools to connect the two; as Raymond Williams (2001/1958) liked to remind us, *culture is ordinary*. This project is what the institution of teaching (as opposed to the institution of schooling) is properly all about. Many of the good teachers I know in the United States have this sort of thing in mind when they complain about administrators and the state. My parents, who were teachers from 1948 to 1982, so often said: "If they would just leave us alone to teach!" It's not going to happen. Teachers must teach *anyway*. And they do—just in the fashion that wonderful works of intellect continue to emerge even in an anti-intellectual society.

Recently, I met a colleague, the superintendent of a small, poor, rural district. She sighed: "Sometimes I feel like I'm just reproducing the system; just propping it up." So do I; the necessity of participation even by objectors is what renders the system *systematic*. When we have real options, both it and we—our children and their children, and yours too, most likely—will be in real trouble. At last.

This statement might seem discordant: I'm thinking, as do many, that "the system" is not going to change (for either good or evil) short of disaster. Disasters always sponsor the most demanding opportunities for agency, but in the meantime, we must tinker and putter and try to do it ourselves: *bricolage*. Necessity is the mother of invention, both now as well as perhaps more urgently later; why not? We need to keep creating works, and valuing them, and teaching such works and much else, especially in rural places. But I'm decidedly not advising or addressing school reform.

So far as I can tell, "school reform," especially (as one very foolish US term has it) "comprehensive school reform," has not merely proven unsuccessful, it's made things worse and worse since at least 1980. And so with bricolage I've got something different in mind; less planned, less coordinated; less ambitious; more incremental; more respectful of local conditions; and more grassroots (see Tye 2000, for a rare compatible perspective, even if she obviously didn't have rural schools particularly in mind).

During the evolution of this chapter, I had been working with a group of colleagues begging for support to establish a project that would take such an interest and cultivate such an idea (in the begging process, a reviewer claimed that "rural is not a national priority"). In actually doing such work—alongside interested teachers—several classes of problems might be relevant, although predicting such matters is dicey:

- Culture of mathematics *blinders* (e.g., mathematics is a set of tools, mathematics has right answers; school mathematics must teach facile computation at every level, etc.);
- Culture of education *constraints* (e.g., accountability and testing, planning time, administrative and material support, belief that projects are best for less able maths students, etc.);
- Local cultural *worries* (e.g., fear of controversy or public exposure, risk of parental rejection, possible threats to job security);
- Curricular coverage *priorities* (e.g., developing activities that sample important knowledge across the maths curriculum—this is a concern I have heard often from maths education colleagues);
- Time management *challenges* (e.g., planning burden, threats to established routines, concerns over "coverage," etc.); and

- Assessment *debates* (e.g., effect on accountability results, defending the educational value of activities, etc.).

Helping educators in rural schools see a new mission and realize opportunities would be difficult and interesting, and necessarily slow work.

Our recent study (Howley et al. 2011) does highlight a number of stalwart rural maths teachers engaging community in varied ways. Educators and community members at one of the seven study sites—an island off the Maine coast—understood, quite clearly, the connections between the existence of the school and the existence of the community, and had struggled for perhaps 20 years, and concertedly for at least a decade, to base much of the school activity in the community. At another site, the superintendent became so convinced of the worth of the high school maths teacher's local vision (he had been a student in our center's doctoral program), that he made the maths teacher the curriculum coordinator. At this site, too, people talked about how the school could contribute to sustaining the town and its enterprises.

De Tocqueville (1848) understood the importance of rural locality to democracy in the United States. He feared that a maturing United States might abandon the source of its democratic strength in locality; and so it has and is. Nonetheless, though now in jeopardy, the local and the rural persist. Moreover, even in the contemporary United States so do aspirations for equality and solidarity—and quite apart from the longings of us comfortable academics (cf. Skovsmose 2010). One has, in short, a little reason to expect more now, and more later, when the necessity of the rural world becomes clearer to those outside it as well as to those within it (i.e., within this imaginative realm of meanings and works recognizable as "the rural"). Wondrous works exist; we have reason to expect better; in part, we teachers and citizens are the reason. We must be.

Notes

For the gift of two constructs, *the institution of teaching* and *the institution of schooling*, the author thanks Patton College students in his Winter 2011–2012 course, *Ideas and Inquiry in Education*: Emily Brindza, Jacob Hinze, Brianna Lauofo, Rebekah Rittenberg, Aaron Smith, Clare Volz, and Zach Wilson. The former construct refers to the purposes of teaching as conceptualized and enacted by teachers, and the latter to the purposes of schooling as conceptualized and enacted by the state. Bless the teachers.

1. Indeed, the field of critical mathematics does exist (e.g., d'Ambrosio 1990; Skovsmose 1994, 2010), and this chapter engages it further along.

2. It's a known fact that very many students and adults, likely a substantial majority, regard mathematics as irrelevant, incomprehensible, and distasteful (Smith 2002). Most of my colleagues in rural education, practitioners and higher education faculty, hold this view. Smith (2002) properly advises that mathematics, though a rarified use of natural language, *is not a language.* It's a different way of knowing and of doing things. It is very much unnatural.

3. But is there something in *mathematics* that necessitates wondrous works, for example, something that will be for the sake of everybody? It's a chicken-and-egg issue. The human (chicken) produces not only the mathematics works, but also the mathematics, including school maths (typically not so wondrous). The wonder that remains to mathematics and the wondrous works of mathematics is human. So is the related evil, and the related devils. So, in my view, there *is* something—not nothing—in mathematics that is for the good of everybody. It's not everything, but it is something, and something wondrous. In this cruel world, that's something indeed.

4. Different from reading the world with mathematics. Reading it in this other way, one can see where Ernest and Skovsmose and Walkerdine are coming from. Humans continue to do a great deal of damage with maths, natural science, and engineering. The natural science bureaucracies understandably fail to grasp this reading of the world!

5. References to maths as a "universal language" in the recent pedagogical literature are nonetheless refreshingly *negative* (e.g., Hoffert 2009).

6. A minority view in this literature held, by contrast, that rural cultures and communities harbored assets worth incorporating into mathematics instruction. Leading the minority in this literature were Ray Barnhardt, Oscar Kawagley, Jerry Lipka, and their colleagues in Native Alaskan communities.

7. See David Gruenewald's works (2003, 2006) for nuanced syntheses of rural place and critical theory.

References

ACCLAIM (Appalachian Collaborative Center for Learning, Assessment, and Instruction in Mathematics), 2002, *Theoretical Framework*, Occasional Paper No. 1b, Athens, OH, http://www.centerforcsri.org/research/improvement.cgi?st=s&sr=SR004395.

Appiah, K., 2006, *Cosmopolitanism: Ethics in a World of Strangers*, W. W. Norton, New York and London.

Arendt, H., 1958, *The Human Condition*, University of Chicago Press, Chicago.

Barzun, J., 2001,. *Simple and Direct: A Rhetoric for Writers* (4th ed.), Harper Perennial, New York.

Berry, W., 1977, *The Unsettling of America: Culture & Agriculture*, Sierra Club Books, San Francisco.

———, 1990, *What Are People For?* North Point Press, San Francisco.

Berry, W., 2010, *What Matters Most: Economics for a Renewed Commonwealth*, Counterpoint, Berkeley, CA.

Burnell, B., 2003, "The Real-World Aspirations of Work-Bound Rural Students," *Journal of Research in Rural Education*, vol. 18, no. 2: 104–113.

Carr, P. and M. Kefalas, 2009, *Hollowing Out the Middle: The Rural Brain Drain and What It Means for America*, Beacon Press, Boston.

Childers, R. and C. Howley, 1994, *Mathematics Activities Manuals: Final Evaluation*, Appalachia Educational Laboratory, Charleston, WV.

Civil, M., 2006, *Working towards Reform in Mathematics Education: Parents', Teachers', and Students' Views of "Different."* Working Paper No. 31, ERIC database (ED495032).

Corbett, M., 2007, *Learning to Leave: The Irony of Schooling in a Coastal Community*, Fernwood, Halifax, NS.

D'Ambrosio, U., 1990, "The Role of Mathematics Education in Building a Democratic and Just Society," *For the Learning of Mathematics*, vol. 10: 20–23.

de Tocqueville, A., 1848, *De la démocratie en Amérique*, Pagnerre, Paris.

De Young, A., 1995, *The Life and Death of a Rural American High School: Farewell, Little Kanawha*, Garland, New York.

Egan, K., 2002, *Getting It Wrong from the Beginning: Our Progressivist Inheritance from Herbert Spencer, John Dewey, and Jean Piaget*, Yale University Press, New Haven, CT.

Eglash, R., 2004, *Black Chaos, White Trash: Order and Disorder at the Intersection of Mathematics and Culture*, Occasional Paper No. 7, Appalachian Collaborative Center for Learning, Assessment, and Instruction in Mathematics, Athens, OH.

Ernest, P., 1998, *Social Constructivism as a Philosophy of Mathematics*, State University of New York Press, Albany, NY.

———, 2010, "The Scope and Limits of Critical Math Education," *Philosophy of Mathematics Education Journal*, vol. 25, http://people.exeter.ac.uk/PErnest/pome25/index.html.

Foucault, M., 1979, *Discipline and Punish: The Birth of the Prison*, Pantheon, New York.

Gruenewald, D., 2003, "The Best of Both Worlds: A Critical Pedagogy of Place," *Educational Researcher*, vol. 32, no. 4: 3–12.

———, 2006, "Resistance, Reinhabitation, and Regime Change," *Journal of Research in Rural Education*, vol. 21, no. 9, https://www.umaine.edu/jrre/archive/21–9.pdf.

Gruenewald, D. A. and G. A. Smith, 2008, *Place-Based Education in the Global Age: Local Diversity*, Lawrence Erlbaum Associates, New York.

Gutstein, E., 2006, *Reading and Writing the World with Mathematics*, Routledge, New York.

Hoffert, S. B., 2009, "Mathematics: The Universal Language?" *Mathematics Teacher*, vol. 103, no. 2: 130–139.

Hofstadter, R., 1963, *Anti-intellectualism in American Life*, Vintage Books, New York.

Howley, C. B., A. A. Howley, and D. S. Huber, 2005, "Prescriptions for Rural Mathematics Instruction: Analysis of the Rhetorical Literature [Computer File],"

Journal of Research in Rural Education, vol. 20, no. 7: 1, http://www.jrre.psu.edu /articles/20–7.pdf.

Howley, C., A. Howley, and E. Pendarvis, 1995, *Out of Our Minds: Anti-intellectualism in American Schooling*, Teachers College Press, New York.

Howley, A., D. Showalter, M. Howley, C. Howley, R. Klein, and J. Johnson, 2011, "Challenges for Place-Based Mathematics Pedagogy in Rural Schools and Communities in the United States," *Children, Youth, and Environments*, vol. 21, no. 1: 101–127, http://www.colorado.edu/journals/cye/21_1/21_1_05 _ MathematicsPedagogy.pdf.

Kantner, M. J., 2008, "The Only Absolute Truth in Mathematics Is the Myth of Mathematics as Universal," *Online Submission*, http://www.eric.ed.gov/PDFS /ED501486.pdf.

Krober, N., 1991, *What We Know about Mathematics Teaching and Learning*. *EDTALK*, Council for Education Development and Research, Washington, DC, http://www.eric.ed.gov/PDFS/ED343793.pdf.

Leopold, A., 1949, *A Sand County Almanac*, Oxford University Press, New York.

Lewicki, J., 2010, *To Know the Joy of Work Well Done: Place-Based Learning and Sustaining School Communities*, coopecology.com, Westby, WI.

Mitchell, R., 1979, *Less Than Words Can Say*, Little, Brown, Boston.

NCTM, 2000, *Principles and Standards for School Mathematics*, National Council of Teachers of Mathematics, Reston, VA.

St. John, M., J. Helms, and A. Smith, 2008, *Findings from Inverness Research Associates Evaluation of the Appalachian Collaborative Center for Learning, Assessment, and Instruction in Mathematics (ACCLAIM)*, Working Paper No. 39, Appalachian Collaborative Center for Learning, Assessment, and Instruction in Mathematics, Athens, OH, http://20.132.48.254/PDFS/ED512643.pdf

Saltman, K. and D. Gabbard (eds.), 2003, *Education as Enforcement: The Militarization and Corporatization of Schools*, Routledge, New York.

Shelton, J., 2005, *Consequential Learning: A Public Approach to Better Schools*, New South Books, Montgomery, AL.

Skovsmose, O., 1994, *Towards a Philosophy of Critical Mathematics Education*, Kluwer, Dordrecht, NE.

———, 2010, "Mathematics: A Critical Rationality?" *Philosophy of Mathematics Education Journal*, vol. 25, http://people.exeter.ac.uk/PErnest/.

Smith, F., 2002, *The Glass Wall: Why Mathematics Can Seem Difficult*, Teachers College Press, New York.

Snyder, T. and S. Dillow, 2011, *Digest of Education Statistics 2010*, National Center for Education Statistics, Washington, DC, http://nces.ed.gov/pubs2011/2011015.pdf.

Sobel, D., 2004, *Place-Based Education: Connecting Classrooms and Communities*, Orion Society, Great Barrington, MA.

Stanic, G. and I. Goodson, 1987, "A Historical Perspective on Justifying the Teaching of Mathematics," in *International Perspectives in Curriculum History*, Groom Helm, London, pp. 209–227.

Stigler, J. and J. Hiebert, 1999, *The Teaching Gap: Best Ideas from the World's Teachers for Improving Education in the Classroom*, Free Press, New York.

Theobald, P., 1997, *Teaching the Commons: Place, Pride, and the Renewal of Community*, Westview, Boulder, CO.

———, 2009, *Education Now: How Rethinking America's Past Can Change Its Future*, Paradigm, Boulder, CO.

Tye, B., 2000, *Hard Truths: Uncovering the Deep Structure of Schooling*, Teachers College Press, New York.

Walkerdine, V., 1988, *The Mastery of Reason: Cognitive Development and the Production of Rationality*, Routledge, London and New York.

Williams, R., 1973, *The Country and the City*, Verso, London.

———, 2001, "Culture Is Ordinary," in J. Higgins (ed.), *The Raymond Williams Reader* (originally published in 1958), Blackwell, Oxford, UK, pp. 10–24.

PART II

Literacy/Pedagogies

CHAPTER 6

Exploring Rurality, Teaching Literacy: How Teachers Manage a Curricular Relation to Place

Phillip Cormack

Introduction

This chapter describes and analyzes an attempt to specifically locate the teaching of literacy in and for rural communities within the context of a university Masters-level course. The course involved practicing, experienced teachers with an interest in literacy education in exploring the potential for utilizing "place" as a curriculum resource for their rural elementary, middle, and high school students. It aimed to help teachers think about the rather slippery notion of "rurality" (Halfacree 1993), moving away from a conventional, realistic understanding to one that emphasizes ways of thinking and meaning. The course sought to link considerations of rurality with a focus on rural places, and on the rural as a space of signification, and introduced the idea of "place-based" or "place-conscious" education and schooling.

My intention here is to consider what can be learned from thinking about their interrelation in an *educational* context. Education is a field with which both literacy and rurality are intricately related. The school has been the place where learning to read and write has been institutionalized since the last part of the nineteenth century—as Muspratt and colleagues (2001, p. 154) note, they are "fellow traveller[s]." Schooling and the literacy project have also been a primary site for carrying modernist or capital-centric (in both senses of the term) conceptions of nation and citizen to the rural as described by Raymond Williams (1973).[1]

Through schooling, literacy has been a means by which the modernist project was expanded to the whole population and through which its practices and ideals have been incorporated into everyday life. In today's late- or postmodern world, literacy continues to be central to the project of educating future workers and citizens and managing their subjectivities (Ball, Maguire, and MacRae 2000), including their ways of thinking and acting in relation to the places they live (Cormack, Green, and Reid 2008). Thus, when place-based education proponent Gruenewald (2003b, p. 646) critiques current education reform processes as promoting "a kind of generic education for 'anywhere,'" an understanding of the history of schooling shows that "anywhere" has a decidedly metropolitan or, perhaps, cosmopolitan bias.

The idea of "rural literacies," therefore, can be seen as a somewhat jarring notion in the context of the schooling project or, perhaps, a nostalgic retreat from its overall scientific and progressive thrust (Cormack and Green 2007). It was in this context that Bill Green and I developed a course on rural literacies for Masters students with an awareness that this concept might sit strangely for many teachers and run counter to accepted curriculum norms. Importantly, we wanted to develop a course that involved *critical* engagement with both "literacy" and "rurality," because working with currently naturalized constructions had the potential for rural literacies to be experienced as a distraction from the main business of schooling standardized forms of literacy ("school literacy"). Instead, we wanted it to be a concept that disrupted accepted ways of doing literacy in schools, especially, but not exclusively, in rural schools.

The Rural Literacies Course

The data for this examination of rural literacies are student responses and assignments in an online course entitled "Rural Literacies." The course was originally developed for trialling with a group of 13 teachers from Newfoundland, Canada, who were studying a single course at the University of South Australia as part of their MEd program at Mount Saint Vincent University, Nova Scotia.[2] The course began with readings and activities that explored various ways of understanding and, importantly, representing *rurality*—that is, the rural as something constructed in discourse. This moved to a consideration of reading and writing the rural, or how the rural is rendered in reading and writing, or literacy. One assignment asked the teachers to collect and analyze local and provincial policy to consider the spaces that are available in the official curriculum for place-oriented study and literacies. Another invited teachers to consider the literacies used in "their place" in different parts of the community and how those literacies matched with the literacies privileged at school. The final, major assignment asked teachers to trial ways of incorporating rural literacies into their teaching and subject curricula.

Understanding the Rural: Perspectives from the Teachers

An early activity introduced the idea that the rural is a relational concept—something that takes its meaning through points of difference from other concepts or—to take up Derrida's (1976, p. 66) theory of *différance,* it is a concept that involves an "articulation" with other concepts. Teachers were asked to brainstorm around the idea of the rural, what it meant to them, and share their thoughts with their peers. Each of the teachers' contributions and responses to one another's contributions and to my comments as course lecturer were analyzed to consider the versions of the rural that were deployed. A typical response was:

> When I hear the word "rural," I think about small communities in the country surrounded by trees and vast land... They are left on their own to be self sufficient. They are close-knit and help each other through times... They are more personal with each other, instead of being a face just walking down the street. It is peaceful in their communities and a more relaxed atmosphere. Their pace is slower because there is no need to rush around. They may not have many attractions like fairs, malls, et cetera, but they offer many other things like scenery and a down to earth feeling!

From such beginnings, a fascinating discussion ensued, as the teachers began to critique and rethink their earlier contributions.

Halfacree's (1993) review of definitions of the rural in what he termed the "'rural' literature" provided a useful starting point for my analysis. Halfacree introduced to the field the idea that discourses actually constitute the rural. He labeled this as "the rural as social representation" perspective as an alternative to two main approaches he critiqued: theories of the rural as "space" and the rural as "locality." Approaches focusing on the rural as space assume that the rural actually exists and seek to provide descriptions of those spaces that are seen to be rural, a strategy that easily runs into problems of competing definition, not to mention circular logic. Another version of this is what Halfacree calls "sociocultural" definitions, which describe how people's characteristics vary according to the space in which they live—a form of spatial determinism that assumes that the space makes people. Locality approaches assume that there are structures operating at the local level that distinguish between urban and rural locations; a problematic assumption in late capitalist economies where scales and borders are increasingly changed and interpenetrated. Such approaches are also often based on assumed polar oppositions between the rural and its Other.

More recently, Halfacree (2006) reiterated the importance of embracing representational and linguistic, or poststructural critiques of these approaches as a way of retaining the rural as a concept (albeit, more fluid) without falling into problems of social determinism or endless debates about definition:

> [R]egarding the rural as an interpretive repertoire, fundamentally destabilizes what is left of any fixity. Any linguistic rural space that is produced through an interpretative repertoire becomes fundamentally and irreducibly contextual and thus highly transient. A ghostly ephemerality is suggested. (p. 47)

The course embraced this representational view of rurality and strongly connected it to literacy, or the representational practices of reading, writing, and viewing, as they played out in the school curriculum. Such an approach allows simplistic representational and determinist binary definitions of what it means to be rural to be challenged and rethought, especially through the way that the representational practices of literacy come to constitute rurality. However, there was no expectation that teachers would have detailed knowledge of these theoretical tools and an acceptance that we would have to work with a combination of lay discourses and those they were learning through the course (Halfacree 1993; Corbett 2000; Gruenewald 2003b). Initially teachers tended to simply describe the places they lived, assuming that they were unproblematically rural. Here is an example:

> First I thought of scenery. Words like countryside, mountains, water, woods and peace came to mind. Then, a sense of community. A feeling of closeness that is associated with smaller places, a sense of caring about others who live there (and of course I thought about the lack of privacy and the busybodies who feel they have the right to know your personal business...but then I went back to peacefulness...Ahhhhh!). And lastly, life's pace came to mind.

Such descriptions focused on both the physical space and on the social interactions seen as driven by the nature of the space—thus social "closeness" arises from "smaller places"—exemplifying Halfacree's point about the social determinism of spatially based definitions. Most responses described the space assuming a priori that it was rural and strongly reading social relations off the nature of that space. Indeed, the descriptions of the physical qualities tended to be quickly dealt with, and social characteristics given more attention. The following gives a sense of these descriptions in relation to Newfoundland:

> First, rural has something to do with surroundings: being in the country or inland (surrounded by trees and hills et cetera), as opposed to being on the coast or by the ocean (lakes, ponds, et cetera, don't count)...The second meaning has to do with size: being relatively small enough in size that you can see or have a clear sense of where the boundaries are of your community, as opposed to being in a larger built up urban center or city. The third meaning of rural for me has to do with a state of mind: a place where you feel a sense of community, belonging, ownership and responsibility that comes knowing most...of the people who live and work around you.

The teachers, probably because of the prompts given in the activity, also took up relational perspectives, acknowledging that the rural could be thought of as something understood in relation to other places, particularly the city:

> The area would have a low population density, work based on a primary industry, for example, fishing, mining, or agriculture, less violent crimes, safer for children to be able to play freely outside, lower cost of real estate, more outdoor activities than larger centers, and a more relaxed lifestyle. Unfortunately, there are other less positive stereotypes that come to mind as well, such as, the residents being less educated, unsophisticated, with more traditional viewpoints on life and religion. Often the "city folks" look down on them.

Such comparative language—less/more, higher/lower—also tended to situate the country and the city at either end of binaries so that the rural tended to be defined in oppositional terms and, often when it came to relative economic advantage, on the lesser end of the binary, although socially a more connected place to be. As in the example above, there was also some evidence of structural definitions of locale, connected to the importance of the economy and the industries that were dominant in a region, in what also might be called a "productivist" view of rurality, as determined by a particular form of production. There was recognition that, generally, rural regions were suffering economically in postindustrial economies, and that behind the rural idyll, presented in tourist advertising and the like, was hard and dangerous work in primary industries. Overall, the teachers' comments fell mostly into descriptions of the space or into sociocultural definitions of the rural. Teachers' comments, however, show that social definitions predominated, as shown in table 6.1.

The comments on the social often referred to "closeness," "community," and a sense of intimacy and sometimes contrasted to what was seen to be possible in the city. The remainder of the comments around tourism, services, industries, and demographic features demonstrates that teachers were also aware of the way that the rural is formed out of other ways of structuring space. Over time, and after reading relevant academic literature, the teachers questioned their earlier views of the rural—in particular, the way that the rural can be romanticized:

> I think it is still true that rural life is not always as glamorous as we make it. This is evidenced in the news yesterday and today of two local fishermen who lost their lives while shrimp fishing (weather related). Surely, earning a living as a fisherman cannot be viewed as relaxed or easy-paced.

Importantly, as one of the teachers noted during this activity, repositioning the rural as a noun rather than simply using it as an adjective, changed the way it could be thought about, and proved a useful distancing device. Also, it made it possible to understand that perspective was important in defining the rural. This provided a useful connection later in the course, when we began to consider the ways in which the discourses of tourism may be shaping the rural through different kinds of linguistic and visual signs.

Table 6.1 Features of the Rural Mentioned by Teachers

Feature	Count
Social	41
Nature	19
Population/demography	12
Leisure or tourism	5
Time	5
Other industries	3
Services	3
Economy	2
Space	2

Curriculum Openings for Rural Literacies

Teachers were next introduced to the concept of place-based education (Gruenewald 2003a; Gruenewald and Smith 2008; Smith 2002), focusing on the local (rural) place of their schools and students' communities as a possible resource for cross-curriculum work, especially in relation to literacy. Teachers responded very positively to the call in this literature "that teachers and children must regularly spend time out-of-doors building long-term relationships with familiar, everyday places" (Gruenewald 2003a, p. 8) because their students were already connected to outdoor environments.

One feature of the place-based education literature is its strong critique of the school curriculum, as inimical to place. Gruenewald (2003a, p. 8) claims:

> In place of actual experience with the phenomenal world, educators are handed, and largely accept, the mandates of a standardized, "placeless" curriculum and settle for the abstractions and simulations of classroom learning.

Similarly, Smith (2007) refers to "the constraining regularities of public school," even while citing examples of teachers and schools enacting exciting curriculum activities in place. As teacher educators, it was important to question this impression that schools and the "standard" curriculum were necessarily hostile to place-based learning. Policy is more fluid than critics and teachers claim, and can often be used as a warrant for exciting work, rather than simply acting as an impediment. For these reasons, the first assignment in the course was to ask the teachers to track down, in some cases from dusty shelves but also, increasingly, online archives, the policies and curriculum guides relevant to their level of schooling and the curriculum area(s) in which they taught. In practice this meant that the elementary school teachers focused on English/Language Arts curriculum materials, as well as broader guides to teaching in the early years, while the middle and high school teachers focused on their main teaching subject or faculty area. The assignment asked the teachers to review these documents to identify possibilities they presented for place-based education.

The review by these 13 eachers did, indeed, find that there was more openness than is implied by place-based educators in their critiques of public school curricula. As one Grade 2 teacher noted,

> As I looked at District policies, school policies and provincial curriculum documents I didn't find anything that would deter me from implementing

a place-based education program with my primary students. In fact, the mission statement of our District is to "embrace, educate and empower every child through quality learning resources and qualified staff using best practices, in a nurturing and safe environment"...The "embrace, educate and empower every child" can have many interpretations, especially the word "empower." I associate it with critical literacy practices and interpret it to mean giving all children a "voice" to question the status quo and work towards equity and social justice for everyone.

Such analysis illustrated that these policies could be used by teachers as warrants for opening up their curriculum offerings. Similarly, a high school music teacher found that graduate outcomes for music were supportive of community connections:

The Guide mentions that "[g]raduates will be able to recognize and assess the significant contribution of music and the arts to the local, national, and global economy"...This would seem to be an impossible task without finding some way of drawing the community into the school or taking the music students out into the community.

When it came to the more specific guides about curriculum content and teaching, teachers also noted that there was a degree of openness that would allow place-based activities to be designed. This was especially the case in the language, arts, and English courses, where a variety of texts and purposes for communication were required by the curriculum. Even in the seemingly more restricted subject—senior high school mathematics—the teacher provided a long list of the ways in which a curriculum unit on banking could easily involve visiting local institutions and clients to conduct research with a mathematical flavor. Furthermore, in some cases, teachers found that the curriculum statements actually encouraged place-based activities—this was the case especially in the natural sciences and the arts.

Barriers for Teachers

An unexpected outcome from analyzing curriculum and policy documents for openings in relation to place-based education in literacy was that it also gave them a standpoint from which to critique those documents. The most prominent barrier identified was the standardized testing regime that had been put in place across the Maritime Provinces, utilizing criterion-referenced testing (CRT) at Grades 3, 6, 9, and 12. Teachers explained that the pressure for children to perform on these tests restricted curriculum diversity. Because students in rural locations typically score poorly on standardized tests, literacy and mathematics *became* the curriculum. As one teacher put it, "there is little interest among our administrators in anything other than improving those CRT scores." Meeting standardized requirements forced teachers to narrow the curriculum (Au 2007; Au and Apple 2010). Teachers reported that the time spent on literacy and numeracy had been increased, meaning that there was less time for those subjects that, as their review had noted, were more amenable to place-based activities.

Beyond these standardizing practices, teachers also mentioned more traditional barriers to innovation, including a crowded curriculum, occupational health requirements that made leaving the school difficult, and in the case of a science teacher, a complaint that many of the required topics, such as pollution and traffic issues, were quite urban-centric. One high school mathematics teacher also revealed a doubt in his own knowledge and skillset to link "real world" issues to the curriculum and find or utilize local resources in addressing them—a reminder of the resourcing and professional development implications of place-based curriculum.

Pedagogical Innovations

For the final assignment, the teachers reported on an investigation into, or curriculum intervention that focused on, the literacies in their local place. The assignment deliberately allowed for teachers to conduct an investigation *with* students, or to develop an intervention *for* them, as this allowed for differing levels of confidence and expertise in the group, and recognized that in some school subjects, simply exploring the possibilities would be a big step forward. In the end, most teachers managed to do both within a four-week period, incorporating a small investigation with the students into local literacies that led to some curriculum work for their classes.

Of the 13 teachers, 5 worked in English/language arts, 4 in social studies, 2 in mathematics, and 1 each in health and music. In what follows, I highlight three key moves that enabled the teachers to develop what proved to be engaging and innovative literacy practices with their students. The first of these is, perhaps, the most obvious and that was moving the learning space from the classroom out into the local area and into students' lives, and treating that as a space that could be "read." The second was to take up an ethnographic stance to the local; that is, to see the local area as a research resource and to learn from their place. This also involved the teachers seeing their students as knowledgeable, or as experts about their place. Finally, it involved moving the balance of the curriculum from text reception to text production so that students became knowledge producers about their places. What these moves have in common is that they disrupt some of the underlying "grammar" of schooling (Tyack and Tobin 1994), which determines that students must be removed from their communities to within the school to learn valued knowledge; that valued knowledge comes from authorized texts; and that the teacher is the key broker and/or creator of the texts students learn from.

The Local as a Literacy Curriculum Resource

An emphasis in place-based education materials is the use of the local as both an inspiration and a resource for student learning. Advantages of local places are that they are relatively quick and cheap to access, and provide a means to link students' everyday lives to their learning of the curriculum. In school, learning to be literate should extend beyond "cracking the code" to helping young people to build bridges between the forms of language and literacy they know and regularly use, and the new forms introduced in school (Dyson 1993, 2003). Such work includes developing new vocabularies, restructuring knowledge held in one form, such as narrative, into others such as reports and explanations (and vice versa), and showing how oral forms are transformed into texts. If such work is done in relation to the knowledges and language/texts of the local, young people in rural communities will have a chance to see that as valued and as a bridge into other learning.

One example of an activity that involved such processes was a local investigation by a Kindergarten teacher into the practice of "mummering" in Newfoundland. Mummering, a Christmas-time practice of visiting neighbors while dressed in a costume that disguised the wearer's identity, brought to Newfoundland by Irish and other immigrants centuries earlier, was virtually unknown to the children, and had all but died out in the community, according to their teacher. This practice, with its costumes, guessing at identity and emphasis on sociability, singing and storytelling, had strong appeal to the young students. The teacher brought to the classroom video and print texts that told about mummering. In addition to facilitating the use of the Internet as a source of information about the practice, the teacher also developed, with her class, a question schedule that the students used as a basis for interviews with older members of the community who had participated in mummering or knew about the practice. Thus, students had information about the practice from a variety of published textual and visual forms and in a local form, from local people who could describe and explain how it worked in a known context. The teacher then created a "scrapbook" with the students, using photographs provided by interviewees plus captions developed by the students to illustrate how mummering worked, incorporating the lyrics from a local song and the descriptions provided in the interviews. One page showing fully disguised mummers led with the question "Guess who we is?" incorporating and valuing local dialect/grammar. Through photographs of the event, the scrapbook also celebrated a class activity where the students themselves dressed up and visited the local senior citizens' home, and experienced a form of the practice with community members with strong memories of how it worked. The work described here represents only part of the language arts unit the teacher developed around mummering.

Place-based work demonstrated that local histories and cultural practices provided the knowledge bases for students to develop multimodal literacies. The literacy work involved multiple transformations of that knowledge into different forms, but always began with the forms closest to these young children's experience of language and texts. Through these curriculum activities, rurality was engaged in as a cultural practice, strongly emphasizing family, history, and tradition.

Students and Teachers as Researchers

The next example involves a high school music teacher who, through this course, came to see music as a form of signification connected to a conception of literacy as a multimodal representative practice that could include music and other sign systems such as music notation. The example involved the teacher as a researcher and demonstrates how more critical perspectives on literacy as a cultural resource influenced the way the teachers thought about the curriculum and their work.

This teacher had been inspired by Pryor's (2004) call to teachers to engage with their students in "modified ethnographies" that, at their core, involve them in observing and listening to their local human culture. He noticed the class-based "choices" students made, driven by issues such as cost of instruments, so that the most affluent students ended up staying in the program, which was strongly built around instrumental music training. In contrast, he noted how important music was in the lives of students and adults in the community generally and wondered why this wasn't reflected in greater participation in the school music program. From this conundrum, the following questions were generated:

- What is the music that children and their families are engaged in on a day-to-day basis?
- What is the music that is valued in the local community?
- Is this music valued by the school music program?
- Is there a way of strengthening the connection between the school music program and the music of the local community, families, and children?

With his senior English class, the teacher designed an interview schedule to take to students who were not enrolled in senior music, to directly tackle the first two questions shown above. The other questions were addressed following the interviews and involved further investigation and reflection by the teacher into the curriculum landscape of the Province and the possibilities within the school. As the teacher explained, some of the students conducted face-to-face interviews, while others contacted their fellow students online, via e-mail and other means, to ask their questions about musical interests, experiences, and attitudes to music. Together with their teacher, the students analyzed the responses to pull together a perspective on these students' views of music and the school music program. The teacher deliberately took a reflexive stance with his students, asking them to think about what they learned, not only about their peers, but also about themselves and the processes of research they undertook, through questions such as

- Did all students surveyed value some form of music?
- How were their rationales for valuing music the same? How were they different?
- What did you learn about interviewing?
- What did you learn about music that was reinforced by the interviews?
- Do you have a different view of music, music styles, and music values because of the interviews?
- How do students who do not take music courses view the music program?

From this review, the teacher learned that music was a vital ingredient in the vast majority of the students' lives, not just as entertainment, but also as a form of communication, for identity formation, and an aid to their learning. For this teacher, "to realise that music has had such an impact on their lives but yet the school music program had no part to play [was] a sobering thought." But more than this, the teacher also reported being "stunned" by an unexpected outcome of the investigation, which was the number of students who provided samples of music they had made themselves. Commenting on the quality of music provided, the teacher noted:

> This has caused me to rethink the value of teaching music theory without the opportunity to practice composition. The goal of the present music program is to learn how to perform music composed by others. Although students have the opportunity to improve their performing and technical skills on a musical instrument there is very little room for creativity. Certainly not the creativity that was displayed in the audio examples collected by the student ethnographers... One student created at least a dozen original compositions including lyrics and music. Even though this student has displayed an interest and talent in the area of music, they would have had difficulty in the present music program which does not place as much value on creativity as it does on high-level performance ability.

Interestingly, it was not traditional Newfoundland music that was the most important in this school's community, as the teacher had predicted, but a range of musical styles, including jazz and popular music. His community informants noted the influence of a nearby postwar US military base that had been closed for decades, but which had left a legacy of interest in a range of musical styles from that country. Another important finding was that students had become early adopters of digital music creation tools. Two students, who had downloaded and utilized programs for creating, recording, and burning a whole CD of tracks that they provided, were reported by a student ethnographer as "very interested and involved in music, [but] don't get involved in the school music program because they don't believe the program cares about what they are really interested in."

These findings demonstrate that a program that was built around the local as a source of knowledge could not only extend the potential connections of the curriculum to place, it could also disrupt any easy assumptions about what the local involved. Historical and contemporary connections with other places, as well as music traditions and music creation tools that crossed borders, demonstrated that rural places are more than simply a locale, and indeed are complexly interconnected with other locales. From a literacy perspective, some of these students were engaging, through music, in new and sophisticated forms of textuality involving reading, writing, and viewing. Their identity was being formed out of the textual tools they had available and the communities within which they could participate. As the teacher noted, however, the school music program had failed to tap into these students' lives, interests, and skills, and a further proposed project (beyond his period in the course) was planned to redesign curriculum to learn from these results.

Other teachers in the group also engaged in research or investigative activities themselves and with their students. An example of a nonethnographic approach was provided by a Grade 8 science and health teacher. She decided to build students' knowledge of their communities, and to help them think about how their place was being represented by undertaking analysis with them of the way their region was represented in tourism texts, specifically tourist brochures. The teacher's design of such projects demonstrated that place could act as a resource for curriculum and as a site where students and teachers become knowledge producers. This was not just because the local was familiar to students. What was at play here was more complex and demanding, because the participants were asked to look at their places through new eyes, through the brochure analysis, or to question the familiar, as in the example of the music curriculum.

From Text Reception to Text Production

The curriculum projects and investigations already described have given examples of the ways that place-based activities shift the typical balance of text reception (reading, viewing, listening) and text production (writing, assembling, creating, speaking) that students experience. As Comber and Nixon (2005) have noted, text production goes along with, and depends on, knowledge production by students, so that they have something to say. Having something to say depends on a larger project, which means that the students are producing texts for purposes that are significant to them and are designed to do work beyond the classroom. That is, the texts produced are more than "dummy runs" for the teacher's eye, but interventions into the world around them with consequences for the authors, with the consequent commitment to quality and appropriateness to purpose. A final example from the teachers' work, in the course, shows that text production was a feature of their interventions, but that it also involved invitations to students to think more critically about their places, and not just engage in celebration.

In this case, an early years teacher working in one of the larger regional centers shared with her students an anthology of children's writing and artwork from the Australian Murray-Darling Basin (Murray-Darling Basin Commission & Primary English Teaching Association 2003), which had been provided as part of her Masters course materials. Her students were inspired by the poetry, stories, and drawings about the Australian interior included in the anthology, and decided that they wanted to write about and draw their own place in a similar way.

Reading her students' writing about their favorite places in the town and nearby areas, the teacher noted both the students' love for those places and the range of places that were included. This was no romantic set of rural retreats the students included, but local leisure parks, the shopping mall, a local store, a car sales yard, or even a backyard. Noting the children's strong connections to these places, the teacher decided to ask them to take their writing further by also thinking about places around them that weren't so high in their estimation. With the students, she labeled the places they had already written about "places to keep" and then asked the students to think about places they wanted to be changed. Thus, the project took a step beyond celebration of place, asking students to think critically about place and imagine themselves as agents in relation to those places. As she reported, students found this a much more difficult assignment, mostly because they weren't used to being asked to think about places in these ways. To help the students, she involved them in gathering images of these places (through drawing or using photographs) and, using the heading "places to change," invited them to write about those places, including what concerned them and what might be done to improve them. Students were able to write about issues of safety and cleanliness, based on their close encounters with equipment, land, and facilities. The writing surprised the teacher in a number of ways, helping the teacher to see places through the eyes of a young person to whom potholes on a footpath can loom large, or to understand how much of their place students knew about and understood.

A final insight from this activity is the power of artwork and personal writing as a response to place. One senior high school English class wrote poetry to accompany their art that spoke eloquently about the all too familiar experience of friends and family leaving Newfoundland, as adults sought work elsewhere. Connection with place, it seems, is intensely visual and personal, and literary and artistic forms of expression prove to be valuable tools for communicating those features to others. Teachers reported that students found such work engaging and, as in the case reported above, this beginning provided a strong basis for other kinds of learning, including the critical.

Conclusions

Green's "3D" model of literacy is a useful frame for thinking about the links between literacy and place, culture, and meaning (Durrant and Green 2000; Green and Beavis 2012). The three dimensions of literacy, according to the model, are the "operational," the "cultural," and the "critical." In the operational dimension, children must learn about how the language works and is realized in signs, and the ways that texts can be structured. The cultural dimension involves learning about the uses to which literacy can be put, and understanding the meanings that may be conveyed. The third, critical, dimension involves learning about the ways that literacy can be used to shape people's lives and the ways we see and act on the world, in the interests of some rather than others. The work these teachers undertook with their students showed that place is a central element in the shape and meanings texts take and make in each of these three dimensions. When students learned the way that tourist brochures about their region were structured and the linguistic elements from which they were made, they were being inducted into the operational aspects of literacy. When students wrote narratives about their place, or interviewed their peers about the music that was important in their lives, they were learning the cultural elements of literacy. This was, perhaps, why ethnographic techniques were so useful for these teachers as an inspiration for their interventions: they were able to tap into the cultural meanings of place, and to help students read and create texts that engaged with these meanings. Finally, when the teachers asked students about the impacts on their own and others' lives of the meanings and patterns they noticed in their place, the literacy work took on the third, critical, dimension.

Some interesting patterns in the teachers' and students' work were discernible from a pedagogical perspective. Student engagement was raised when the teachers allowed into the classroom aspects of students' lives connected to their place. This was particularly so in the cultural dimension of literacy, where activities gave a space in the curriculum for meanings and experiences that were part of the children's community commons. Parents and community members, too, could be given an authoritative place within such curriculum activities. Clearly, then, as claimed in the place-based education literature, schools and learning can benefit from allowing place past the school gate and into the classroom, or by taking the classroom beyond the school. However, to say this would only be to report half of what happened in these classrooms. This is because the school literacy curriculum was able to be brought into *critical* engagement with place to develop new insights and learning for the students. When students examined their town's website and brochures, they learned not only about a textual form, they also learned that texts shape places by making some features visible, while ignoring others. When the teacher asked the students to go beyond celebratory writing and drawing about their favorite places, students were helped to develop critical faculties that are not only important to successful academic achievement in the "standard" school curriculum, but which are also important to their role as place-makers (and future citizens) in their lives beyond school.

The teachers' work demonstrated that to see schooling and the school curriculum, as represented by literacy education, as necessarily antithetical to place is to create a false opposition. Yes, schooling can be improved by being more open to place but, equally, forms of school literacy, particularly those committed to a critical approach, can lead to future place-makers having a better understanding of the ways that places are made in and through texts. This work illustrates that Halfacree's call for rural research to adopt a more discursive understanding of place as significantly involving practices of representation is highly suggestive for the relations between schooling and place, *and* for rethinking rural literacies. More than this, it shows that such work can go beyond the academy and into the lives of even very young students and their classrooms.

Notes

1. For a useful discussion of the implications of Williams' ideas for rural education, see Johnson and Howley (2000).
2. The course continues to be offered some seven years after it was first offered. In the year following its introduction, the course was reshaped as "Literacy and Place," to be more inclusive of the range of teachers, including many from urban areas, who were undertaking the Master's program.

References

Au, W., 2007, "High-Stakes Testing and Curricular Control: A Qualitative Metasynthesis," *Educational Researcher*, vol. 36, no. 5: 258–267.

Au, W., and M. Apple, 2010, "Testing, Accountability and the Politics of Education," *Educational Policy*, vol. 24, no. 2: 421–433.

Ball, S. J., M. Maguire, and S. MacRae, 2000, "Space, Work and the 'New Urban Economies,'" *Journal of Youth Studies*, vol. 3, no. 3: 279–300.

Comber, B. and H. Nixon, 2005, "Literacy Moves On: Using Popular Culture, New Technologies and Critical Literacy in the Primary Classroom," in J. Evans (ed.),

Reading Isn't Just about Books: 21st Century Approaches for 21st Century Children, David Fulton, London.

Corbett, M., 2000, "Book Review: Struggling for the Soul: The Politics of Schooling and the Construction of the Teacher," *Journal of Research in Rural Education*, vol. 16, no. 2: 141–151.

Cormack, P. and B. Green, 2007, "Writing Place in English: How a School Subject Constitutes Children's Relations to the Environment," *Australian Journal of Language and Literacy*, vol. 30, no. 2: 85–101.

Cormack, P., B. Green, and J-A., Reid, 2008, "Making Sense of Place: Exploring Concepts and Expressions of Place through Different Senses and Lenses," in F. Vanclay, J. Malpas, M. Higgins, and B. Adam (eds.), *Making Sense of Place: Exploring Concepts and Expressions of Place Through Different Senses and Lenses*, National Museum of Australia, Canberra.

Derrida, J., 1976, *Of Grammatology*, trans. G. C. Spivak, Johns Hopkins University Press, Baltimore.

Durrant, C. and B. Green, 2000, "Literacy and the New Technologies in School Education: Meeting the L(IT)eracy Challenge?" *Australian Journal of Language and Literacy*, vol. 23, no. 2: 89–108.

Dyson, A. H., 1993, *Social Worlds of Children Learning to Write*, Teachers College Press, New York.

———, 2003, "Popular Literacies and the 'All' Children: Rethinking Literacy Development for Contemporary Childhoods," *Language Arts*, vol. 81, no. 2: 100–109.

Green, B. and C. Beavis (eds.), 2012, *Literacy in 3D: An Integrated Perspective in Theory and Practice*, Australian Council for Educational Research, Melbourne.

Gruenewald, D. A., 2003a, "Best of Both Worlds: A Critical Pedagogy of Place," *Educational Researcher*, vol. 32, no. 4: 3–12.

———, 2003b, "Foundations of Place: A Multidisciplinary Framework for Place-Conscious Education," *American Educational Research Journal*, vol. 40, no. 3: 619–654.

Gruenewald, D. A. and G. A. Smith (eds.), 2008, *Place-Based Education in the Global Age: Local Diversity*, Lawrence Erlbaum Associates, New York and London.

Halfacree, K. H., 1993, "Locality and Social Representation: Space, Discourse and Alternative Definitions of the Rural," *Journal of Rural Studies*, vol. 9, no. 1: 23–37.

———, 2006, "Rural Space: Constructing a Three-Fold Architecture," in P. Cloke, T. Marsden, and P. Mooney (eds.), *Handbook of Rural Studies*, Sage, London.

Johnson, J. D. and C. B. Howley, 2000, "Review of 'The Country and the City,'" *Journal of Research in Rural Education*, vol. 16, no. 2: 146–151.

Murray-Darling Basin Commission & Primary English Teaching Association, 2003, *Spirit of Place*, Murray-Darling Basin Commission/Primary English Teaching Association, Canberra/Marrickville.

Muspratt, S., P. Freebody, and A. Luke, 2001, "Technologies of Inclusion, Geographies of Exclusion: Schooling and Literacy in Small Rural Communities," in P. Freebody, S. Muspratt, and B. Dwyer (eds.), *Difference, Silence, and Textual Practice: Studies in Critical Literacies*, Creskill, Hampton Press, New Jersey.

Pryor, A., 2004, "Deep Ethnography: Culture at the Core of Curriculum," *Language Arts*, vol. 81, no. 5: 396–405.

Smith, G. A., 2002, "Place-Based Education: Learning to Be Where We Are," *Phi Delta Kappan*, vol. 83: 584–594.

———, 2007, "Place-Based Education: Breaking through the Constraining Regularities of Public School," *Environmental Education Research*, vol. 13, no. 2: 189–207.

Tyack, D. and W. Tobin, 1994, "The 'Grammar' of Schooling: Why Has It Been so Hard to Change?" *American Educational Research Journal*, vol. 31, no. 3: 453–479.

Williams, R., 1973, *The Country and the City*, Oxford University Press, New York.

CHAPTER 7

Rural Boys, Literacy Practice, and the Possibilities of Difference: Tales Out of School

Jo-Anne Reid

Introduction

My son Jon was a skateboarder, one of those annoying kids on boards who skated and jumped off driveways and slid along cement edges in public car parks. We lived in Armidale at that time, a small regional city in northern New South Wales. We'd told the children when moving that Armidale was "half way between Brisbane and Sydney," but it looked small and pretty isolated on the map. Less than a month after our arrival, the youngest, Andrew, claimed we'd misled them, pointing out: "Mum, it's actually halfway between *Guyra* and *Uralla*!"–two even smaller rural highway towns, for which Armidale served as a larger "sponge city" (Argent et al. 2008).

We had moved when the children were 11, 13, and 15, and the kids that Jon, the eldest, began to hang out with were nice kids he'd met at school whose out-of-school activities were focused on skating, heavy metal rock music, and deep hanging out. In the schoolyard, he and his group were seen as cool enough to keep out of trouble, with their black trench coats, dreadlocks, and good grades. As the "black coats," they sat with older boys on the "Year 11 lawn" at lunch time, separated from other groups of adolescent "petrol heads," "footy boys," "rodeo riders," and the racially marked "Koori kids." Girls divided their attention among these groups, or sat in their own segregated girl-groups that the boys did not differentiate by name.

After being pulled over by police for skateboarding on a main road, Jon decided to join with a group of other kids to lobby the local council to build a skate park down in the creek lands, where skaters, boarders, and bikers could legally meet and practice. The kids wrote letters, attended council meetings, worked with the local youth officer, spoke on local radio, held a skate competition to raise money, and were ultimately successful in achieving their aim. As a parent *and* teacher educator, I was impressed at the range of "authentic literacy experiences" that were being taken up by these young people as they shared skillsets and energy in achieving what was, for them, an engaging, purposeful social activity. For me, it looked just like what I was describing to my preservice teacher education students at that time as a "Rich Task." This concept, introduced along with the idea of "productive pedagogies" (Hayes et al. 2006) as part of the Queensland New Basics curriculum, is described by the Department of Education and Training, Queensland (2001) as "transdisciplinary activities that have an obvious connection to the wide world."

This story offers substantial challenge to views of literacy then (and still) on offer in NSW schools—where literacy is seen as a set of functional skills and tools for reading, writing, talking, listening, and viewing—hierarchized into a Syllabus whose outcomes can be regularly tested, so that, as Green notes in Chapter 1, "literacy is what gets assessed."

Literacy Practice In and Out of School

In this chapter, I rehearse and reframe an old argument—that there is a real need for literacy educators in school settings to attend to the out-of-school lives and experiences of their students in order to ensure that rich, meaningful literacy experience is incorporated into standardized and regulated curriculum (Nyland 2001; Bigum et al. 2003). Further, I argue that because state literacy curriculum pays so little attention to place—to locational diversity—as it attempts to demonstrate educational performance at state, national, and global levels, it gives little real attention to the situation or diversity of learners who populate the schools. The need for attention to place is particularly acute in rural settings, where poverty and the often overdetermined social positioning of particular forms of gendered subjectivity mean that too many rural adolescent males are unable to connect with and engage in literacy activities in school settings, with either pleasure or success. Where a lack of literacy proficiency (and associated disinterest) causes disengagement with school literacy practices across the curriculum, there is a strong chance that schooling will fail to connect with the complex needs, experiences, and potential of rural boys (Alloway and Gilbert 1997; Broughton and Manuel 2007; Corbett 2007; Sanford and Madill 2007).

Certainly in the Australian context, as around the world, educational expectations and aspirations for boys are significantly lower than for girls—or for boys who grow up in major cities (Kraak and Kenway 2002; Baxter et al. 2011). Life is tough all round for working-class rural males *and* females in contexts of poverty and ecosocial decline, such that mental illness, self-harm, violence, and suicide are growing issues for many rural settings in the Australian context (Pease 2011)—and these are compounded significantly for some by the added "disadvantage" of Aboriginality (see Greenwood 2009). Working with the concept of *rural social space* (Reid et al. 2010) as a construct that situates and constitutes the subjectivities available to young people in rural communities, my aim here is to explore the potential of school (multi)literacy activity to support young people to construct possibilities of different sorts of social space for their own and future generations.

In what Kenway et al. (2006, pp. 18–19) describe as the paradoxically integrative and fragmentary effects of globalization on local cultures, it is not difficult to understand why so many rural youth in Australia are positioned, and constitute themselves, as "marginalized" within a range of discourses that privilege dominant metropolitan, Anglo-European constructions of successful gendered subjectivities. While the "petrol heads," "footy boys," and "rodeo riders" might have dominated the high school yard in the rural community I have introduced here, these subject positions were neither fully inclusive nor all that was available for the young males in this community. This particular rural social space had been constructed over decades of introduced acceptance of the value of academic labor as a means of making a living, as its associated support needs had led to the university becoming the largest employer in the town. Without the interplay of this social and economic history, there would have been little room for the adolescent "black coats" with their marked affiliation with global metropolitan youth formations around heavy metal music, street talk, and skater culture. Kenway et al. (2006, p. 5) note that rural places are increasingly pressured by the collision of traditional forms of masculinity and the effects of globalizing cultures that provide "more open, and sometimes more appealing or more threatening, identity positions" in young men's lives. It is easily seen that the Anglo boys were more powerful in this regard—they had the capacity, within limits, to shift positions and perform a range of different "selves" from time to time, season to season, and to fashion themselves across several of these overdetermined categories for young rural males.

The social space of this community meant that, after race, it was social class that was the greatest limitation on the range of masculinities available to them. There were no "cricketers" at this school, for instance, even in summer. There was no school band, although the "black coats" included arty and dramatic types. Some of the Koori kids might mix with and identify themselves, from season to season, with the "footy boys," taking up powerful positions in this group according to their skill with the ball. However, the history and construct of this particular rural social space (Reid et al. 2010) means that none of the Koori kids would be made team captain, no matter how good they were.

The playground politics carried over into the classroom, and, had the teachers known the playground identities ascribed to the particular groups of boys in their classes, they would very likely have been able to rank the groups according to their academic success. Black coats consistently did well at school, rodeo riders and footy boys did far less well, and the petrol heads and Koori kids tended to leave school just as quickly as they could, for trade training at TAFE or juvenile justice facilities, respectively.

But as others have argued (Bigum et al. 2003; Cole et al. 2010), there is room here to challenge the inevitability of these distinctions, and to do school literacy differently, in ways that challenge conventional stereotypes of rural masculinity. There is no reason why rural boys should continue to have lower educational aspirations (Baxter et al. 2011) and success (Alloway and Gilbert 1997) than girls, or boys in cities. It is clear that dominant discourses of schooling, and school literacy in particular, work alongside film, television, music, and other media to actively represent the rural youth subject in particular ways, and that these constrain or enable young people in rural locations. Donehower (2007) argues that literacy is a resource that can help to renegotiate relationships among rural people in order to support the sustainability of rural communities. In a context in which the children and adolescents of such communities are less likely to achieve success in schooling, such a rethinking of school literacy practices in rural schools is imperative.

Edgy Literacy Engagement—Activity on the Margins

In line with a range of studies (Nyland 2001; Cole et al. 2010) that highlight the importance of engagement, I turn now to another case of integrated literacy activity that began at the skate park, after school.

Along with a group of Koori kids and others that he did not know, Jon and a friend were handed a brochure inviting them to talk about making a movie. This film sought to bring together young people who actually lived marginalized lives, to help explain what being a young person in rural NSW is actually like, as part of a national violence prevention strategy for young people in rural and remote locations. Interested, Jon and some of the others went back after school the next day. And the next. And the next.

After nearly seven months, they brought home the first cut: two hours of grainy color and black and white footage, which we all watched keenly so that Jon could show us "his scene"—a mood shot of large brown autumn leaves piled high and shifting, stirring in the wind on the edge of the road. It was a fine shot, and it produced just the mood of impending cold, dark loneliness that the episode it was part of demanded. I was impressed, but also dumbfounded by what I was seeing in the other scenes of the film. How had this happened? What had been going on in the weeks of afterschool and holiday hours he had spent doing this? It was a wonderful achievement, but how come he'd kept so quiet about what they were doing? "That's the ethics," he explained. "We agreed to keep faith with the people whose stories we did."

That was the limit of my involvement in the film that is the focus of this chapter. I did not participate, understand, or set out to research what was going on: I was the mother of a kid who took part, and who was presented with a completed artifact that I now go on to study, for what it is, for what it means, *and* for what it can teach me as a literacy teacher educator. I may not even have found it so interesting if we had not been invited to the Armidale premiere screening of the film six months later. It was cut now to one hour, ready for national release on the SBS television channel. The film was stunning. The Town Hall was full. Almost all of the Koori families in town were there. I kept looking around for a school principal, a drama teacher, somebody who I knew would appreciate, like me, just what we were seeing, and just what had been achieved by these kids. But there were no teachers. Talking to one of the organizers after the screening, I learned that, as far as he knew, none of the kids had talked about what they were doing at school, and none of their teachers knew anything about it. The point of the activity for them seemed to be that this was NOT school, and that they could never do anything like this at school.[1]

From this perspective, then, I present an analysis of just one part of this *out-of-school* literacy experience that successfully brought together hundreds of young people, over time, and supported them to work collectively to express and communicate meanings about key issues in their lives. Over several months and across multimedia formats, they worked together to tell, scribe, script, act, and re-create stories from their lives on the edge of rural social spaces. They have produced a lasting artifact (Crawford and Priestly 2000) that challenges many of the assumptions that categorize, marginalize, and sometimes institutionalize many of them as failures, both in terms of standardized literacy tests, school, and social success. The representations they produced are powerful and critical accounts of the rural social spaces they inhabit and continuously reconstruct as they struggle to make sense of their lives without support (or even acknowledgment) from their schools or the official literacy curriculum. This work went on in the marginal times and places around the edges of the school day, highlighting the disconnectedness between student life and school literacy. Yet, it seems clear that attention to stories of such out-of-school experience would assist teachers to conceptualize and design different sorts of literacy curriculum that may work to counter dominant, unitary forms of masculinity and femininity on offer to young people in disadvantaged rural locations, and continue to limit their educational success and aspiration.

Film as Social/Literacy Work—The Case of *HURT*

The AFI award-winning feature film *HURT* was professionally produced, under the artistic direction of Philip Crawford's Big hART, though it was not designed as a commercial release. Instead, government funding enabled it to be screened on national free-to-air television and at the International Film Festival in Cannes in 2000. Its cover describes it as a docu-drama where young Australians from rural areas tell their own stories, with their images, in their own words. Its few reviews highlight the involvement of "youth at risk" and the more sensational aspects of the content of the film:

> *HURT* is a docu-drama like no other. 250 young Australians from rural areas and small towns have been given the opportunity to tell their own stories with their images in their words. Challenging, haunting and ultimately uplifting, *HURT* recounts episodes in the lives of young people whose faces have been marked with lines of experiences beyond their years. Cruelty, beauty and isolation seen through young eyes. The cast and crew included 15 car thieves, 23 homeless young people and 9 young people with mental illness. There were 200 camera operators, 98 sound recordists and 85 performers. *HURT* includes 50 portraits, 8 stories, 11 image based

scenes, 3 songs, 2 docu-drama scenes, 2 comedy scenes and 1 connecting narrative. *An outsider film.*

Funded by the NSW Government as part of an anti-violence strategy, *HURT* is not only worthy television, it's also fascinating, revealing, cathartic stuff. The problem with much "youth" TV is that it's either cynical or patronising, or both. The beauty of *HURT* is that it lets young people tell their own stories. In all cases, young people were operating cameras, recording sound, art directing and performing (interestingly, though, each performer was acting, rather than merely telling about a personal experience). In other words, the person on screen is not usually telling his or her own story.

And the result is somewhat surprisingly, nicely polished. The original music is raw and excellent, the stories are wonderfully interwoven and the performances are captivating. (Molitorisz 2002)

While the film itself is worthy of study,[2] as a teacher educator, I approach it here with questions about the potential of a "rich" literacy event such as this, as a model and provocation for rethinking literacy curriculum in schools. Literacy understood as cultural practice, and the actual practice of culture, rather than as functional skills and content to be taught, learnt, and tested, means that "rich literacy tasks" should form the context for the teaching, practice, acquisition, and learning of skills and content in more meaningful ways (Gee 1991). With a focus on youth (here, young males) as subjects, and working with poststructuralist accounts of the constitution of human subjectivity as multiple, fluid, and always in process, I move now to examine *HURT* as an artifact and an event that assists me to understand the forms of subjectivity that participants in the project of education might take up, explore, and practice, in and out of formal institutional settings.

Masculinities on the Edge

While *HURT* deals with violence in the lives of both boys and girls in rural communities, my concern here is to produce an interpretive account of a self-representation of male rural youth that speaks back to dominant discourses of rural youth and masculinity. I argue that, through its development, it produces a counterdiscourse (a contradiction) that makes available for young people an ultimately positive and hopeful position in the world. As both a mother and a teacher of boys, my own reading position in relation to the text is also contradictory—boys are "trouble" in many classrooms (Mills 2007), for teachers, *and* for their female classmates (Martino and Pallotta-Chiarolli 2005, p. 124).

Yet it is clear that outside of the classroom, *all* boys are not so trouble-some. At home, for instance, with their mothers, sisters, aunts, cousins, friends, and grandmothers they are certainly not always or, indeed, even regularly, "trouble." Many boys are sensitive to the feelings of girls and women, caring, supportive, funny, kind, loving, and lovable.

Yet these more sensitive forms of masculinity are not valued in domi-nant discourses of maleness, particularly in rural locations. There are few outlets and opportunities for many young men to produce them-selves as nurturing and loving human beings. This is what makes one particular section of *HURT* so intriguing and worthwhile to examine in more depth, where one young man chose, initially, to tell a story that produced a representation of a loving, caring, sensitive masculine self within a day-to-day context of male violence and anger.

Each of the young people, who wrote, filmed, or performed in the production of *HURT* is memorable in his or her own way. There are many segments that could have been selected as registers of ubiquitous forms of rural social space that construct abjection and marginality for some people as normal (Kenway et al. 2006):

> Perhaps one key characteristic of rurality—or rather its influence in human capital development—is the notion of shared social space. If members of small rural communities share the same social space, the potential risks in stepping outside that space are considerably higher than that of their urban counterparts. (Atkin 2003, pp. 512–513)

"Knowing one's place" in rural social space is far more possible and prob-able than in larger population centers. When everyone knows you, and knows about how and where you are situated, spatially and socially, in the community, it is difficult to mistake or to misrepresent your posi-tion, or your perceived potential as a human being in that place. A sub-stantial episodic account of the cultural initiation ceremony provided for a Koori youth by his uncles, after his mother had caught him stealing, buying grog, and missing school, is strung through the film, for instance, and produces another view of gender relations in places characterized by disintegration, defiance, and the overdetermined limits placed on the youth of traditional Aboriginal communities in despair.

In the transcript presented below, however, I focus on a story written, shared, and scripted by a non-Aboriginal youth, whose membership of a poor white agricultural family produces an equally, but differently, lim-ited set of discursive possibilities within which he can constitute himself as a subject of school and, as a male.[3] This adolescent's vulnerability and dreams for the man he would like to become are startlingly—painfully—open to an analysis that speaks clearly to the aims of this chapter. His capacity as a sensitive, literate male is not as limited as his career performances on school literacy assessments would indicate.

My challenge is to show this in a way that acknowledges his achievement, and respects both his situation and the ambiguities of his dreams, his love, and his sorrow, while simultaneously arguing that the dominant discursive constructions of masculinity available to him may be insufficient for him to become the person he is dreaming here. His account provides the viewer with a privileged access to this young man's imagination of himself becoming somebody who is different from what he is able to be, in this place, with this education, and these limited prospects. In examining this segment as a researcher, though, I acknowledge that work from who and where I am:

> It is an impossible task to avoid the place of the subjective in research [...] instead of making futile attempts to avoid something which cannot be avoided, we should think more carefully about how to utilise our subjectivity as a feature of the research process. (Walkerdine 1997, p. 59)

In this case, as a mother and as a teacher of rural youth, I bring to, and use in, my reading of this segment my own maternal and pedagogical knowledges, understandings, and beliefs about love, affection, and resilience for the healthy growth of a child. These shaped me as a woman who grew up in a conservative "small-town" environment, but who left it eager for the promise of what else was available outside the safety of that circle, and angry with the self-satisfied bigotry of many of those who wanted to keep it secure. As Soja (1989, p. 6) argues,

> We must be insistently aware of how space can be made to hide consequences from us, how relations of power and discipline are inscribed into the apparently innocent spatiality of social life, how human geographies become filled with politics and ideology.

In my own hometown I knew no Aboriginal people at all, and did not understand this as a fact worthy of reflection and interrogation. Like many in my generation, my education did not raise this as an issue (Burney 1997), and I understood it as problematic only when I had moved outside this particular space. The young people in *HURT*, of course, have not moved away—they have been constituted as subjects within the norms and truths of the particular forms of rural social space in which they are growing up. And, as I have explained above, the social space of Armidale, produced out of its particular history, is different from that of Moree, or Walgett, Narrabri, or Tamworth, or indeed my own home town—further north again. Growing up some*where* is a key aspect of growing up *someone*. While Wexler (1992, p. 10) noted that, for students in school, the "central and defining activity" of young people is their systematic engagement in the "symbolic interactional labour through which they become somebody," it is through this work that they "establish at best the semblance of an identity. In turn, that image further organises the course of their lives. [...] Students are not victims but symbolic workers in the identity production process." *Where* they do the work of becoming somebody, though, just as *when*, makes all the difference.

Australian studies such as that by Smyth and Hattam (2001) have discussed this concept of identity production as the "work" of young people, and McLeod and Yates (2006) have also taken up the notion of "becoming someone" as both project and process. Following Foucault, they argue that human subjectivity is constructed in discourse, embodied, involving unconscious as well as conscious desires, fears, and dispositions. Subjectivity is produced in "dreams and ambivalence—and accumulating life histories shape how subject positions are negotiated and subjectivity is fashioned" (p. 87). They also note: "All accounts of subjectivity are partial and incomplete...and the challenge for us as researchers is to read different perspectives against each other, not to settle for a single, all-encompassing account [...] of what is really happening" (p. 88).

A Story of What Might Have Been

This is my challenge here, because I cannot claim to know what is "really" happening in the life of the young man I focus on, in the story he tells:

34.40
Mum was pregnant, about 4 months pregnant when she found out it was a girl a baby girl, and Mum was all excited—went out and bought all baby stuff and a new pram and girls clothes. And I was pretty happy cos it was all boys, there was me and William and Joshua, but Mum always wanted a girl, and so she was pregnant with her...

34.59
Then when it come to about 6 months pregnant...Mum went into labour and they sent her up to John Hunter hospital, by airplane, and she had

labour there, she gave birth to her. And we called her Saffra. And she lived for about seven hours and died.

35.28

Everyone was really hurt by it. Josh was only a baby so he didn't really understand. William was crying a lot. And Mum come home and we got sent away for about 6 months—me and William sent away for foster care sort of thing. Mum had a nervous breakdown, so I never really got to see Mum, very much after that...

35.51

And then when I moved back in I said sorry, and I felt pretty lonely at the time, didn't know what to really do. I felt very angry with myself. I never seen her, I never got to really touch her until when I went to the funeral...

36.43

If she did live, I dunno, might have been, dunno... different hair, she might have been small, might have been tall, I would have took her places when I got my licence, would have had fun, taking her to parks, play games with her. She would have had, like, her own little toys, for girls. Would have been, probably, good at school. Would have been different having a girl around, listening to girl music...and she might have had red hair, or she might have been a tomboy, might not have been. Could've been happy, could've been sad. I could have been like her best brother, or maybe not—some of my other brothers might have been. Would have made Mum happy having a girl...

37.31

And that's about it.

HURT (transcript)

Big *h*ART Inc, 1999

This is an intensely moving episode for me, as a viewer. I feel strongly for the narrator, a young man poised on the slippery roof of a poor farm house in a dry and dusty paddock—poised in-between birth and death, man and boy, the softness and hope of his boyish love for his mother and his dreamed-of baby sister, and the reality of the harsh dry masculine world that he has to deal with, alone.

All that I know for sure is that, just like my Jon, and 249 other kids, he was hanging around some public place in his rural town one afternoon and was "picked up" as maybe interested in making a movie. I know that he responded to the invitation to tell something about violence that he'd seen, heard, or experienced with a story from which violence is absent, yet its effects haunt, echo, and menace throughout—a story that is masterfully oblique, yet hits us as an anthem for doomed youth.

I know, too, that the kids who heard this story accepted it, talked about it with him, and that one of them wrote it down as he told it, so that the collective was able to keep it safe for reuse and reworking on another day. His characterization of his longed-for baby sister as "probably, good at school" strongly suggests that he already lives by a storyline in which he has constituted himself (because he is a boy?) as someone who is not. Yet I know that the group came back to reread each other's stories several times, talked about them again, and chose this one as important enough to workshop, to interrogate, to understand and elaborate sufficiently well that they could transform it from a memory into something else, something new, using different forms of storytelling. In this way, the project leaders had designed a process that will resonate with English teachers everywhere—for me, echoing the powerful tradition of a personal language curriculum base that had shaped the field of English and literacy education in recent history.

These are Michael Halliday's (1975) approach to the study of language and text in his "language in use" workshops, James Britton's (1970) theoretical articulation of the move from expressive language to transactional or poetic forms, and James Moffett's (1981) range of writing workshops such as the "memory monologue" process from *Active Voice*. I had worked with these approaches to writing in my own teaching, and still know their power for assisting writers with the generation and crafting of text for particular purposes and audiences. The transcript from the film sequence provides a sense of the story, although the full impact and affect are best provided in the filmic mode. As the work of the *HURT* participants continued through the sharing of existing skillsets and the practice of new skills, the problem of this transformation became a real, and very rich, literacy task for the kids involved. The point of the *HURT* project, in the rural locations in which it was carried out, is that this literacy event potentially offered and enabled participants to try out, practice over time, and know how to take up new and different subject positions within their own lives—and thereby recognize themselves differently.

Transformative Literacy Experience for Becoming Somebody in the Bush?

Pease (2011) notes that the rural idyll is a myth for many people in rural communities, and that there are a number of sociocultural aspects of rural areas that may have implications for gender relations, in particular: "greater social and political conservatism; stronger enforcement of gender rules and traditional; roles in the family; a strong belief in the privacy of family matters; a mythology of mateship among men and reinforced patterns of female subordination" (p. 155). As McLeod and Yates (2006, p. 87) note, "non-rational aspects of subjectivity are often poorly captured in exclusively narrative- and discourse-based accounts of subjectivity or in views of subjectivity that represent it as a cluster of subject positions." Instead:

> [S]ubjectivity is embodied and emotional—desires, dreams, ambivalence—and accumulating histories shape how subject positions are negotiated and subjectivity is fashioned.

Deciding on the mode of presentation and representation of this story involved considerable high-order thinking, critical use of vernacular knowledge of film and film technique, and explicit instruction in creating and evaluating visual, sound, and narrative effects in the film medium. As with every sequence in the film, the *HURT* participants were not left alone as they used their existing skillsets and were taught those "operational" (Green 2002) skills that they needed to continue and complete the task with which they had become so "involved."[4] As noted above, the project provided expertise and support from a range of Aboriginal and non-Aboriginal actors, directors, and musicians. The literacy demands of real-world skills such as storyboarding, casting, deciding on location, time for shooting, the choice and preparation of appropriate and evocative sound, decisions about contextualizing background and lead-in shots, collecting and arranging the material props they needed, planning shots and camera angles, sequencing and timing shots were all meaningful and necessary to develop within the "cultural dimension" (ibid.) of filmmaking practice. So too were the "critical" (ibid.) literacy skills of considering and deciding on the style and pace of, and then directing, rehearsing, and timing the reading of the voiceover text (above) after editing.[5] In this way, participants, involved in an ongoing, sustained literacy experience over time, were being taught and were practicing and operationalizing new skills and knowledge within a discourse and practice community that, I argue, following Gee (1991), set up the conditions for mastery of this "secondary discourse" through practice that involves both "acquisition" and "learning." My reference here to Green's "3D" model of literacy, where the "operational-technical" and "critical-reflexive" dimensions of literacy are learned in and through "cultural-discursive" practice, highlights the powerful and substantial benefits of such an approach as a curriculum model for literacy learning in school settings (Green 2012).

This power resides in the transformational dimensions of meaning-making, for real purposes and audiences—arising from the articulation of personal and local experience and story—and reshaping this experience through collective discourse and transformation across modalities. At the simplest level, the focus on personal oral language as the starting point for literacy learning and the supported transformation of meaningful ideas from talk to text, and, here, to film, video, music, or other medium, becomes a model for school literacy practice that can supplement and complement mandated versions of literacy. While I am focusing on the "aesthetic" as a form of (self)-production here, the same process applies to the production of more "efferent" dimensions of literate subjectivities, as evidenced in my introductory tale of Jon and his mates working to get themselves a skate park in their local community.

It is this sort of literacy curriculum that is particularly important for schools in educationally "disadvantaged" locations, where the range of secondary discourses available to young people can be limited or constrained by their positioning in the particular forms of (rural) social space in which they live and learn about themselves and the world. The strong binary association of school success and femininity in this boy's story is important for teachers. It makes available an understanding of the space he has to do the work of constituting himself as a man. The intimated yearning for a place for himself in school, evident in his words; the associated visual shot of him closing a children's book, as his sister's death closes the possibility of him reading to her, suggests the pleasure he had known as his mother had read to him in the unlit kitchen of his home, and discloses his regret at the potential loss of literacy as a source of pleasure without the "excuse" that a baby girl might have provided him. For me, this particularly highlights the importance of schools attempting to think carefully about ways in which rural boys might find a place to explore other forms of pleasure in and through their involvement in rich and rewarding literacy practices. Following the theoretical literacy curriculum pathways forged by Britton, Gee, and Green, and the parallel practical approaches to literacy instruction offered by Halliday and Moffett, the importance of school literacy providing rich, personally involving, rewarding, and intrinsically pleasurable tasks for students, to supplement (if not replace) the "thin gruel" of mandated curriculum from elsewhere, is clear. To follow Michelle Fine (1991), this means that if the lives and subjectivities of low-income adolescents are to be taken seriously as an issue of social justice in education, the boundaries and concerns of (literacy) education in schools must be stretched by their teachers to incorporate that which is central to their lived experience. Shirley Brice Heath has similarly discussed the value of creative work with images for literacy learning, arguing that "young people engaged in a highly participatory arts-based programme leading to performance and product development, have multiple opportunities to take part in joint problem solving and critique" (2000, p. 126).

Conclusion

When the success of projects such as *HURT* and the sorts of activities Heath talks about here is focused out of school, there is an immediate issue of whether the school situation can accommodate such complex and engaging forms of literacy practice. Each of the situations I have discussed here has taken place outside of school—and for the most part, would not have been seen as involving literacy at all. The kids were involved in doing something in the world—their learning was not prearranged by the teacher to meet learning outcomes that were predetermined by the Syllabus. They learned together as they worked together to complete something they saw as worthwhile:

> In non-school situations, where time flows beyond the usual limited number of minutes available for [...] classes within schools, young people work collaboratively toward maintaining the organisation, preparing and producing the work of the group and assessing success or failure. (Heath 2000, p. 126)

Certainly there are real constraints on teachers wishing to program for such rich tasks within current school subject and timetable structures. Teachers themselves rarely get to participate in such activities, and it may be unrealistic to expect that they will design authentic literacy curriculum when they themselves are not engaged as intellectuals in literacy events. Reflection on the success of the enterprise of *HURT* as a literacy event allows us to see how such work could be conceived. These young people worked to a limited timeframe, and they worked episodically, sometimes with month-long breaks between activities as the production team moved from town to town, and left for the city to transcribe, locate equipment, and edit film. They were able to regroup, refocus, reread, and replan, and move forward as the activity played out over time. They did not choose their own task or topic, though it is important to note that they worked with a *whole* task that allowed them to imagine a clear end point and then solve the problem of how to get there, and from a topic that was open enough to allow all contributions to be valued and new skills to be learned and practiced.

There are many such tasks and topics available to teachers with a conceptual understanding of rural social space and knowledge of the affordances and constraints of the ways that rural social space constitutes and subjectivates young people. If teachers are to make a difference in the lives of the young people they teach, we must make room in even the most crowded curriculum to negotiate and work with literacy as cultural practice in the school setting.[6] As Barbara Kamler (2001) writes, there is a need for literacy pedagogies to take a lead toward "relocating the personal," in supporting young people to make themselves up as literate subjects inside, as well as outside, school settings.

The value of this work *inside* school is that teachers' professional expertise can support students to make the connections between their cultural-discursive practice and the associated acquisition and learning of operational skills and technical understandings about language, text, and modes of meaning. Teachers would have confidence that young people can be trusted to be able to fill in a curriculum space constituted as an "invitation" or "question" rather than simply a "command" (Green 1990). Teachers' expertise can support these forms of literacy practice within critical-reflexive frames that matter in the sociospatial situation of educational practice, so that students are offered ways of reading their place, and their position in it, differently.

Where school systems have organized themselves in ways that place such rich tasks "outside" rather than integral to the literacy program, we are in danger of providing such narrow understandings of literacy that we cannot see the evidence and potential of enlisting literate behaviors more appropriate to the particularities of the people and places they serve.

Notes

1. See Corbett and Vibert (2010), for a discussion of perceived literacy hierarchies in school and nonschool literacy activity.
2. http://www.daybreakfilms.com.au/hurt/.
3. The introductory frame to this boy's story is included as the second segment of the online representation of the film at http://www.daybreakfilms.com .au/hurt/.
4. See Kim Donehower (Chapter 2) for an account of the importance of emotional and intellectual satisfaction and pleasure that resides in this sort of involvement in a task.

5. Only the final editing of each sequence was not done by the youth participants themselves.
6. See Reid (1992) for another example of sustained literacy-focused classroom
practice.

References

Alloway, N. and P. Gilbert, 1997, "Boys and Literacy: Lessons from Australia,"
Gender and Education, vol. 9, no. 1: 49–58.

Argent, N., F. Rolley, and J. Walmsley, 2008, "The Sponge City Hypothesis: Does It
Hold Water?" *Australian Geographer,* vol. 39, no. 2: 109–130.

Atkin, C., 2003, "Rural Communities: Human and Symbolic Capital Development,
Fields Apart," *Compare: A Journal of Comparative and International Education,*
vol. 33, no. 4: 507–518.

Baxter, J., M. Gray, and A. Hayes, 2011, *Families in Regional, Rural and Remote
Australia,* Fact Sheet 2011, Australian Institute of Family Studies, Melbourne,
Victoria, http://www.aifs.gov.au/institute/pubs/factssheets/2011/fs201103
.html.

Bigum, C., M. Knobel, C. Lankshear, and L. Rowan, 2003, "Literacy, Technology and
the Economics of Attention," *L1-Educational Studies in Language & Literature,*
vol. 3, nos. 1–2: 95–122.

Boomer, G. (ed.), 1982, *Negotiating the Curriculum,* Ashton Scholastic, Sydney.

Britton, J. 1970, *Language and Learning,* Penguin Press, London.

Broughton, M. and J. Manuel, 2007, "What Do Australian Boys Think about
Reading?" *Literacy Learning: The Middle Years,* vol. 15, no. 1: 9–16.

Burney, L., 1997, NSW Aboriginal Education Consultative Group President's
Statement 1996, NSW Department of Education and Training, Aboriginal
Education Policy.

Cole, B., M. Mooney, G. Munns, A. Power, W. Sawyer, and K. Zammit, 2010,
Engaging Middle Years Boys in Rural Educational Settings, NSW DET, Sydney,
NSW.

Corbett, M., 2007, *Learning to Leave: The Irony of Schooling in a Coastal Community,*
Fernwood, Halifax.

Corbett, M. and A. Vibert, 2010, "Curriculum as a Safe Place: Parental Perceptions
of New Literacies in a Rural Small Town School," *Canadian Journal of Educational
Administration and Policy,* no. 114, http://umanitoba.ca/publications/cjeap/pdf
_files/comm2-Corbett-Vibert.pdf.

Crawford, P. and M. Priestly, 2000, *HURT,* Big hART & The Omni Group, SA Film
Corporation, Adelaide.

Department of Education and Training, Queensland 2001, The Rich Tasks, http://
education.qld.gov.au/corporate/newbasics/html/richtasks/richtasks.html.

Donehower, K., 2007, "Rhetorics and Realities: The History and Effects of
Stereotypes about Rural Literacies," in K. Donehower, C. Hogg, and E. E. Schell,
Rural Literacies, Southern Illinois University Press, Carbondale.

Fine, M., 1991, *Framing Dropouts: Notes on the Politics of an Urban Public High School*, SUNY Press, Albany, NY.

Gee, J., 1991, "What Is Literacy?" in C. Mitchell and K. Weiler (eds.), *Rewriting Literacy: Culture and the Discourse of the Other*, Bergin and Garvey, New York.

Green, B., 1990, "Imagining the Curriculum: Programming for Meaning in Subject English," *English in Australia*, no. 94: 39–58.

———, 2002, "A Literacy Project of Our Own," *English in Australia*, no. 134: 25–32.

———, 2012, "Literacy in 3D: Contextualisation and Commentary," in B. Green and C. Beavis (eds.), *Literacy in 3D: An Integrated Perspective in Theory and Practice*, Australian Council for Educational Research (ACER), Melbourne.

Greenwood, D. A., 2009, "Place, Survivance, and White Remembrance: A Decolonizing Challenge to Rural Education in Mobile Modernity," *Journal of Research in Rural Education*, vol. 24, no. 10: 1–6.

Halliday, M, 1975, *Learning How to Mean*, Edward Arnold, London.

Hayes, D., M. Mills, P. Christie, and B. Lingard, 2006, *Teachers & Schooling Making a Difference: Productive Pedagogies, Assessment and Performance*, Allen & Unwin, Sydney.

Heath, SB 2000, "Seeing Our Way into Learning," *Cambridge Journal of Education*, vol. 30, no. 1: 121–132.

Kamler, B., 2001, *Relocating the Personal: A Critical Writing Pedagogy*, SUNY Press, Albany, NY.

Kenway, J. A. Kraak, and A. Hickey-Moody, 2006, *Masculinity Beyond the Metropolis*, Palgrave Macmillan, London.

Kraaak, A. and J. Kenway, 2002, "Place, Time and Stigmatised Youthful Identities: Bad Boys in Paradise," *Journal of Rural Studies*, vol. 18: 145–155.

Martino, W. and M. Pallotta-Chiarolli, 2005, *Being Normal Is the Only Way to Be: Adolescent Perspectives on Gender and School*, University of NSW Press, Sydney.

McLeod, J. and L. Yates, 2006, "Becoming Someone as Project and as Process," in J. Mcleod and L. Yates, *Making Modern Lives: Subjectivity, Schooling and Social Change*, SUNY Press, Albany, NY.

Mills, M., 2007, "Issues of Masculinity and Violence and the Current Boys' Debate in Australia," *Redress: Journal of the Association of Women Educators*, vol. 16, no. 2: 21–25.

Moffett, J., 1981, *Active Voice: A Writing Program across the Curriculum*, Boynton/Cook, Montclair, NJ.

Molitorisz, S., 2002, "Show of the Week," *Guide, The Sydney Morning Herald*, viewed March 24, 2011, http://www.documentaryaustralia.com.au/da/case Studies/details.php?recordID=33.

Nyland, B., 2001, "Language, Literacy and Participation Rights: Factors Influencing the Educational Outcomes of Boys," paper presented at the 12th European Reading Conference, Dublin, Ireland, July, 1–4.

Pease, B., 2011, "Reconstructing Violent Rural Masculinities: Responding to Fractures in the Rural Gender Order in Australia," *Culture, Society & Masculinity*, vol. 2, no. 12: 154–164.

Reid, J., 1992, "Negotiating Education," in G. Boomer, N. Lester, C. Onore, and J. Cook (eds.), *Negotiating the Curriculum: Educating for the 21st Century*, Falmer Press, London and Washington.

Reid, J., B. Green, M. Cooper, W. Hastings, G. Lock, and S. White, 2010, "Regenerating Rural Social Space? Teacher Education for Rural-Regional Sustainability," *Australian Journal of Education*, vol. 54, no. 3: 262–276.

Sanford, K. and L. Madill, 2007, "Understanding the Power of New Literacies through Video Game Play and Design," *Canadian Journal of Education*, vol. 30, no. 2: 432–455.

Smyth, J. and R. Hattam, 2001, "'Voiced' Research as a Sociology for Understanding 'Dropping Out' of School," *British Journal of Sociology of Education*, vol. 22, no. 3: 401–415.

Soja, E. W., 1989, *Postmodern Geographies*, Verso, London.

Walkerdine, V., 1997, *Daddy's Girl*, Macmillan Press, London.

Wexler, P., 1992, *Becoming Somebody: Toward a Social Psychology of School*, Falmer Press, London.

CHAPTER 8

Reconfiguring the Communicational Landscape: Implications for Rural Literacy

Kathryn Hibbert

[L]et me say what I have discovered through the acts of reading and writing... that language that carries weight in our culture is very often fuelled by a search for home, our rather piteous human groping toward that metaphorical place where we can be most truly ourselves, where we can evolve and create, and where we can reach out and touch and heal each other's lonely heart.

Shields (2003, p. 262)

Locating the "Self"

Claiming that we research who we are, Cole and Knowles (2001) suggest examining "segment[s] of one's life written for purposes of understanding oneself in relation to a broader context" (p. 49). In this chapter, I revisit a study that marked my foray into research in the virtual world and the subsequent creation of a national network for students and teachers entitled, *The Salty Chip: A Canadian Multiliteracies Collaborative.*[1] Through this work, I explore the "expanded spaces" for learning (Gutierrez and Larson 2007) created outside of rural or urban geographies, by rethinking the affordances of the virtual space. In particular, the chapter will consider the implications of a changing communicational landscape (Jewitt 2010) as theories and practices of multiliteracies come together with recent thinking about rural education to consider a notion of "rural literacy," and how such a notion might afford or limit as we go forward. To move forward, it is sometimes necessary to begin by looking back.

Meditation 1

Although I have lived exclusively in urban spaces for the past three decades, I was born and raised in rural Ontario, and still consider my rural roots as "home" in a way that has never emerged in the various cities we have lived in. Perhaps it is true that you can take a girl out of the country but you can't take the country out of the girl. As I write this chapter, I try to reconcile tension between the urban "land of opportunity" and the rural "land of my youth." My recollections of childhood in a rural space are complex. Certainly my siblings and I hold a strong connection to the land; we understood well the relationship between our labor and our economic survival; we participated fully in the significant daily tasks required to work the land, grow crops, and care for livestock. It was customary for city dwellers to take a drive out to the country on the weekend, stopping at the corner abattoir for meat and freshly made cheese. A half-mile off the highway, they would stop at our farm to buy sweet corn and mushrooms, and further down the road they would purchase eggs. Despite this seeming abundance, we knew that our primary objective was to get an education so that we, too, could move to the "land of opportunity."

Three decades later as I visit the family farm (figure 8.1), I am struck by its beauty, but saddened by a new reality; of those living in the homes all along our road, few, including my family, continue to farm their own land. The shift to the "factory farm" model has meant that many living in rural spaces are employed elsewhere. It seems that the "land of opportunity" has come to the farm. I worry about the competing demands of nature and economics (e.g., the increasing compromises in food safety). This, in a context of regulations (e.g., pesticide controls and education) designed to improve the health and welfare of our farm families, the land, and the produce. It is a changing landscape; one focused on end products and bottom lines, and I wonder about the long-term implications for our future. How do we engage in serious dialogue about these issues in ways that will promote respect for the land and the health of our citizens?

In proclaiming the years 2003–2012 the "literacy decade," UNESCO acknowledged the vital role that literacy plays in ensuring full participation in society (np). The proliferation of multiple forms of text, and the affordances that new "literacies" have for meaning-making, offer expanded opportunities for literacy to be understood as a social practice, concerned with how "people make sense of their everyday lives" (Barton and Hamilton 1998, p. 4). Our everyday lives, as my little vignette demonstrates, are changing. In their work on *Local Literacies*, Barton and Hamilton (1998) have observed that "within a given culture,

Figure 8.1 The Family Farm.
Courtesy: Photo by J. Dill.

there are different literacies associated with different domains of life" (p. 9). Learning about the home literacy domain can present challenges; literacies created in one space (e.g., the home) do not always translate well into what counts as school literacy (Heath 1983). When we consider who is producing and legitimizing certain forms of texts, and who is consuming and assimilating them, we begin to see more clearly the effects of "urbanization, rural outmigration and the subsumption of spatial peripheries into the social, cultural, economic, and political spheres of the urban core" (Schafft and Jackson 2010, p. 1). The objective of reforming rural schools was to make them "look more like urban schools: larger, bureaucratized, run by educational professionals rather than locals, and informed by the latest pedagogical knowledge" (p. 2). Over the past two decades, education in Ontario, Canada, as elsewhere, has embraced this line of thinking, ushering in standardized curricula and provincial assessments (complete with teacher "training") while consolidating township school boards into larger administration units under the

Fewer School Boards Act—all despite research documenting a negative impact on rural communities (Fredua-Kwarteng 2005); and ignoring the way that "placed resources" "become dysfunctional as soon as they are moved into other places" (Blommaert, cf. Prinsloo 2005, p. 96).

In the rush to compete on a global scale, leaders at all levels have failed to examine old assumptions about individuals and communities in these changing times. Author Daniel Pink (2009) argues that the business-managerial models of the past will not serve the needs of the present generation. Pointing to deep human desires "to direct our own lives, to learn and create new things, and to do better by ourselves and our world" (p. 10), he underlines the incommensurability of these desires with managerialist approaches. The path to success, Pink explains, is to understand that what motivates people is deep personal satisfaction gained by participating in a life in which one has autonomy, mastery, and purpose. The managerialist approaches currently governing our lives, he argues, favor compliance.

Unpacking the "Rural"

Meditation 2

I pause here, to think about why his work resonates so strongly with me. When I think of rural, I think of the land—living interdependently with nature, animals, families, and neighbors. We used to give tours to school children on our farm so that they could better understand the process involved in bringing food to their tables. The care needed to create a suitable, rich growing environment, the work of planting, cultivation, and tending to crops or caring for livestock are invisible to the average consumer, interested only in the end product. I realize, however, that I give little thought to other "ruralities" that I have not embodied and I begin to grasp the power of embodied knowledge on our worldview. Rural is not simply "farming"—and yet some would see it as "anything other than urban." The definition seems to have more to do with the lack of a critical mass. Urban "sprawl" suddenly becomes a physical manifestation of how dominant discourse "unnaturally" silences imagination or understanding through place-less policies and practices. Perhaps rural refers then to the understanding, valuing, and respecting of "place" and the unique processes associated with the local. Perhaps rural refers to difference; to attending to the whole of something rather than parts disconnected. If this is the case, there are many people, like me—still rural in my imagination and desires—struggling to thrive despite dwelling in the poor growing conditions afforded by urban spaces. How might we reclaim this space to revitalize our thinking? How might reconceptualizing the "rural" as a resource instead of a problem help us begin this process?

A change of century often marks a time of reflecting upon the past and excitement about the future. In the early twenty-first century, we have witnessed profound technological advancements coupled with unprecedented labor mobility. At the same time, we have witnessed the collapse of large Western cities and their gradual return to nature.[2] Residents of Detroit, United States, for example, describe the events that led to the downfall of the once powerful manufacturing industry as a very slow decline (figure 8.2). The rebuilding of a sustainable community emerged as people worked together for a common purpose; in this case, to eradicate hunger. It is a project that acknowledges that people had become "alienated from their ground...When we reconnect people, it helps [build] responsibility, and...a greater love for who we are" (Booker 2011, np).

Booker's comments offer insight into how notions of rurality highlighting the connection of rural people to "their ground," and the affordances of new literacies allowing them to connect and speak authoritatively from what they know, may offer educators a means to reclaim their intellectual ground, build fertile learning communities, and rediscover their passion. First, we must become aware of "urban sprawl" and its effects on how literacy is defined and enacted in rural Canadian classrooms. Although not constructed of bricks and mortar, the artifacts of urban (policy) sprawl

Figure 8.2 Banksy, Detroit, 2010.
Source: Green Celebrity; http://www.flickr.com/photos/greencelebrity/4697673815/

and subsequent neglect of communities can be seen to have operated in a parallel fashion. Learning outcomes have been "misappropriated to serve in the development of a system that is more suited to modern management techniques, and to survival in a competitive market economy" (Hussey and Smith 2002, p. 231). Such practices "guided by neoliberal ideology . . . extend their reach . . . into local levels" (Sloan 2008, p. 572). The time has come for rural students and teachers to "redefine place as something other than local geography, to craft alternative identities other than those imposed on them, and to encourage them to imagine worlds beyond their own" (Schafft and Jackson 2010, p. 4).

New Literacies Studies

As Ontario was introducing standardization to a shrinking but increasingly powerful school board bureaucracy, a group of ten academics from the UK, Australia, and the United States (a.k.a. the New London Group) were meeting and theorizing about the multiplicity of communication channels and diverse modes of representation and expression afforded in today's wired world. Concerned with the application of a market-economy mindset to an educational context, they argued that local diversities (social, cultural, and economic) should be respected as economically attractive assets. Their 1996 manifesto, *A Pedagogy of Multiliteracies: Designing Social Futures,* stressed notions of democratic pluralism and productive diversity (rather than singular standardization) as the means to achieving social equity in addition to economic development (New London Group 1996). The ensuing pedagogy of multiliteracies sought to situate learning in the lives of learners. As Brooks (2011, p. 111) explains, "if you can surround a person with a new culture, a different web of relationships, then they will absorb new habits of thought and behaviors."

Setting the Context

Ontario is Canada's most populous province with a population of over 13.1 million. Of those, 2 percent have identified as Aboriginal (North American Indian, Metis, or Inuit), and an additional 15 percent of the population is considered rural. Projections to 2036 see growth in urban areas, but significant declines in the rural areas. The provincial capital, Toronto, is one of the most multicultural cities in the world. The rural spaces are also diverse; with many farms owned or worked by immigrants. Ontario is home to several francophone communities, black settlements founded by descendants of the Underground Railroad, and 127 First Nations communities.

Like other jurisdictions, Ontario has undergone significant reform and consolidation measures in an "accountability era" (Gross Stein 2001) that promotes "economic efficiency" and alignment of educational "voice" (Grumet 2010). At the turn of the century, the population in rural Ontario was shrinking, contributing to the closure of rural schools. For vulnerable communities in rural Canada, resource depletion and shifting global commodity prices challenged residents to consider ways to diversify and stem the rural youth "outmigration." Geographically speaking, deterritorialization and reterritorialization leads to an alienation of place and loss of situated control over local resources and practice—as well as a loss of what was local to those holding the "loci of power" (Swyngedouw 2000), a point that resonates with my experience.

Consolidation and centralization were economic responses to shrinking resources with little or no consideration that such moves effectively extinguished rural schools and rural ways of knowing and acting in community. Gallagher (1995) observes:

> This approach . . . larger (and therefore more efficient) units of administration . . . sets aside the . . . real costs of further distancing parents and other community members from what once were their schools. In truth, many school boards, particularly in the larger school districts, are already as remote from the people they represent as provincial and regional governments are. (p. 71)

Miller (1995), who views the "community *as* curriculum" (p. 2), laments the loss of the rural school as a hub to the community for lifelong learning, as it limits his ability to build the community capital needed to sustain inhabitants. His sentiments mirror Schafft and Jackson's (2010) claims about "the *interrelationship* between school and community, and how that interrelationship is shaped by the global-local context in which it is embedded" (p. 3, emphasis added). The loss parallels the erosion of the family farm alongside the erosion of respect for the local knowledge of all of those, including teachers, who live and work in rural spaces. Yet, rural literacies scholars, Donehower, Hogg, and Schell (2007), contend that it is a vital component of "the complex global economic and social network" (p. xi).

Within this context, discourses of community and citizenship have emerged, as educators are challenged to achieve "a different kind of citizenship—an active, bottom-up citizenship in which people can take a

self-governing role in the many divergent communities of their lives"
(Cope and Kalantzis 2009, p. 172).

Virtual learning was introduced in large part to ensure access to
teachers who resided in rural and remote areas of the province, or were
working full time and caring for children. It was an unabashed success
in eliminating traditional barriers to continuing education. According to
Corbett (2006, p. 111), "communication and transportation technologies
have shrunk both geographic and social gaps between rural and urban."
Might the communications technologies of the virtual world—a new
kind of sprawl—provide educators a place to come together, to build a
new kind of "intellectually fertile" community and in the process reclaim
their "ground"? Might this serve to reconfigure "rurality" as resource and
a standpoint rather than deficit? Against this backdrop then, I review
and reconsider data gathered within a virtual learning environment.

Planting the Seeds: Teachers' Literacy Understandings in an Online Course

In an online Reading course for teachers, 20 teachers and 2 instruc-
tors (with a range of classroom experience), from Boards that spanned
15 different school districts, assembled seeking a specialist designa-
tion. Many were located along the southwest or southeastern parts of
Ontario—reflecting the population distribution: 14 taught in rural[3]
areas (map 8.1).

Unlike district or provincially run professional development, the
virtual classroom offered a reconfigured communicational landscape
in which *place* is less tangible or immediately obvious. In the virtual
classroom, teachers were learning alongside others working across the
province and often in other parts of the world. What happens to conversations about literacy when teachers are *dis-located* from regional or
provincial constructs of knowledge? Does *location* still *matter* (Green
2012) in the same ways?

Barton and Hamilton (1998) claim that their approach to understanding and developing local literacies in the UK was "strongly shaped by the
insistent voices of practitioners and adult students... who reject definitions of literacy in terms of skills, functions and levels which do not fit
their experiences, nor their visions of the power of literacy in everyday
life" (p. 5). As I reviewed the narratives generated from the participants, I
found almost universal alignment and compliance with mandates. I wondered, has *place-less* pedagogy disempowered the local agency of rurally
placed teachers and learners? If so, how might the virtual environment

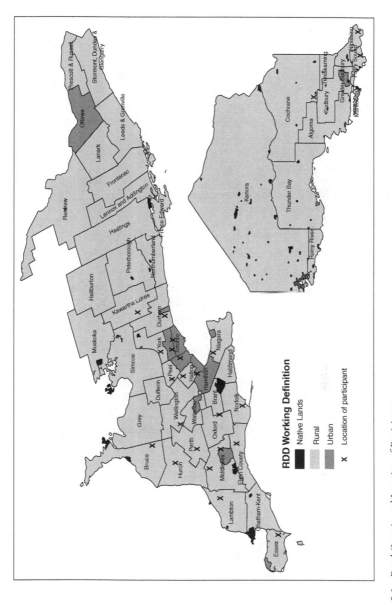

Map 8.1 Rural Ontario and Location of Participants.

Source: Ministry of Agriculture, Food and Rural Affairs © Queen's Printer for Ontario, 2012. Adapted and reproduced with permission.

serve as a space to rebuild community and *re*vision the local? I begin by offering a glimpse into the stories told in this study.

Narrative: Doing "My Level Best"

Ariana[4] was a conscientious and enthusiastic participant in the course. Working in a community located just beyond the border of a large urban area, her participation in course discussions mirrored her desire to be a "good" teacher. Deeply embedded into her conscience about good teaching, however, was the institutional story embraced by her school board:

> Many schools...have committed to Balanced Literacy programs. This is very progressive because they have backed the talk with funding, support materials and staff,...Reading Recovery Teachers, book rooms full of leveled text and release time to conference at each level...We will be creating a book room soon, and will begin to define our programs closer to what they do in the District.

Despite the benefits of an approach that requires a differentiated pedagogy based on the needs of the child rather than a pre-set curriculum, there are dangers in what is described here. What was not mentioned was that the support amounted to *place-less,* "purchased pedagogy"; essentially, *training* in the use of commercial products (Hibbert and Iannacci 2005; Hibbert, Heydon, and Rich 2007). A subsequent posting by Erin, a classmate working for the same Board (but located even further from its urban loci of power), revealed a different experience: "my school does not have a literacy coordinator, or any of the great things that you talked about." The expressed desire in Erin's comment appeared rooted in a consumerist ethos; to improve or legitimize one's literacy program, it appeared essential that one had to "buy into" particular programs, policies, and products. Under pressures associated with a relatively new "audit culture," boards were spending considerable funds on commercial packages that claimed to meet the needs of all students—regardless of place, culture, or learning need. Such moves, in effect, further alienated educators from their role, their responsibility, and their ability to act as decision makers.

To offer an example of this, I share excerpts from the online course discussion surrounding the "leveling" of texts—a key feature of this approach. The seemingly simple idea about matching readers with "appropriate" texts was spun into a publishing industry complete with guiding lists for leveling (and guided purchase suggestions of preleveled resources). Many school boards have linked initiatives in a mandated commercial assessment (Developmental Reading Assessment [DRA]) with the added expectation that *all* classroom and library texts be leveled. Before long, this "tool" essentially usurped complex information gathered and utilized by both readers and teachers as they learn to choose appropriate texts. In an attempt to disrupt the "leveled text" discourse, I shared the following:

(Late yesterday afternoon, I met my husband at a local shopping center to purchase a family gift. While chatting with the storeowner, her son and husband arrived en route to a sports activity.)

Mom: Hello "Johnny." Are you ready for the game?

Son: I'm a little nervous, but yeah.

Mom: Did you remember your math book and your AR? [Accelerated Reader]

Son: Oh. I got the math, but I didn't bring the book.(Dad and son proceeded to the back of the store to fix a snack).

Mom: [To me] Is it normal for students to test out at a level that is lower than the year before?

Me: That depends. Are they using the same test? Are you referring to a particular publisher's level? Did he read over the summer?

Mom: I don't know what they are using, but he's really upset that he's not in a higher level. He's very competitive. [Calls to son] Johnny—did you read today?

Son: yeah.

Me: What do you like to read? Who is your favorite author?

Son: Oh, I guess I would have to say Gary Paulsen. I like all the Brian stories. And guess what mom—the teacher moved me up a level today!

Mom: Really!

Son: Yeah! Now instead of being 4.2–5.9, I am 5.3–6.4!

Mom: Is Harry Potter in that level?

Son: Just the first one [in the series].

Me: Are you looking forward to reading Harry Potter?

Son: Oh I've read them all already. I'm just not in the level where I can read them in school.

(I went on to discuss the books with him, to discern whether there was a suspicion of comprehension weaknesses etc. He was more than able to discuss all the books, draw links to others he had read outside of school etc., but neither mother nor son seemed to see the irony in what I have quoted you.)

After a marked "silence," Jayne (a teacher in an affluent, urban center) explained,

There is such a push now to be accountable for your marks and I find that parents are questioning more and DO want to see written work to justify why their child is not at their grade level in reading.

Teri (a teacher in a rural north central community) added:

> The amount of assessment we are doing . . . is taking some of the joy and fun
> out of learning . . . the ongoing joke is that by the time all the paperwork
> and assessments are completed, we barely have time to teach the kids!

Up to this point, no one had discussed the purpose for the assessments or
the leveling—the strengths or limitations, the relationship, relevance or
cultural appropriateness for their students, or the way it could be useful
and/or misused. We had reached a place in our relationship with each
other where we could finally unpack teacher agency and educational ideals, and how even within the limits of the institution there was a *place*
and a *space* for teachers to act and a rich discussion ensued. It was somewhat surprising then, to find a realignment with leveling books resurface
in the final weeks of the course—in spite of the stories these teachers
told us all about what they know to be good teaching—that seemed to
underscore the power of the dominant narrative. For example, Rachel (a
teacher in a very small rural school in Southwestern Ontario) provided
the following direction to her colleagues:

> First go to http://www.newton.k12.ks.us/dist/curr/bp/lit/levels_of_read-
> ers.htm. Here you will find a chart that compares various leveling sys-
> tems . . . you will need this. Then go to http://www.leveledbooks.com/
> booksearch.html. Here you can type in the names of recent books and
> series to get a reading recovery level (which you can then reference to
> Fountas and Pinnell A, B, C, etc.).

Rachel's post revealed a core commitment to the leveled books process in
her practice in spite of her evolving understanding of where she and her
students were situated within a discourse of accountability. What vision
of education or of children lies behind such practice? How might we
foster a sustained critical literacy stance in such an essentialized environment? How do we encourage more "rural minded," holistic thinking in
such a context? Might the leveling of text mirror the hierarchy of "place"
implied in the relationship between urban-rural ways of knowing? Will
the local interests and situated knowledges of Rachel's students be over-
looked as she fits them into the received structure?

Rural Literacy in the New Economy

Historically, it seems, much has been made about how to *fix* or *accommodate* the rural literacy "problem." According to Graff (2011, p. 43),

schooling and literacy education were the first steps in re-ordering the values and customs of rural populations entering the Industrial Age...Literacy was not...by itself a vehicle for economic advancement, but rather a means of inculcating values and behaviors in the general population that made large-scale economic development possible.

An overemphasis on particular types of "literacy for school" has altered educators' vision and understanding about what gets lost in the narrow view. As Eppley (2011, pp. 88–89) notes,

attention to matters of place...is out of bounds in high-stakes teaching environments that seek to normalize children and teachers because context contradicts standardization...By their nature, these policies attempt to ignore place, but place always matters...Place-conscious pedagogy...understood as a means of resisting inequitable literacy practices...is explicitly learner-centred and in its most mature form seeks democratic participation spiralling from the local to the global.

Mindful of Wenger's (1998, p. 10) observations that "our designs are hostage to our understanding, perspectives and theories," my reanalysis of the conversations looked for the way language functioned in the various discussion areas, and the role our understandings, perspectives, and theories played in the design of the online Reading course. I gleaned a number of things from this process. Using Halliday's (1973) *Functions of Language* to categorize the postings, I discovered a lack of opportunity for participants like Rachel to develop and use "imaginative" thinking. Could such a design flaw in the way the course structured space to discuss these issues explain, in part, why teachers were less inclined to think of possibilities beyond the status quo? Taking a functional approach, I conducted a cross-data analysis to learn "how the form of language has been determined by the functions it has evolved to serve" (Halliday 1973, p. 7). I learned that despite significant efforts to foster community, the modular format of the online course, and the pedagogy imported from a "bricks and mortar" world, may have perpetuated an essentialist approach, serving to further reify the place-less pedagogies it sought to disrupt. Where did we make space in the course for teachers to tell us about the uniqueness of place and how their own literacy experiences and resources informed their pedagogy? Where could Rachel have been helped to imagine a practice that extended her pupils' reading through interest and purpose, rather than formulaic level? How could the professional learning space assist her to gain authority in her own school community?

Digging Deeper

Eppley (2011, p. 94) suggests that "we make sense of the world through our discourses, but discourse also speaks through our self-representation, thus making discourse an important consideration in how teachers understand children." I began to think about Wenger's (1998) concept of *reification* in relation to Halliday's (1973) functions of language and the impact that these two concepts have for rendering an interpretation. Wenger (1998, p. 61) cautions that the "evocative power of reification . . . is also its danger." For example, centralized place-less mandates may have generated the initial form, with negotiation of meaning occurring within its confines. For Wenger, reification "shapes our experience" (p. 59) and is tied very closely to participation. The way in which we participate in the world is very much related to identity, and tied up in issues of gender, class, culture—and perhaps increasingly of place. In the negotiation of meaning, it is important to attend to the interplay of participation and reification; the way in which we represent place—our self, our practice, formal and informal, tacit and explicit. The powerful discourses about literacy instruction universally positioned "best (place-less) practices" as the gold standard; implicitly positioning those in rural areas as somehow deficient and in need of "catching up."

In the context of discourse communities that represent historically powerful and legitimized institutional ways of knowing, the metaphor of urban sprawl again comes to mind. Those on the periphery are simply "annexed" and overtaken. Is it possible, given the dominance of "space-blind" policies (Green and Letts 2007) produced in urban-centric places, for anything nonurban to thrive?

In the "virtual space" of an online environment, it can be possible (at least initially) for some of the dominant social cues to be less visible (e.g., rural/urban, class, gender, age). As in the case considered here, the interplay of self and experience as participants related to others began with the articulation of shared experiences. Although initially the backward and forward process appears to cancel out geographic distance or the specificity of place, the discussion eventually draws on discourses that participants identify with, or that are dominant in the various other communities they may belong to. One instructor, for example, positioned herself not as an "absolute authority" but a colleague, with one set of knowledge and expertise to bring to the discussions. She held a "big picture" understanding of the course, and was charged with the responsibility for building community and fostering interaction among participants. However, the instructor was also a school principal tasked with ensuring alignment with centralized policies. She had grown up in, and now taught in, the rural context—however, her positioning as a leader overrode any values she may have brought with her from her rural upbringing. Principals are often *placed* in rural settings early in their administrative careers; the schools are smaller, giving new members an opportunity to become acculturated into their new roles. Well-performing leaders see subsequent placements in larger urban settings as a form of promotion, rendering alignment with centralized policies and dominant discourses a professional incentive. As we have seen in Rachel's case, institutional identity and institutional knowledge trumps personal or local knowledge. It is a dichotomy that new literacies may help us redress.

Reclaiming "Place" through Digital Affordances

The New London Group (1996) has argued that the purpose of education "is to ensure that all students benefit from learning in ways that allow them to participate fully in public, community, [creative] and economic life" (p. 9). Multiliteracies teaching and research engages new literacies that are changing the ways in which teachers and students interact with learning and increasingly how they collaborate. Challenges faced by educators include how to harness what are often seen as disruptive technologies, in powerful ways that reposition rural students and teachers from consumers of monolithic texts to designers of representational texts. The ability to localize, contemporize, and individualize learning is "mobilizing a strong movement" (Casserly and Smith 2008, pp. 261–262), and calls upon participants to share their unique and local identities. Could the professional reading group on which I am focusing provide more opportunities for participants to build on local knowledge and critique the centralized discourses and practices if it was designed to allow the affordances of multiliteracies pedagogy?

According to Davidson and Goldberg, (2009, pp. 1–2), "the single most important characteristic of the Internet is its capacity for world-wide community and the limitless exchange of ideas," a comment that appreciates the richness of the diversity in the exchange. With respect to rural education, this means legitimizing the work of refocusing attention on the places within which we live and work; on the relationships between people, their livelihoods, and their communities (Theobald 1997) rather than purchasing decontextualized curricula. Rural, place-conscious education offers teacher and students a way to reconnect to their community in ways that motivate them to "imagine the world as intradependent...and develop a richer sense of citizenship and civic action" (Brooke 2003, p. 6). As this reimagining unfolds in an increasingly digital environment, we need to be mindful of what happens when "people move texts across contexts" (Barton and Tusting 2005, p. 23). Rural teachers and learners can bring their knowledge "home" by creating and re-creating online representations for their embodied knowledge.

The Salty Chip: A Canadian Multiliteracies Collaborative (figure 8.3) is an example of a different design for teacher learning. It is a network that reflects this place-conscious thinking; an attempt to reconnect students and teachers to the places where they study and work. It was conceived as a dynamic network, where teachers and students could connect, share, collaborate, customize, and improve upon *multiple literacies* including Web 2.0 tools, in meaningful and *locally relevant* ways. Would such a network motivate teachers to locate their own community's interests and identity within the broader national and international communities in ways that develop a stronger sense of rural citizenship? *The Salty Chip* was designed to support teachers and students to plan together, gather feedback, and build upon each other's ideas. It serves to scaffold the teachers' knowledge about using the tools; something often found to be somewhat behind the knowledge of their more technologically savvy students (see, for example, Prinsloo 2005). The expanded community allows us all to learn more about unique cultural identities and ways of engaging with all forms of text. As our knowledge and experience of "multiliteracies-in-use" grows, so too will our collective abilities to design relevant, engaging experiences with and for our students. Learning about the rural in relation

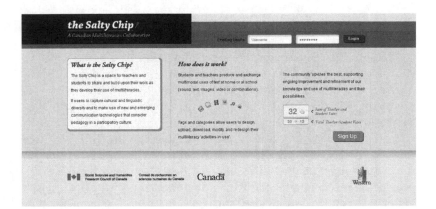

Figure 8.3 The Salty Chip: A Canadian Multiliteracies Collaborative
Source: www.saltychip.com

to other communities may help both teachers and students "construct understanding about the world" (Theobald 1997, p. 138).

Using Virtual Affordances to Reclaim Rural "Ground"

The sense of disconnection I describe at the beginning of this chapter seems to mirror the disconnection that teachers and students have been increasingly experiencing with regard to an authentic sense of their place in the world; their responsibility in relation to each other and their notions of the future. My own life offers an example of the movement from the rural to the urban—the changing nature of both the rural sociogeographic landscape and the digital-communicational landscape. Gruenewald and Smith (2008) suggest that place-based education is "the educational counterpoint of a broader movement toward reclaiming the significance of the local in the global age... It seeks to resist the erosion of place resulting from economic globalization's negative impact on communities" (cf. Eppley 2011, p. 97), an approach that place-conscious teachers can certainly apply. Multiliteracies intersects with the rural and an agenda concerned with social justice by offering a means for all learners to participate more fully in civic life in ways that represent their unique identities and values.

The ways in which the teachers like Rachel "recomposed" their experiences through participation and reification in a virtual community of professional practice showed some promise, but it is impossible to appreciate the long-term effect on their thinking. The flashes of interdependence evident in the data recalled the interdependence of a typical farm community when you relied upon one another to survive. In virtual spaces like *The Salty Chip*, everyone is tethered to a common curriculum. As they develop relationships with one another and begin to form a community, the potential for this space to become "place conscious" and challenge what has been "normalized" is palpable. However, the virtual world, too, can be co-opted to serve various purposes. Corbett (2006) suggests that the

> struggle for space takes the form of the concentration of control of resources into the hands of fewer and fewer economically powerful interests. In rural areas, this has meant that the resources people have traditionally harvested become commodities to be bought and sold. (p. 116)

In the design of an online course, it is important to recognize and make visible the power that policies and regulations have on limiting learning and/or participatory space. How did the board and provincial policies surrounding "leveled text" rewrite the literacy landscape in schools? It served to uproot and *displace* teachers from the intimate knowledge of students and books that stems from interacting as readers—in favor of those suggested by generic, formulaic knowledge that can be *bought and sold*.

Multiliteracies approaches offer new pedagogical tools, and new ways to mediate relationships. Prinsloo (2005) suggests that new literacies function as artifacts; "as signs that are embedded in local relations which are themselves shaped by larger social dynamics of power, status, access to resources and social mobility" (p. 96). Bringing "multiliteracies" together with understandings about "the rural" helps create new ways of knowing ourselves and reconnecting to what matters deeply. According to Wesch (2011), we are witnessing a type of "cultural inversion": the trend to express individuality is paired with a counter trend toward valuing community. We must remember that advances in technology are *built around people.* And people are increasingly developing networks and those networks determine how people influence one another as they work toward a valued purpose. Recalling Pink's (2009, p. 10) claim that humans are motivated by the desire to "direct our own lives, to learn and create new things, and to do better by ourselves and our world," it would seem that a reinvigorated rural literacy is one that aims to reclaim that deep personal satisfaction gained from *participating* fully in a life that values *place.*

Multiliteracies theories allow us to reclaim the rural as part of an agenda aimed at improving participation by all citizens. Reconsidering the teachers' narratives in the Reading course has led me to believe that virtual spaces of learning, appropriately configured, can be an ideal space to serve this purpose. However, recalling Halliday (1978), opportunities for constructing a virtual space that makes this possible must be explicit by design; we must invite teachers engaging in these spaces to first reconnect with their "place-based" knowledge and experiences and those of their students in order to position local ways of knowing next to those privileged in centralized curriculum and assessments. Raising awareness of this positioning may help educators advocate better for local needs and knowledge. Making the local "visible" may help reestablish communities around these marginalized ways of knowing and perhaps persuade others of their value. Prinsloo (2005) has argued that such "connectivity makes possible a level of economic and social integration at a world level that would have been impossible otherwise" (p. 88). Explicitly employing a multiliteracies approach to teaching in the virtual world may function to persuade participants of the value of "ruralities" in a way that previous pedagogies lacked. Employing various modes and media can enhance our ability to communicate in powerful ways. A virtual community built around people (Hibbert and Rich 2006) offers enormous potential to disrupt monolithic forms of knowledge. People have enormous capacity in their diversity for meaning-making. It is time to make a "place" for them to do so. Reconfiguring the communication landscape afforded by the virtual space allows teacher learners an opportunity to reflect deeply on their own ruralities in ways that may help them open up new spaces in their classrooms.

Notes

1. "The Salty Chip: A Canadian Multiliteracies Collaborative," http://www.saltychip.com.
2. See the example of the Urban Farms Project in Detroit, http://www.urbanfarming.org/.
3. Defined according to the Ontario Ministry of Agriculture, Food and Rural Affairs, http://www.reddi.gov.on.ca/images/Slide2.jpg
4. All names are pseudonyms.

References

Barton, D. and K. Tusting, 2005, *Beyond Communities of Practice: Language, Power and Social Context*, Cambridge University Press, Cambridge.

Barton, D. and M. Hamilton, 1998, *Local Literacies: Reading and Writing in One Community*, Routledge, London, UK.

Booker, C., 2011, *Urban Farming: Global Food Chain*, http://www.urbanfarming.org/.

Brooke, R. E., 2003, *Rural Voices: Place-Conscious Education and the Teaching of Writing*, Teachers College, Columbia University Press, New York.

Brooks, D., 2011, *The Social Animal: The Hidden Sources of Love, Character and Achievement*, Random House, New York.

Casserly, C. and M. S. Smith, 2008, "Revolutionizing Education through Innovation: Can Openness Transform Teaching and Learning," in T. Iiyoshi and S. V. Kumar (eds.), *Opening Up Education: The Collective Advancement of Education through Open Technology, Open Content, and Open Knowledge*, MIT Press, Cambridge, MA.

Cole, A. L. and G. Knowles, 2001, *Lives in Context: The Art of Life History Research*, AltaMira Press, Lanham, MD.

Cope, B. and M. Kalantzis, 2009, "Multiliteracies: New Literacies, New Learning," *Pedagogies: An International Journal*, vol. 4, no. 3: 164–195.

Corbett, M. 2006, "What I Might Have Said: Rural Education and Globalization," *Our Schools, Our Selves,* vol. 16, no. 1: 109–119.

Davidson, C. N. and D. T. Goldberg, 2009, "The Future of Learning Institutions in a Digital Age," John D. and Catherine T. MacArthur Foundation Report, http://www.scribd.com/doc/13476078/The-Future-of-Learning-Institutions -in-a-Digital-Age.

Donehower, K., C. Hogg, and E. Schell, 2007, *Rural Literacies*, Southern Illinois University Press, Carbondale.

Eppley, K 2011, "Teaching Rural Place: Pre-service Language and Literacy Students Consider Place-Conscious Literacy," *Pedagogies: An International Journal*, vol. 6, no. 2: 87–103.

Fredua-Kwarteng, E., 2005, "School Closures in Ontario: Who Has the Final Say?" *Canadian Journal of Educational Administration and Policy*, vol. 46: 1–26.

Gallagher, P., 1995, *Changing Course. An Agenda for REAL Reform of Canadian Education*, OISE Press, Toronto.

Graff, H. J., 2011, *Literacy Myths, Legacies & Lessons: New Studies on Literacy*, Transaction, London, UK.

Green, B., 2012, "Literacy, Place and the Digital World," *Language and Education*, vol. 26, no 4: 337–382.

Green, B. and W. Letts, 2007, "Space, Equity and Rural Education: A 'Trialectical Account,'" in K. N. Gulson and C. Symes (eds.), *Spatial Theories of Education: Policy and Geography Matters*, Routledge, New York.

Gross Stein, J., 2001, *The Cult of Efficiency*, House of Anansi Press, Toronto.

Gruenewald, D. A. and G. A. Smith (eds.), 2008, *Place-Based Education in the Global Age: Local Diversity*, Lawrence Erlbaum, New York.

Grumet, M., 2010, "The Public Expression of Citizen Teachers," *Journal of Teacher Education*, vol. 61, no. 1: 66–76.

Gutierrez, K. D. and J. Larson, 2007, "Discussing Expanded Spaces for Learning," *Language Arts*, vol. 85, no. 1: 69–77.

Halliday, M. A. K., 1973, *Explorations in the Functions of Language*, Butler and Tanner, London.

———, 1978, *Language as a Social Semiotic: The Social Interpretation of Language and Meaning*, Pitman Press, Bath.

Heath, S. B., 1983, *Ways with Words*. Cambridge University Press, Cambridge.

Hibbert, K. and L. Iannacci, 2005, "From Dissemination to Discernment: The Commodification of Literacy Instruction and the Fostering of 'Good Teacher Consumerism,'" *Reading Teacher*, vol. 58, no. 8: 2–13.

Hibbert, K., R. Heydon, and S. Rich, 2007, "Beacons of Light, Rays, or Sun Catchers? A Case Study of the Positioning of Literacy Teachers and Their Knowledge in Neoliberal Time," *Teacher and Teaching Education*, vol. 24, no. 2: 303–315, doi:10.1016/j.tate.2007.01.014.

Hibbert, K. and S. Rich, 2006, "Virtual Communities of Practice," in J. Weiss, J. Nolan, and P. Trifonas (eds.), *The International Handbook of Virtual Learning Environments*, Kluwer Academic, Dordrecht, The Netherlands.

Hussey, T. and P. Smith, 2002, "The Trouble with Learning Outcomes," *Active Learning in Higher Education*, vol. 3, no. 3: 220–233.

Jewitt, C., 2010, *Challenge Outline: New Literacies, New Democracies*, Scibd, http:// www.scrib.com/doc/31645645/Future-Learning-New-literacies-and-new-democ racies#

Miller, B., 1995, "The Role of Rural Schools in Rural Community Development," Eric Digest No. 384479, http://www.ericdigests.org/1996–1/rural.htm.

New London Group, 1996, "A Pedagogy of Multiliteracies: Designing Social Futures," *Harvard Educational Review,* vol. 66, no. 1: 60–92.

Ontario Government, 2011, *About Ontario,* April, http://www.ontario.ca/en/about _ontario/index.htm.

Pink, D., 2009, *Drive: The Surprising Truth about What Motivates Us,* Riverhead Books, New York.

Prinsloo, M., 2005, "The New Literacies as Placed Resources," *Perspectives in Education,* vol. 23, no. 4: 87–98.

Schafft, K. A. and A. Youngblood Jackson, 2010, "Introduction: Rural Education and Community in the Twenty-First Century," in K. A. Schafft and A. Youngblood Jackson (eds.), *Rural Education for the Twenty-First Century: Identity, Place and Community in a Globalizing World,* Pennsylvania State University Press, University Park, PA.

Shields, C., 2003, *The Arts of a Writing Life,* Turnstone Press, Winnipeg, Manitoba.

Sloan, K., 2008, "The Expanding Educational Services Sector: Neoliberalism and the Corporatization of Curriculum at the Local Level in the US," *Journal of Curriculum Studies,* vol. 40, no. 5: 555–578.

Swyngedouw, E., 2000, "Authoritarian Governance, Power, and the Politics of Rescaling," *Environment and Planning D: Society and Space,* vol. 18: 64–78.

Theobald, P., 1997, *Teaching the Commons: Place, Pride and the Renewal of Community,* Westview Press, Oxford, UK.

UNESCO Literacy Decade, http://www.unesco.org/en/literacy/why-the-literacy -decade.

Wenger, E., 1998, *Communities of Practice: Learning, Meaning, and Identity,* Cambridge University Press, Cambridge.

Wesch, M., 2011, Keynote address, Canada 3.0, Stratford, Ontario, April 2011.

PART III

Place and Sustainability

CHAPTER 9

Thinking through Country: New Literacy Practices for a Sustainable World

Margaret Somerville

Introduction

In *The Country and the City*, Raymond Williams (1973) complains that the images of English rural life he is exposed to in his Cambridge University education are not the images of the specific rural places where he grew up in Wales. His is a specific country(side). He develops the thesis that *the country* and *the city* are relational categories that can be understood only together. In the vastly greater movement of transposing the English rural to the Australian landscape, processes of colonization produced both material and discursive effects. The country and the city were inscribed onto an old and fragile continent with deep prior symbols and representational practices in which cities did not exist and the country was not rural.

My aim in this chapter is to disrupt the binary thinking through which the category "rural" is created, by taking Country as a location from which to think. In doing this, I explore the methodology of 'thinking through Country' developed in collaboration with U'Alayi researcher Immiboagurramilbun,[1] as fundamental to the production of knowledge. Thinking through Country is produced from the space of mutual entanglement between settler and Aboriginal knowledges, languages, and practices of representation. To think through Country fundamentally disrupts the way that we understand the relationships between language and land, literacy and representation. Habitual binary thinking prevents deep engagement in the questioning of knowledge systems and their representational practices in relation to ecological sustainability.

Understandings and practices of literacy are embedded in the nature of knowledge. Western knowledge systems privilege abstract, generalized knowledge over local, embodied, and emplaced knowledges (Haraway 1991). These hierarchical systems of knowledge are constituted through binary structures of language and thought that separate human subjects from their embeddedness in the natural world and its ecological processes (Rose and Robin 2004). Australian scholars, both Indigenous and non-Indigenous, have engaged with Indigenous place knowledge since first settlement (Carter 1987). It is commonly understood that for Australian Indigenous people, Country as a concept differs from the many terms such as environment, nature, land, and country that constitute our relationship to the natural world (Rose 1996). Such scholarship, however, tends to leave each knowledge system intact and separate, failing to address the effects and responsibilities of our mutual entanglement.

Indigenous knowledges and practices of representation have fundamentally changed since white settlement. In these changes, core knowledge concepts have been translated into English, bending the English language to serve the purpose of Indigenous understandings, as in the concept of Country. Cultural practices based in singing the country through ceremony have been radically translated into new art forms in which sacred knowledge and symbols are transformed from ephemeral body and ground designs onto canvas and boards. Ceremonial body performance has been translated into new forms of dance and body movement. These new representational practices have emerged from the space between Indigenous cosmologies and Western forms, and have the potential to disrupt binary structures of knowledge. However, structures of Western knowledge are dominant and remain intact, a seemingly indestructible force in their capacity to induce planetary destruction.

Literacy is an important site of transformative change both in terms of its conceptualization and its practices (Freire 1996). It is through particular literacy approaches and pedagogies that language practices are formed and potentially transformed. If our relationship to place is constituted through language and story, literacy practices are a crucial site for the transformation of our relationship to the natural world. Current practices of literacy in schools have evolved within Western language systems that separate human beings from the ecological processes and the natural world. Literacy practices in schools continue to privilege narrow concepts of literacy as reading and writing despite a decade of scholarship that emphasizes the importance of multiliteracies and new literacy technologies (Cope and Kalantzis 2000).

Recent research in literacy has identified the potential of connections between literacy and place to extend the field's attention to the more-than-human world (Green, Cormack, and Nixon 2007, p. 77) and to better connect with the life worlds of children (Comber 1997). Realizing this potential is increasingly challenging, however, under the current conditions of "rampart standardization" (Comber 2011, p. 343), emphasizing literacy benchmarking through standardized testing and reporting. Literacy is an important site of struggle for Indigenous peoples in Australia because Indigenous children are the single most disadvantaged group under current literacy regimes. On the other hand, Indigenous local knowledge of Country is widely accepted as a key to environmental sustainability. How can these two apparently irreconcilable ideas be thought together? How do our understandings of "rural as Country" *and* of "literacy" change through bringing these ideas into conversation with each other?

In this chapter, I take the idea of place or Country as a starting point, and literacy as a process of meaning-making through representational practices, to explore what literacy practices or knowledges we need to create a sustainable world (Donehower, Hogg, and Schell 2007). While I take up Donehower et al.'s argument for the connection between rural literacies and sustainability of rural places and communities, my interest is in a more radical reconceptualization. I want to move beyond the rural/urban binary to take our relationship to Country as the fundamental focus, and to foreground literacies based in local places as a starting point for ecological sustainability.

Thinking through Country

Thinking through Country is a conceptual and methodological framework developed in a research collaboration between Chrissiejoy Marshall, an Aboriginal doctoral student, and myself, as a non-Indigenous place researcher. Chrissiejoy is a U'Alayi[2] speaker who grew up on the Narran Lake in western New South Wales (NSW). When she was with her Aboriginal family she was called Immiboagurramilbun, Immi for short, the name she prefers when referring to her Aboriginal knowledge. When white people were around, she was known as Chrissiejoy Marshall, named after her father, the property owner. She grew up learning the deep knowledge of Noongahburrah (water people) culture, a small clan of the larger U'Alayi language group specific to the Narran Lake area.

Chrissiejoy struggled against academic language and knowledge struc-tures. To be able to proceed at all she had to develop a methodology of Country, even though her research was not about developing a con-flict resolution training package for Aboriginal communities. In order to think at all, she recognized that she had to think through Country, particularly the specific County of the Narran Lake. Country was not a generalized place but rather a specific place with particular material (geographical) characteristics and cultural stories.

Chrissiejoy's identification with the Country of the Narran Lake is not about essentialist origins but represents complex processes of translation, language, and literate practices. Her grandmother was an Erinbinjori woman from north Queensland; her grandfather and uncles were Noongahburrah people of the U'Alayi language group from the Narran Lake; and her father was a white station owner. She learned Erinbinjori, U'Alayi, and English languages and claims all of these iden-tities and knowledge traditions. It is the Narran Lake, however, the place of her growing up, that she identifies as the location of her thought and knowledge. It is the way that she makes meaning of the world, the struc-ture of her literate subjectivity. The Narran Lake is foundational to her ontology and epistemology; it is her text.

The necessity to engage with the development of an alternative methodology that sits between Western knowledge traditions and her Aboriginal[3] knowledge of Country meant that she was particularly reflex-ively aware of the process. The methodology was developed in visual, oral, and written forms. She produced a painting and an accompanying oral story that structured and informed each cluster of meanings, or chapters, based on her knowledge frameworks of Country. The paint-ings were digitally photographed and her stories digitally recorded and presented on a DVD to her doctoral colleagues as an assemblage of forms and meanings. By moving between the paintings, the oral storytelling, the writing, and consciously reflecting on the development of a radi-cal alternative methodology, Chrissiejoy was able to express meanings that would otherwise have been unsayable in written academic English alone. In this way, new modes of literacy were generated from the space in between knowledge systems, languages, and forms of representation. One of her paintings, for example, reflexively explores an alternative ontology described in the following quote from her oral performance and recorded digitally on DVD (Immiboagurramilbun 2003):

The swans *(Byahmul)*—One swan is the *Mulgury (Mingin)*[4] [totem] of my mother, *Karrawanna*, who died within a couple of hours of my birth.

The second swan is for *Noongahburrah*, my grandfather's mob who lived around the Narran Lake, *Terewah*, is where this *Mulgury* belongs—to that land and those people.

Erinbinjori is the largest and most powerful of the crocodiles. He was in the *Belin* of my people and very important to our land and people. Crocodile is the *Mulgury* to that land and people.

The dots are all linked to show the continuous connection of everything—depending on the closeness of the dots as to how connected the object or person is to my being.

Wardook/Bohrah (kangaroo) and *Jindi/Dinawan* (emu) are both *Mulgury* to us of the Erinbinjori mob. The *Wwardook* is of the men (note the closeness of the dots) and the *Jindi* is of the women. These two are also very important to our *Belin*.

Bandabee (The Kookaburra) is the Mulgury of my grandmother (Yoon-garlin). Ticalarawillaring—Erinbinjori mob.

The Albatross is the Mulgury of my son.

Chrissiejoy communicates this ontology using a mixture of U'Alayi, Erinbinjori, and English naming practices as well as through the performance of oral storytelling and digital images of her paintings. These multiple acts of translation offer her non-Aboriginal audience the possibility of entering a space where these knowledges can begin to be accessible and meaningful. While these ideas are drawn from Aboriginal knowledge traditions, they do not exist in Aboriginal cultures in this form. Bringing them into articulation in this way is already to enter the liminal, an act of translation between specific Aboriginal traditions, contemporary Aboriginal cultures, and Western forms of English language and painting. These multiple acts of translation necessarily include the series of computer-generated digital images of her paintings and their accompanying oral stories such as those quoted above, which are incorporated into her performance. The representation of this knowledge as literate practice is multimodal, contemporary, and hybrid, while drawing on traditional knowledge and practices of Country. This act as a practice of literacy places Chrissiejoy in an ontological relationship to the natural world and all of its creatures, to her relatives by blood and kinship, and to Country. I propose this understanding as the foundation of thinking through Country as literate practice.

Local Place Literacies

Thinking through Country offers a conceptual and methodological framework for reconceptualizing the relationship between literacy and ecological sustainability because it is founded in local place knowledge. In order to explore the nature of local place literacies as the basis of Aboriginal knowledge systems, I draw on a series of partnership projects with Gumbaynggirr people on the mid-north coast of NSW. In these projects, we developed new resources for language, literacy, and place learning (Somerville and Perkins 2010). These projects can be conceptualized in terms of proceeding through a series of questions about the nature of place knowledge. In the first project with a single clan group of Gumbaynggirr people on the mid-north coast of NSW, we asked: What constitutes Indigenous knowledge of this local place and how can this knowledge be understood in contemporary language and forms of literacy? The second project, which extended throughout Gumbaynggirr Country, investigated how Gumbaynggirr knowledge moves from local to regional knowledge without losing the specificity and the materiality of local place literacies. The third project asked: How do Australian Indigenous knowledge systems move beyond the boundaries of local and regional knowledges in relation to water in the Muurray-Darling Basin, and what literate practices represent this more-than-regional knowledge of Country?

In the first project about local place knowledge in Gumbaynggirr country, I worked in partnership with Gumbaynggirr elder Tony Perkins and the community in the Garby (rock wallaby) elders clan territory of the Corindi-Red Rock area (Somerville and Perkins 2010). Tony initiated the project with archaeologists and oral historians to research their local place knowledge for their ecotourist enterprise. For Gumbaynggirr people, local place boundaries are important because they signify identity and knowledge in Country. A sense of the boundaries of one's Country is constructed from within, from the center of one's being. Learning the boundaries of their clan's local Country began with familiarity with the places where they habitually traveled and camped: "We can put lots of dots on a piece of paper within a certain area, but outside that area you might find only a coupla dots, but they're more ceremonial type camping areas when you're traveling from one area to another."

Knowledge of the extent of local clan territory is linked to story knowledge that was "passed down . . . when the Old People were around." This applies to places they may never be able to visit, but because there are so many stories of those places of belonging and identity, they become familiar with their Country. When young Gumbaynggirr people moved far away to the city, their parents and grandparents took the responsibility of teaching them about their identity in place. Even without going to Country, they learn "where to go, who to see and what languages were spoken." This knowledge, communicated through language and story, is a way of mapping Country through relationships and connections.

Tony said that Gumbaynggirr people are frequently asked to represent this knowledge as "lines of a map." He said it is a new way of representing boundaries as knowledge of Country and caused many problems. "Lines on a map," he said, "hem people in" because they are contrary to a sense of local Country defined from within. These lines do not conform to Country as it is understood through the delicate negotiations with others involved in boundary work: "A lot of time we had to spend with people from Yamba and Maclean trying to work out a line running from there at Minnie Waters and them places. We're tryin' to work out a line. Where will it run? How do we get that line?" To understand a relationship to Country that is not defined by print literacy is to understand Country through other knowledges: through walking and camping; eating from a place; oral stories; spiritual intensities; relationships; connections; and negotiations.

We recorded stories of local places with the Garby Elders and the community from the Red Rock-Corindi Beach area to produce a series of small books called "Yarrawarra Place Stories." Eventually Tony and I compiled all the stories into a book, with Tony adopting the role of oral storyteller and myself the work of the writer. These are then used as resources for teaching both the local community and the broader public. In these processes of moving from oral to written forms, new local place literacies were produced. Three substantive domains of local place knowledge emerged that together constituted local place literacies: the material translations of No Mans Land; the food ecologies of eating from place; and stories of spirits in places. These stories were told orally, transcribed verbatim, and structured into written text eventually. Within each of these domains, the collective of transcribed stories structured the text. A key story was chosen for each section, which was either collectively produced or representative of that section. These stories were represented as scanned lines following the rhythm of the oral story at the beginning of each section.

No Mans Land

Them times
you find a lot of camps
along the back of the beaches
or headland
along the edge
of a creek or lake
'cause they all jumped over

the other side
of the fence
No mans land
that's what they call it.

Stories about No Mans Land literally mapped their new lives by the Corindi Lake where a small group of Gumbaynggirr people came to live after the fences of white settlement forced them from their lands. These stories located the places where different families built their camps around the Lake, the structures and placement of the camps, the materials they used for building and in their daily lives. The structures of sociality through which they lived their lives in Country were translated through the materialities of the Lake. In No Mans Land, we follow the material/spatial and related epistemological translations that produced new place literacies when this group of northern Gumbaynggirr people came to live outside the fences of encroaching white settlement at Corindi Beach.

In the narrow coastal strip they called No Mans Land, Gumbaynggirr people negotiated the terms of their engagement with white culture. Here, on the other side of the fences, they believed they were free of government and church intervention, continuing to speak their language and enact cultural practices. They built shelters, improvised all of the necessary household objects and artifacts, made new music and sang new songs. It was through these material improvisations within the liminal space of No Mans Land that their old cultural practices made new stories. Through this process of cultural translation, local place knowledge, including its language and stories, changed to incorporate the radically different context of their new relationship to Country. In this sense, it traces the ontological and epistemological translations, including those of language and literate practice, which enable a contemporary cultural practice of Country.

Eating Place

Just along the beach
beautiful blue beach in there
mullet come in the mouth
of the Lake
a terrible lot of them
mostly big sea mullet,
along the beach for pipis and things,
we ate lilly pillies, wild cherries, raspberries,
five corners, they're nice,

and just along the beach
you get them little white berries
we used to eat those,
geebungs, another one,
rolypolies, gooseberries,
you're never short of things
to eat.

The second domain of local place knowledge is about eating food from local places. Stories of finding, gathering, preparing, and cooking food from their local places were by far the most common stories told by northern Gumbaynggirr people. When these seemingly diverse stories were clustered to explore what they meant in terms of local place knowledge, it became clear that they fell into natural groupings according to the local place ecologies, where these foods came from. Yarrawarra people lived on prawns, crabs, and fish from the estuary; turtles, swamp hens, and eels from the swamp; pipis, gugumbals, and abalone from the intertidal zone; mullet, tailor, jewfish, and so on from the sea; kangaroos, possum, and porcupine from the surrounding bushlands; and turtles, ducks, and cobra from the river. In between all of these places, they ate native fruits such as lilly pillis, wild cherries, nyum nyums, and pigface as they walked through the dunes and coastal heathlands. Each of these places is known in its intimate detail—the bodies of the foods formed within that place, and the knowledge of collecting, preparing, cooking, eating, and sustaining their life forms—and is a fundamental part of a complex literate practice.

When people tell stories about eating all of these foods, they talk about them in terms of the qualities of the places where they come from, their local food ecologies. This intimate, embodied knowledge of particular local places through eating food is the economic basis of knowledge of Country and of caring for Country through ceremony. In Eating Place we learn the nature of an ecological identification with land through sustaining life by eating what the land provides. This is a two-way process whereby those whose lives (and cultures) are sustained are also inextricably tied to the necessity to sustain the ecologies within which the food source is produced. It is through language and story as literate practice that these knowledges are represented and communicated.

Spirits in Places

There's different times
through the year

you could be peggin' out clothes
or just walk out
on the front verandah
there's a breeze blowing
you just feel real close
this is when I really miss
the Old People,
specially all the grand aunts and mum,
it must be just the change of season
or something.

Spirits in Places begins with ordinary, everyday stories of "the Old People," those extraordinary people who bridged the time before and the time after white settlement. They were initiated into the highest level of knowledge of Country and made conscious decisions about the changing nature and transmission of this knowledge. These stories are about the spirit presences and powers of the Old People, about special places, and about initiation as the highest form of cultural learning of Country. The special places of initiation and ceremony are known only through story as they are no longer accessible for ceremony. Story, as literate practice, becomes even more essential as these knowledges are translated into language (and silence). An understanding of local place knowledge through spirit stories is perhaps the most complex and untranslatable of the three domains. It is the realm where Chrissiejoy necessarily turned to multiple modes of expression in her attempts at translation.

In Spirits in Places, we see the ways that cultural practices of initiation involve the highest form of learning Country, and continue to embody the intensely material and local in stories of ritual and ceremony. This is contrary to the processes of Western knowledge formation where the highest form of knowledge is transcendent, erasing traces of local, embodied, and material connections to place. The highest form of local Indigenous knowledge was expressed in multiple forms in ceremonies in and about specific local places. These forms included dance, music/sound, body and ground designs and symbols, the particular local shapes of the land, and lines of connection to other places. It is the intersection of multiple modes of representation in place that gives rise to the necessity for multimodal forms of literate practice as translation of knowledge of Country. The higher the level of local place knowledge the greater the arcs of connection to other places. In this way, the knowledge of Spirits in Places underpins the movement from local to regional place knowledges.

Moving from Local to Regional Knowledge and Literacies

Through language and story, contemporary Gumbaynggirr people learn about connections between local places that cross their Country in linking trails. Linking trails were the walking tracks that connected local everyday living places to special ceremonial places, *mirral*, and ceremonial places to each other, throughout Gumbaynggirr county. Linking trails are also songlines, the lines of connection that inscribe on Country the deepest cultural stories that connect people to those places. Songlines are a series of small stories of events in the lives of the creation ancestors that occurred in particular places and are linked to each other through walking trails. The larger storyline tells of the events in the journeys of the great ancestral beings as they traveled through the landscape creating the shapes of the terrain and all the living creatures. These storylines become songlines through the ceremonies in the special places. Cultural knowledge of the lines of connection and mobility is as important as the knowledge of each of the separate places in the storyline:

> Lots of people believe that we're only connected to a very small area. They say, yeah but you fellas only based at Red Rock, and they're pretty happy cause it's just that little area of Red Rock, that keeps them happy. Well that's right in one sense but then you gotta go out on that long journey on knowing how the law and how the custom, how it works for Aboriginal people living at Red Rock, then you start to understand why it's important to know about the links from Yamba right through to the Nambucca area, across to Armidale, all them places so it becomes a bigger picture. It's far greater than just a small area, it links up, it might not be used today, that sort of linking trails, there's reasons behind that, but it's part of history and it's a part of our culture and it's part of our heritage, that's what it is and that'll never go away, whether we use it or not it's part of our lives. (Tony Perkins)

The "long journey" that Tony talks about is both a physical and a metaphysical journey. It is a journey that anyone is invited to undertake, a long process of coming to know Country. In the old days, the journey was undertaken literally through walking the tracks that connect vast areas of Country associated with the process of coming to know the highest forms of cultural knowledge. In contemporary times, the knowledge of linking trails as storylines is understood through creative processes of map-making as a new form of literacy that includes digital technologies.

In collaboration with the Muurrbay Aboriginal Language and Culture Cooperative, we recorded contemporary, historical, and creation stories and mapped them onto Country. We mapped Uncle Martin Ballangarry's memory story of walking from Bowraville Mission to Stuart Island in the Nambucca estuary, recording his story and marking the story places of his journey on the map. It was only later, in the process of writing, that I recognized that Uncle Martin Ballangarry's walking story followed part of the linking trail of the creation hero, Birrugan, which we had also mapped as a creation story.

To map Martin's walking story is to enter a world of knowing Country through walking. It begins as a journey from one place to the other, and like all good traveling stories departs in the middle with a digression about cobra ecologies ("I'm a guggurr man"), revealing the intricacies of walking knowledge and intersecting trails. Martin oriented himself to the map by finding the river and then the different places along the way. Place is infinitely detailed as he marks Wirriimbi Island, a white-owned farming property they walked through, a little creek that flows into the river, and a flat where they met up with the women and children after the boys had been taken aside by the older men. The boys (and the girls too, but this is Martin's story) were already learning special knowledge as they walked with the Old People. They learnt to hunt, spear, and collect wild fruits: "The Uncles of me, they taught me to do the spearing—how to do things." As the walking proceeds, stories are told about the past and the present as story places open up along the way. We pass an area that Martin describes as a "no-go zone" because it is marked by a "diamond tree," a sacred tree that "maybe there was a massacre site there." Stories of linking trails contain symbolic and intricate deeply coded references to other places and place knowledge.

Walking trails story the dynamic interactions between people and place over large tracts of Country. Martin's story of walking through Country, where food is collected, places are learned, histories are recorded, where all of the places are storied and marked, is the quintessential linking trail. The mapping of Martin's walking trail gives us insight into the basis of the songlines that criss-cross Gumbaynggirr Country. A songline is a walking trail that links the story events, the path that the creation ancestors followed as they did the same, walking through Country, collecting food, and living out the events in their lives that are marked forever in the landscape. When grids of roads and buildings transform the outward appearance of the place, the story remains as a mnemonic reminder of deep connection. Each of the special places along a storyline has a song that evokes all the other aspects of the ceremony. Songs are connected in a songline through the linking trails. It is through these linking trails that local place knowledge becomes regional knowledge, connected across Gumbaynggirr Country and beyond, always retaining the connection to the material specificity of each local place.

The songlines that followed the linking trails are no longer walked, but were taught as stories by the Old People: "because we never got the chance to do all the old traveling ways." These stories were also recorded by linguists when the old initiated men sought white linguists to record their stories in times of turbulence and change. Significantly, the Old People also recorded some of the songs that embodied the highest level of ceremonial knowledge of the special places on the linking trails. In deep mapping with cultural knowledge holders and language workers from the Muurrbay Language and Culture Centre, we mapped layers of place stories through time. We mapped storylines of the places where Gumbaynggirr people live now, where they lived in the historic past, and the deep-time creation stories of the ancestors. It is the deep-time mapping of creation stories that generated the term *deep mapping* and reveals the translation of regional place knowledge as contemporary literate practice.

In deep mapping interviews, we recorded oral place stories, simultaneously marking the places on a road map to link the story to the geographical location. In making visual representations from the mapping interviews, we scanned the road maps onto the computer and removed all the roads and towns using photoshop software. Story text and images were then inserted onto the map to show the events in the stories and images of the places where these events happened. The creative act of deep mapping is a symbolic reversal of the processes through which the grid of roads and towns was laid over earlier memories and story places. It is a process through which the relationships between place, story knowledge, and mapping as a literate practice are made visible.

Deep mapping replicates the ongoing cultural work that reconnects people, language, story, and Country at Muurrbay Aboriginal Language and Culture Centre. It is a process of repatriation whereby Gumbaynggirr histories, memories, experiences, and stories are reinscribed on Country. Intensive language work drawing on archivally recorded material reveals the connections between story and Country in the translation of Gumbaynggirr into English. The process is also developed as a pedagogy in which groups of Gumbaynggirr learners go to the special places in the storylines where the Elders and knowledge holders tell them the story. The learners write, paint, and produce artworks in relation to these places and their stories. The work of connecting language and story back to Country is ongoing. It continues the process of imagining landscapes through layers of stories that were already present in the language work that Uncle Harry Buchanan began with white linguists and which Gumbaynggirr people continue today. It is the process whereby a storyline, the skeleton of a story, becomes a songline again and through which regional knowledge and literate practice of sustaining Country is renewed. When language, story, and Country are reconnected, we again open up the possibility of singing the Country and sustaining the life forms there through contemporary literate practices.

More-Than-Regional or Global Place Knowledges

In developing representational tools that move beyond more-than-regional-knowledge boundaries of Country, contemporary Aboriginal people in Australia have created powerful multimodal and symbolic representations. The most well known of these, Western Desert art, for example, has created contemporary symbolic languages through which worldwide audiences can conceptualize a different relationship to Country (Grosz 2008). Creative forms of expressing such concepts, including performance and digital modes, are central to these translations. Having experienced ceremony with Western Desert women in their very early days of their contact with white settlement, I have learned something of this codified ceremonial knowledge of Country in an experiential, embodied way without having the language resources to translate their meanings. Western Desert art began in this liminal time/space as a symbolic translation of ephemeral ground paintings and body designs that were part of the synchronous intersection of multimodal performance in Country, including song, dance, sound, music, vibration, earth, story, collectivity, totemic ancestral relationships, and so on. The symbolic representations in Western Desert art draw on all of these modes and express what is inarticulable in purely explanatory or verbal forms.

The act of expressing knowledge of Country that connects local, regional, and global place knowledge into art forms in the water project[5] drew on a similar array of ontological and epistemological translations to shape new literate practice. Australia had over 200 distinct Aboriginal languages with around 600 different dialects at the time of white settlement, and each of these constituted a different country. The portion of the linguistic map of Australia that is labeled the "Riverine" language group shows 40 patches of different colors of variable sizes and shapes outlined with an irregular line of dark pink to indicate their linguistic coherence. The pink line that delineates the territory of the Riverine Language Group overlaps almost exactly with the map of the Muurray-Darling Basin. The fuzzy lines where the different patches of color meet and merge indicate that language territory boundaries are determined by complex ecological relations and negotiations.

The artworks produced within this project about water in the Murray-Darling Basin can be read as maps of Country. Maps, as previously stated, are perhaps the most taken for granted of literate practices that shape our relationship to Country and for this reason are an important site of learning and transformation. In the water project, five artists from different language groups throughout the Muurray-Darling Basin produced artworks about their relationship to water Country. Each artist produced works that map Country in very different ways. The maps can be seen on the website that accompanies the book from this series of projects, *Water in a Dry Land: Place Learning through Art and Story.* Through the artworks, stories, digital images, and text, new literacies are produced from the space between Aboriginal and Western practices of literacy. These are displayed on the website that accompanies Routledge's Innovative Ethnography Series: http://innovativeethnographies.net/water-in-a-dry-land (Somerville 2013a), because these literacies are necessarily digital and multimodal.

The first artist/researcher, Chrissiejoy Marshall, mapped the overall framework of thinking through Country in a jigsaw of images each representing different aspects of the methodology. In her oral presentation on DVD, she begins with the piece in the center top of the painting that she describes as "a mud map of the Noongahburrah country." The black lines are the rivers that mark the boundaries of this Country, and the black orb in the center represents the Narran Lake, described as the most significant and sacred site for "all the other peoples of the nation that spoke the U'Alayi language as well as several other nations of Aboriginal people within bordering countries" (Immiboagurramilbun, in Somerville 2013). Each jigsaw piece is elaborated and later expanded into an image of its own, covering the elements of ontology, epistemology, methods, and representation, mapping the space between her identity as Chrissiejoy Marshall and her identity in Country as Immiboagurramilbun. It offers a new framework for a literate practice of Country.

Daphne Wallace, a Gomaroi artist from Lightning Ridge, painted a bird's eye view of the land surrounding the Narran Lake with differently colored squares of cultivation—the green, gold, red, brown of cotton, sorghum, pasture, and ploughed ground. Traversing and disrupting these geometrical divisions marking the private ownership of land, the shimmering water of the Lake and rivers that feed into it, winds in and out, through and across the squares of divided country. Both water and land are marked by cultural stories, with water carrying the symbols of Gomaroi water stories, flowing across the geometrical divisions of land into exclusive private space. This painting maps the mutual entanglement of settler and Aboriginal cultures in water and land.

Paakantji artist Badger Bates' lino print of "Iron Pole Bend, Wilcannia" on the Darling River is structured around the Ngatyi, or rainbow serpents, who play a central part in the creation storylines. The flow of waters bursts forth from the Ngatyis' mouth, their bodies create the shape of the rivers and travel with the waterways. The waters of the river are alive with the river's creatures—cod, catfish, shrimp, yabby, and mussels. Around the edges of the water, we can see the mythical creatures whose movement and storylines link to other places. The artwork conceptualizes the spaces and places of these stories differently from the way space and place is understood and represented in Western knowledge frameworks. It produces a new way of seeing and knowing and new literacies in the development of new processes of representation.

Yorta Yorta artist Treahna Hamm maps the creation story of the Murray River on possum skin cloaks using ochre from the sacred Barmah Forest. In the cool climates of southeastern Australia, possum skin cloaks were important for everyday warmth—babies were wrapped in them and people were buried in their cloaks. They were used in ceremony to signify identity in Country. Treahna participated in the revitalization of the tradition of inscribing possum skin cloaks with Aboriginal communities across Victoria and all along the Murray River. In inscribing the marks of identity in Country on a possum skin cloak, Treahna said: "Imagine the river without a map . . . this is my Country, where I come from, you could wear it as a cloak and use it as a map, together."

Extensive knowledge that crosses the boundaries of Country is held in map-like images that follow the lines of story across the material terrain of the landscape. Through this mapping, a different relation to global place knowledge is constructed that maintains its links to the local and is translated into new forms of literacy. Lines on a map are a construct of a Western culture of writing, and maps are perhaps the most taken for granted of literate practices that represent a particular relationship to knowledge and to Country. To disrupt the process of map-making through which the Australian landscape "was explored, its map-made emptiness written over, cross-crossed with explorers' tracks and gradually inhabited with a network of names" (Carter 1987, xx–xxi) is the most crucial initial process of making new practices of literacy. Through these new processes of representation, we reverse the literate processes whereby

Australia was created as a blank slate, the white sheet, to be named in the settlers' language, stories, and images.

The processes of literacy-place-making that I have traced in this chapter follow the practices that Aboriginal people in Australia have been engaged in since colonization began. They are generated in the space of relation between Aboriginal and settler languages, cultures, and countries. My work has been motivated by the enduring question of what we need to learn from the world's longest surviving culture inhabiting the planet's oldest and most fragile continent. For me, literacy has always been the most important site of this work since I facilitated literacy classes of Aboriginal students returning to study and observed their most extraordinary progress from oral to print literacy as we developed literacy pedagogies together. In this chapter, I have arrived at my latest work, taking the idea of Country as a starting point, and literacy as a process of "naming the world," to explore what literacy practices or knowledges we need for planetary ecological sustainability. I have articulated the translations from traditional indigenous knowledges and representational practices to the new literacies and literate practices through which our relationship to Country and literacy can be transformed. I have observed and analyzed how these pedagogical processes of literacy-place-making shape new literate subjectivities in Country in a primary school setting, but that is another story.

Notes

I would like to acknowledge the Indigenous knowledge holders whose thinking and ongoing work is crucial to the formation of these ideas, particularly Immiboagurramilbun (Chrissiejoy Marshall), whose conceptual framework is central to this chapter. I acknowledge the Australian Research Council's contribution for their financial support of the three projects on which this work is based. Ursula Kelly, as another chapter author, provided insightful feedback that assisted in the development of this chapter.

1. Immiboagurramilbun is Chrissiejoy Marshall's Aboriginal name, which she prefers when referring to her Aboriginal knowledge.
2. Yuwaalaraay is standard orthography, U'Alayi Immiboagurramilbun's preferred spelling.
3. Chrissiejoy prefers the use of the term Aboriginal to Indigenous.
4. Mulgury and Mingin are U'Alayi and Erinbinjori language words for the concept that has been translated inadequately into English as dreamtime/totem.
5. "Bubbles on the Surface: A Place Pedagogy of the Narran Lake," funded by the Australian Research Council, 2006–2009.

References

Carter, P., 1987, *The Road to Botany Bay: An Essay in Spatial History*, Faber & Faber, London.

Comber, B., 1997, "Managerial Discourses: Tracking the Local Effects on Teachers' and Students' Work in Literacy Lessons," *Discourse: Studies in the Cultural Politics of Education*, vol. 18, no. 3: 389–407.

———, 2011, "Making Space for Place-Making Pedagogies: Stretching Normative Mandated Literacy Curriculum," *Contemporary Issues in Early Childhood*, vol. 12, no. 4: 343–38, www.wwwords.co.uk/CIEC.

Cope and M. Kalantzis (eds.), 2000, *Multiliteracies: Literacy Learning and the Design of Social Futures*, Routledge, London and New York.

Donehower, K., C. Hogg, and E. E. Schell, 2007, *Rural Literacies*, Southern Illinois University Press, Carbondale.

Freire, P., 1996. *Pedagogy of the Oppressed*. Revised edition, translated by Myra Bergman Ramos, Penguin, London.

Green, B., P. Cormack, and H. Nixon, 2007, "Introduction: Literacy, Place, Environment," *Australian Journal of Language and Literacy*, vol. 30, no. 2: 77–81.

Grosz, E., 2008, *Chaos, Territory Art: Deleuze and the Framing of the World*, Columbia University Press, New York.

Haraway, D., 1991. *Simians, Cyborgs, and Women: The Reinvention of Nature*, Routledge, London and New York.

Immiboagurramilbun (Marshall, C. J.), 2003, "Talking up Blackfella Ways of Knowing through Whitefella Magic," DVD produced by Young Australia Productions and presented at Doctoral School, University of New England, Armidale, New South Wales.

Rose, D. B., 1996, *Nourishing Terrains: Australian Aboriginal Views of Landscape and Wilderness*, Australian Heritage Commission, Canberra.

Rose, D. B. and L. Robin, 2004, "The Ecological Humanities in Action: An Invitation," *Australian Humanities Review*, nos. 31–32, http://www.australianhumanitiesreview.org/archive/Issue-April-2004/rose.html.

Somerville, M., 2013, *Water in a Dry Land: Place-learning through Art and Story*, Routledge, London and New York.

———, 2013a, *Water in a Dry Land: Place Learning through Art and Story*, Routledge Innovative Ethnography Series, http://innovativeethnographies.net/water-in-a-dry-land.

Somerville, M. and T. Perkins, 2010, *Singing the Coast: Place and identity in Australia*, Aboriginal Studies Press, Canberra, ACT.

Williams, R., 1973, *The Country and the City*, Oxford University Press, London and New York.

CHAPTER 10

Literacy, Place-Based Pedagogies, and Social Justice

Lyn Kerkham and Barbara Comber

Introduction

Our long-term program of research has considered the relationships between teachers' work and identities, literacy pedagogies and schooling, particularly in high-poverty communities. Over the past decade, we have worked with teachers to consciously explore with them the possible productive synergies between critical literacy and place-based pedagogies, and the affordances of multimodal and digital literacies for students' engagement with the places where they live and learn. These studies have been undertaken with teachers working and living in various locales—from the urban fringe to inner suburban areas undergoing urban renewal, to rural and regional communities where poverty and the politics of place bring certain distinctive opportunities and constraints to bear on pedagogy for social justice. There is now wider recognition that "social justice" may need rethinking to foreground the nonhuman world and the relation between people and politics of places, people, and environments in terms of "eco-social justice" (Green 2010; Gruenewald 2003b) or spatial justice (Soja 2011).

In this chapter, we explore place as a site of knowing and as an object of study as developed through the *Special Forever*[1] project by teachers in schools located in the Murray-Darling Basin bioregion. Putting the environment at the center of the literacy curriculum inevitably draws teachers into the politics of place and raises questions concerning what is worth preserving and what should be transformed. We consider how the politics of place both constrains and opens up possibilities for pedagogy for eco-social justice and review the pedagogical work that one teacher, Hannah,[2] undertook with her upper primary class. We show how her engagement with place as curricular afforded significant opportunities for the students in her class to develop critically literate practices, to expand their repertoires of multiliteracies, and to develop an eco-social justice disposition.

From Social Justice to Eco-Social Justice—A Framework for a Pedagogy of Place

A range of approaches to social justice has informed education policy-makers and researchers. Generally social justice is concerned with people's rights and interrogating existing systems and practices to consider whose interests they serve. In education, social justice has focused on questions of access, opportunities, and outcomes for different groups of learners—typically in terms of class, gender, race, ethnicity, disability, and other factors, including more recently rurality and remoteness (place-based categories), which might impact on learning, educational, and long-term work trajectories.

Early work on critical literacy was inspired by Brazilian educator Paulo Freire (Freire 1972; Freire and Macedo 1987) who argued that reading involved more than decoding words. Rather, it should involve interrogating how things were organized in the world to privilege some groups over others. In advocating adult literacy campaigns he was interested in repositioning poor workers as analysts, hence he campaigned for an education that fostered questioning of the ways things were and imagining how they could be made just. Ideally this consciousness-raising through proper education would lead to a form of liberation whereby workers would have the freedom and the knowledge to argue for their rights and avoid exploitation and alienation. However, feminist theorists (Gore 1993; Weiler 1991) and people of color questioned the universality of this model of social justice, disputing its representativeness of diverse people's everyday experiences. Theories of social justice based mainly on socioeconomic matters ignore the invisible and unpaid work that is done, particularly by women, to keep systems running and maintain white male privilege.

In the 1990s in Australia, Connell's (1993) work on "curricular justice" in the context of poverty and education (through the Commonwealth Disadvantaged Schools Program), feminist poststructuralist textual analysis (Gilbert 1993; Mellor, Patterson, and O'Neill 1991), and critical discourse analysis (Fairclough 1989, 1993, 1995; Janks 1993, 2010) were also influential in designs of literacy pedagogies and curriculum infused by social justice principles. Comber (1994, p. 661) sought to capture the combined spirit of these moves in the following principles for critical literacy:

- Repositioning students as researchers of language;
- Respecting student resistance and minority-culture constructions of literacy; and
- Problematizing classroom and public texts;

These principles focus on language and literacy practices and did not explicitly locate teachers or students in place. However, as our work is situated mostly in sites of high poverty, we continually noticed the ways in which class, culture, language, and locale were intricately related. We began to consider how theories of space (Gulson and Symes 2007) and place (Gruenewald 2003a, 2003b; Somerville 2007) might inform our research and collaborative inquiries with teachers about literacy and social justice, and also to review work that foregrounded context (Seddon 2003), neighborhood (Lupton 2005), region (Green 2010), and so on. Two important contributions to our understanding of pedagogy for eco-social justice are Gruenewald's (2003a) critical place-based pedagogy and the different but complementary "pedagogy of responsibility" originally proposed by Bowers (2001, 2005) and subsequently taken up by Martusewicz and Edmundson (2005).

To focus on the local places where students (and teachers) live and learn is at once a critical and a generative pedagogical act. It takes seriously the importance of experiential learning in nurturing an attitude of care and a deep connection with particular places, and of identifying cultural and ecological aspects of local places and environments where the damaging imprint of human activity might call for restorative action. Abstract curriculum that has been designed and written elsewhere is inadequate to the task of "learning to live well" within the limits and possibilities of specific places, and of understanding the cultural and political processes that shape what happens there (Gruenewald 2003a, p. 9).

What might be entailed in an education that has place-consciousness as its goal (Gruenewald 2003b; Smith 2002), and is, by its very nature, located in specific places? There are many different curriculum pathways to nurturing mutuality between students, their environments, and their communities, as Gruenewald (2003b) and Smith (2002) describe. These include cultural studies informed by student research into community histories; nature studies in local places; "real world problem solving" that involves students in identifying and engaging in school or community issues; internships and entrepreneurial opportunities; and induction into the decision-making processes of communities. A critical place-based pedagogy, however, also emphasizes the "transformation of oppressive elements of reality" (Gruenewald 2003b, p. 5). Its two complementary goals, "decolonization" and "reinhabitation," were inspired by Freire's liberation pedagogy as well as postcolonialist work. Gruenewald (2003a, p. 9) writes that reinhabitation involves learning to live well socially and ecologically in places that have been disrupted and injured; while decolonization involves learning to recognize disruption and injury and address their causes. Thus, relations between people and place are made central to a curriculum that "[admits] critical social and ecological concerns into one's understanding of place, and the role of places in education" (p. 9). Gruenewald's eco-justice framework recognizes that discourses of both critical pedagogy and place-based education are needed to inform a pedagogy that focuses on localized social and environmental action and works toward socially and ecologically sustainable communities.

The metaphors of decolonization and reinhabitation are paradoxically one of the strengths of a critical place-based pedagogy and its nemesis. They carry with them the intentions and connotations associated with a Freirean worldview that presumes critical praxis and social transformation as universally accepted and acceptable goals. Bowers (2008) takes a different view: seeing critical pedagogy and place-based education as entirely divergent. For Gruenewald, Freire's commitment to social justice, his insistence that human beings are subjects and not objects of history, and his argument for a dialogical, problem-posing education, are not at issue. Bowers (2003, 2008), on the other hand, argues that Gruenewald and other advocates of a critical place-based pedagogy are caught in "double binds" while they never question the concepts and practices that have developed from Freire's critical pedagogy with its allegedly anthropocentric view of the relationship between humans and nature. In addition, Bowers roundly castigates these theorists for their inability to disentangle their thought from the "root metaphors" of Western thought and science mechanism, change as a positive and progressive force, and individualism (Bowers 2001, p. 404)—which, as he argues, are embedded in Freirean approaches.

These concerns are central to Bowers' cultural-ecological framing of a "pedagogy of responsibility." In this respect, a pedagogy of responsibility "exists in the tension between two necessarily ethical questions: what do we need to conserve and what needs to be transformed?" Further it asks "what are my just obligations to this community?" before asking, "what are my oppressions (or my students' oppressions) from which to be liberated?" (Martusewicz and Edmundson 2005, p. 79). Obligations are emphasized here, rather than the rights of oppressed peoples. In response, Gruenewald (2003a, p. 10) acknowledges that because transformation is strongly emphasized in critical pedagogy the question of what needs to be conserved "takes on special significance to a critical pedagogy of place." Bowers, moreover, acknowledges that the limitations and inequalities that cultural traditions and practices may produce deserve critical attention. From the standpoints of the most disadvantaged, questions about how things have come to be the way they are, who benefits, and how might things be otherwise, need to be asked (Connell 1993).

In summary, both Gruenewald (2003a, 2003b, 2004) and Bowers (2001, 2004, 2005) argue that the domination of nature and the domination of oppressed groups are two sides of the same coin, and a manifestation of an unjust and unequal society. Given much of the complementary nature of their work, we take a position that wants to avoid the pitfalls of critical theorists without abandoning the notions of decolonization and reinhabitation as goals in specific places and communities. These terms are abstract but not immutable: while they have been conceptualized in one historical moment and place, they are appropriated, reframed, and rendered open to reinterpretation in response to actual acts of thinking, reading, and writing at other times and in other places. Further, these metaphors speak to the politics of place—a dimension that is absent in Bowers' pedagogy of responsibility—as well as the social and ecological dimensions of place. As such, we argue that decolonization and reinhabitation are important for a critical pedagogy of place that has place-consciousness and eco-justice as its goals.

We turn now to a discussion that brings ecological and social issues that are so central to a critical pedagogy of place into dialogue with literacy studies.

Literacy, Place, and the Environment

A small number of literacy researchers has worked across the boundaries of scholarship in literacy and environmental education, with a specific focus on regional and rural communities (Bishop 2003; Comber, Nixon, and Reid 2007; Cormack and Green 2007; Cormack, Green, and Reid 2007; Donehower, Hogg, and Schell 2007; Edmondson 2001; Green, Cormack, and Nixon 2007; Nixon 2007; Reid 2007; Somerville 2007). As Green et al. (2007) explain in their introduction to a special themed issue of the *Australian Journal of Language and Literacy*, the essays collected in that issue focus on the MDB at a time when the region was firmly in the Australian national consciousness as ongoing debates about the access, rights, quality, and sustainability of its waters were intensifying. The essays reflect some of the work undertaken in the *River Literacies*[3] project and its interest in "bringing literacy-educational scholarship to bear on the environmental challenge that looms large in all our lives." This work gives impetus to recent research in the "nexus between literacy work and environmental learning and more broadly . . . ecosocial sustainability" (Green et al. 2007, p. 80). In what follows, we outline some of the theoretical work that has contributed to making connections between literacy studies and environmental, place-based education.

Taking the environment as "an object of literacy" brings two contexts together: the geographical locations of particular MDB communities, and the literacy-rich integrated curriculum in which young people (and teachers) might learn about environmental sustainability (Green et al. 2007, p. 78). This was a central concept for the *River Literacies* project, which documented the ways in which teachers engaged their students in research and communication, through a range of media, focused on their local places in the MDB and the environmental issues that confronted them. The project also sought to involve teachers (and students) in tasks that encouraged them to communicate about their environment in ways that stretched the boundaries of traditional literacy practices. This communication aspect of the project parallels the conceptual work of Andrew Stables and colleagues (Stables 1996, 2004; Stables and Bishop 2001; Stables et al. 1999). Their argument for an approach to environmental education that is informed by a well-theorized framing of literacies takes reading and writing practices well beyond decoding and encoding printed texts.

In their discussion of "functional-cultural-critical" (environmental) literacies, Stables and Bishop (2001) speak directly to the question of what constitutes a text and, in the context of environmental literacy, what it means to "read" the environment. These are questions that have shaped debates in the literacy field but have been peripheral to environmental education. Their broad view of environmental literacy as an "essentially semiotic relationship with the biophysical world . . . a view too broad to be properly considered a mere subset of 'environmental education'" (Stables and Bishop 2001, p. 91), has its origins in Saussure's work on signs and the meaning of cultural practices (Hall 2003; Stables 2001, 2004). It provides the basis for a strong conception of environmental literacy where "the environment *itself* is invested with textuality" (Stables and Bishop 2001, p. 92, emphasis in the original). In other words, an effective environmental education, while including experiences that teach students to live productively, responsibly, and sustainably, takes as its starting point the notion of environment *as* text. Put another way, we "read" the rivers, gardens, ridges, forests, rocks, farmlands—the land-scapes that constitute the environment—and simultaneously construct their meaning in words, sounds, and images.

Responsibility and care for place, representations of place, and embod-ied connection between people and place are key themes in Somerville's (2007) exploration of a pedagogy for place literacies. Her "search for pedagogies that will change the way we relate to our places" (p. 151) is a response to the need to fundamentally rethink how we live locally and in relation to the natural world in a time of environmental and social crisis. Calling to mind Gruenewald's (2003a) work on "decolonization" and "reinhabitation," she brings into play the notion of multiple and contradictory narratives of places that explain and constitute relation-ships with the land and waters of Australia. She writes that "the process of making visible the contradictory and contested stories of 'connection, exploitation and care' is a step towards new place literacies" (p. 156). The elements of a place pedagogy that she proposes foreground the complex relations between people and place, cultures and environments:

- place learning is necessarily embodied and local;
- our relationship to place is communicated in stories and other rep-resentations; and
- place learning involves a contact zone of contested place stories. (p. 153)

Somerville's argument signals the need to work on and with literacy practices—ways of reading and writing the world—as they intersect with place-responsive pedagogies in order to contribute to sustainable communities and environments, and to understand what places can teach us.

In what follows, we consider the literacy practices and place-based ped-agogy of one primary school teacher who was actively involved in *Special Forever*. We first locate Hannah in her place, as a teacher, farmer, and activ-ist, before introducing her environmental communications curriculum.

Hannah's Place History

Hannah lives on a river about 50 kilometers from Tindale, the hub of a cattle-farming region. She and her husband bought a mixed farm in the district more than 20 years ago, the same district where her family "have been making a living off the land for generations." She also holds shares in the homestead that has "been in the family for about 100 years." On her way to school each day, the road she travels takes her past sheep and chicken farms, paddocks of lucerne, cattle properties, and through a landscape that is a "green oasis" in winter, but in the summer months is dry, dusty, and drought-stricken. Hannah's place stories are stories told from multiple perspectives: teacher, rural woman, farmer, and environmentalist. As described below, she draws on each of these identities as she recounts her experience of taking a stand on a local environmental issue.

A comment she made about her own farming practices to indicate why and how she positioned herself in relation to that particular issue serves as a preface:

> Whatever we do on our farm, well really, we're only there for 50 years or whatever, and it goes on to someone else, and if you haven't planted trees, you haven't looked after it, what have you got to hand on? Just a degraded bit of ground, as some people think that they own everything, top of the ground and under the ground and, you know, do what they like with it. I mean there's a lot of adults like that. I don't believe you can do what you like with it. You've got to look after it; it's got to be better. No, I feel very strongly about that.

Imbued in these comments is a sense of custodianship, a reciprocity with the place that sustains her life and livelihood, echoes of which will be found in her environmental communications curriculum. Custodianship, or "looking after it," entails, from Hannah's point of view, planting tree lines and bird corridors, conserving the river bank, not overgrazing, and not burning crops. It is possible, she argues, to "have a farming enterprise and still be able to look after the environment." Here is a glimpse of the interanimation of her identities as a farmer and a teacher.

Speaking Up for the Environment

The local council had plans to redevelop a horse arena that was used for drafting,[4] camping activities and leisure riding into a football ground with a new stand. The redevelopment would include bulldozing trees that were 100–150 years old. In her account, Hannah positions herself in relation to people "on [her] side" and "on the other side" regarding an issue that "caused a huge rift in the community." She "came to be appointed as spokesperson for the whole of that valley, and for the people who were against the football club." In her recount, she speaks first as a farmer whose livelihood depends on the land, about poor land management practices, and the destruction of trees up river that would exacerbate flood damage and erode river banks on properties along the river, including her own:

> People just couldn't understand why I'd want to save trees, and why I'd worry about whether there was going to be erosion, but really the thing that matters to us was our property was only not far downstream, and it could have had a huge effect on our livelihood, plus the two properties above us, and honestly we'd seen what this flood could do; it ripped through huge areas of land.

At the same time, Hannah's reference to the age and stature of the trees suggests they should be protected for their intrinsic value, that they are more important in the landscape than a football ground and football stand. Her use of verbs such as "bulldoze [a huge area]," "demolish [trees]," and "flatten [everything]" powerfully evokes the violence of the actions proposed by the developers. In contrast to the power of nature in the flood that "ripped through huge areas of land," the deliberate intention to destroy the trees for a football ground, for Hannah, is a moral provocation, at the heart of which are competing social and political interests.

As her narrative unfolds, she constitutes herself as both a farmer and an environmentalist. She describes the "huge effort" she put in to being spokesperson for the valley: she canvassed councillors and approached "Land Care people...water resources people, bird-watchers which at the time I didn't know existed...all those sort of people" who would support her argument for the environment and against the redevelopment of the football ground. Hannah prepared her case methodically, drawing together documentary resources and the expertise of "professional groups" to present a convincing case to the council and to the community.

Her campaign was successful: the trees would not be "demolished" and the arena would not be redeveloped, which "meant [the football club] had to plant grass each year after the camp drafting people ripped it up." After the meeting, the "leader of the other side" congratulated her. Hannah reflected that she had "done a lot of research" and had worked at "[getting] a lot of professional people on our side." Yet this success was not without cost to Hannah. Others in the school, she explained, were on "the other side," "unbeknown to me until I went to that meeting."

In this moment, the success of the campaign *outside* the school context is tempered by one of the consequences of "taking sides" *in* the school where sides continued to be taken after the event. Although the issue was neither centered on the school nor related to teaching, and indeed fundamentally concerns the question of what needs to be conserved, Hannah's response suggests the professional implications of speaking out on issues that overlap personal and professional life in the microcosm of the school. Further, it hints at the politics of place that unavoidably shape community expectations about teachers and teaching, even among the profession and immediate colleagues. Hannah's account hints at the difficulty of articulating the boundary of teachers' work as she calls on professional resources to engage fully in the debate, but it also suggests that competing agendas and a politics of difference are in play: difference in power relations around professional competence and status that she speaks of in terms of "being prepared."

Hannah concluded her account with a comment that implied her stance as a farmer and environmentalist, articulated through her self-as-teacher, and she made explicit the connections between being a teacher and being a credible model for practicing what she teaches:

> Well one reason why I did it was because I *was* a teacher, because I'd learnt that, I'd always taught the kids that if you believe in something you've got to stand up for it, so the kids saw me standing up for it, because it was a huge media issue at the time, yeah, so everyone in the community certainly knew which side I was on. (Hannah's emphasis)

This is a crucial point for directing the listener/reader about how to hear and understand Hannah's narrative from her point of view as a teacher. As a teacher, she took a risk by participating in the campaign and making her position public. Her public stand involved her in recruiting a variety of experts more broadly in the community. As she commented, although it was "kept out of the school grounds... everyone in the community would have known which side I was on." She represented herself in that sense as a willing, and unavoidably public, figure in the debate. From the beginning, the community was divided on this issue. Hannah's account of how this rift is played out brings sharply into focus the political processes that shape what happens in a local community as well as the risky and complicated business of making judgments about how one ought to act at a given moment, and in relation to others with whom there are ongoing professional and other relationships.

Hannah speaks from multiple positions in this narrative, making farmer, environmentalist, and teacher selves salient at different times. This multiple and complex positioning is iterated in her comments about being involved in environmental education:

> A lot of people think you're just a greenie. I am a greenie, but I'm not a radical greenie, I'm dead against radical greenies because my family have been making their living off the land for generations, [and] see the importance of looking after the environment and planting more trees, and having a good balance.

This positioning in relation to place and "place-consciousness" (Cameron 2003a, 2003b; Gruenewald 2003a) resonates with an eco-social justice framework and the notion of custodianship, an ecoethical identity, that pervades the pedagogic work Hannah undertakes as part of her environmental communications curriculum.

The Politics of Place and the Curriculum

Hannah is aware of the political nature of the decisions she makes about the kinds of local issues that can and should form the centerpiece of a project for an environmental communications curriculum. Each year, she "looks at what issue will raise its head...something the kids can have a real impact and involvement in." Like other issues, coal mining is "hugely political" and she makes opportunities for engaging the students in learning to read different perspectives, values, and standpoints. For example,

> Even though some people might think "Oh yeah, we're getting involved in political issues," yes we are, because these children are going to be the leaders of our next generation...I took them down to *An Inconvenient Truth*, because we'd been learning a lot about global warming, and it was interesting. We took about 100 children to it, but mine really had the background knowledge about global warming. All the kids watched it, but when it came to where, you know, they were stating that Australia and the United States were the only ones that hadn't signed the Kyoto Agreement, a lot of people cheered and thought that was a good thing...My children turned around said "They don't understand," so they've learnt a lot along the way about the environment, many different issues.

Her pedagogical moves encourage the students to become critical readers, and to understand that reading and writing is always about "reading and writing the world." At its simplest, this can be seen in the way Hannah and the students collect news articles from various sources, and read them against each other. The students discern the differences between the metropolitan *Morning Herald* and the local paper, and have "become very critical in the way they talk about articles written by politicians." She considers that students should learn first about local issues, and that will contribute to the students' awareness of "bigger issues in the world":

> I can't see the point in learning about, you know, Antarctica or the rain forests in Brazil, when they don't even know that there's going to be a coal mine under their backyard. I mean it doesn't make sense.

Hannah's environmental communications curriculum embraces the principles of place-responsiveness and deliberately seeks to present students with multiple perspectives on issues that matter to them. It makes available opportunities for students to engage with knowledgeable adults in the community, and addresses both the "cultural commons" that is so important in the concept of a pedagogy of responsibility and the politics of place that is integral to a critical pedagogy of place. These features, as well as what we recognize as decolonization and reinhabitation, are incorporated in the *Birds in our Backyard* project. This project evolved over several months and engaged the students, and Hannah, in learning about the diversity of birds that share their place and the local environment. Our research with teachers indicates that the teacher's history, identity, and current positioning impact on the design of literacy curriculum and pedagogy (Kerkham 2011; Kerkham and Comber 2007). The short classroom examples that follow illustrate how one teacher assembles a range of material and discursive resources to exploit the pedagogical affordances of her place.

Environmental Communications

Birds in our Backyard was prompted by some of the students' observations of birds in the schoolyard, a serendipitous beginning to what became a major curriculum focus with Hannah's upper primary class over several months. Hannah began by turning to people in the community "with more skills than [her] on a particular topic" to support her teaching, in part because she acknowledges the importance of students "seeing real people in the classroom regularly, no matter what the program is...we get out and find people, challengers basically." She "tracked down" a local ABC radio presenter, "Mr. Twitchers," an expert on birds in the region, and invited him to speak to her students about local bird species and the art of bird-watching. In preparation for his visit, she and the students gathered resources: they commandeered library books and bird charts, located an 80-year-old egg collection and brought a variety of bird nests into the classroom. She asked the students to identify birds in their backyard or the school ground in order to help them generate some questions for "Mr. Twitchers." Not all the students could name the birds they saw, and some said that no birds visited their yard, but their interest was piqued. "Mr. Twitchers," intrigued with their preparations and questions, and their enthusiasm for finding out about the birds in their locale that this activity sparked, bought an illustrated field guide for the class. He also provided them with bird-watcher's checklists and leaflets about the local bird routes.

From October 2005 through to February 2006, the students used the checklists to record their observations of birds in the schoolyard, identifying those that were permanent residents, migratory birds (such as Dollar birds from New Guinea), and birds that used the school as a "flight path." They kept records of birds that visited the park next to the school, as well as those they saw along the river nearby, building up their knowledge of birds, their habitats, and seasonal patterns of presence and absence. Over time, like accomplished ornithologists, they also learned to identify birds by listening to their calls, recorded some themselves, and downloaded others from the Internet.

The visit by "Mr. Twitchers" opened up a broader audience for students' writing: he was keen to publish some of their work in the *Bird Observer* magazine. Further, he invited Hannah and the students as special guests to the local Botanical Gardens for the launch of the guide for bird routes in the local council area.[5] This excursion afforded Hannah an opportunity to make contact not only with people at the Botanical Gardens, with whom they developed a reciprocal and ongoing relationship, but also with two Aboriginal elders from the local Aboriginal community, who she invited to the class to share their knowledge of birds in the area.

Over several months, Hannah engaged the students as researchers in and of their place: they carefully and methodically observed, listened, recorded, and read. She and the students made several visits to the Botanical Gardens over the following weeks to observe birds and their habitats, and experience firsthand the sensory world of a bird-watcher. Hannah adapted observation sheets from environmental education sources that the students used to note such things as

The habitat (ground, bushes, tree trunks, treetops, river, swamp, etc.)
What the bird was doing (feeding, building a nest, etc.).
Feeding: insects on plants in the air, in the water, seeds, nectar, etc.
Movement on the ground: hops walks, stands on one leg, etc.
Flight: fast, slow, straight, undulating, gliding, hovering, aerobatics, etc.
Call: describe in words
How many of this type of bird did you see while observing?
Is the bird native or exotic?
If exotic, which country?
What are some of the bird's enemies?
Is the bird tame or timid?
How has this bird adapted for its way of life i.e. its survival?
Other special observations.

The task for the students on these occasions was to assume the stance of bird-watcher:

> Work by yourself or in pairs. You must remain very quiet. Find a comfortable spot to sit so you will not have to move, because sudden movements and noises scare birds away. Wear dull, bush colored clothes so that you blend with the surroundings. Write down your observations straight away.

In order to structure what the students attended to, Hannah provided sound and sight maps (see figure 10.1) for them to note where and what they saw and heard:

> Sitting at a point, facing North, be very quiet. Record the sounds you hear, for example, bird, motor, wind, et cetera. Use the lines as direction

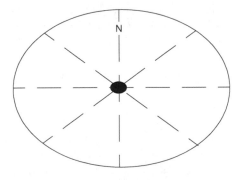

Figure 10.1 Sound Map.

Source: Produced by teacher being discussed—recorded during research fieldwork by author.

guides. Put sounds you judge to be close near the centre, and distant sounds near the edge of the sound map.

Hannah also approached a local finch breeder to show his collection of Australian finches to the students. On this visit, the students learnt about and observed at close hand, the beak structure, feathers, tails, markings, and colors of a variety of finches.

To this point, we have outlined the ways in which Hannah's classroom practice draws on community knowledges and regards the "cultural commons" held in both Indigenous and non-Indigenous communities as rich resources for situated learning in and about the local environment. There is also an important sense, however, in which the students become particularly attuned to the multiplicity of relations between people and place.

In order to communicate what they were learning, the students produced a range of texts. For example, they worked in pairs to desktop publish a number of picture books—fiction and nonfiction—based on what they had learnt about birds and waterways in the district for the Year 2 class; they wrote poetry for a competition that was organized in a nearby district; they worked individually and collectively on class collages and paintings. Hannah and the students familiarized themselves with software such as *Audacity* that they then used to create multimodal Photostories and Powerpoints, embedding recorded birdcalls and adding text to images on the slides. Hannah jointly constructed a scientific report on a pelican with the class, explaining and demonstrating the linguistic structures and features of the genre. The students then independently wrote a report on a bird of their choice. Their writing reflected their familiarity with the report genre, as well as their knowledge of the layout and conventions of the illustrated field guide that was a constant source of information in the classroom.

There are two points to make about the textual work Hannah asks of the students. First, Hannah engages them in a process of building their knowledge of the field—not just from reading books and field guides in the classroom but "actually being out there in the environment," as she observes. Producing texts enables the students to build both their knowledge and their communicative repertoires over time. Through such a process of semiotic engagement with the environment (Stables and Bishop 2001), the students developed a multiplicity of ways of knowing the environment and communicating what they had come to know.

The second point relates to Hannah's work in assisting these young writers to use the words of others for their own purposes. They were learning the scientific discourse of bird-watching and the language of specialized texts, and were putting to work the words they were becoming accustomed to reading in the illustrated field guide, the words they had heard in exchanges with "Mr. Twitchers," and the words they used to complete their observation checklists. In their print and multimodal texts, the students appropriated these words to communicate not only their knowledge, but also their understanding of their responsibility for the environment, the birds, and their habitats.

For the students, learning about their place is not just an academic exercise, nor does it entail memorizing facts and regurgitating ideas. They are in the process of understanding the local effects of globalizing environmental problems, in this case through monitoring seasonal bird populations and their changing migration patterns in relation to extended drought and habitat depletion. As a result, Hannah explained:

> They were able to ascertain themselves, after an issue looking at what birds visited our playground, they realised that we didn't have a habitat for smaller birds, so therefore they were going to be able to do something about it, and they were going to be able to do something about it with the assistance of adults . . . we went up and photographed the shrubs and . . . the understory up there at the park, and then came back and thought "Yes, we can do that here at our school," and they had a huge input into the grant application that we put in. They had to do their own designs about what our garden might look like, and last week we found out that we were successful with that grant.

They are learning to listen to their place and the environment *and* take action. Hannah takes the students outside the school and classroom, and outside themselves. She enables them to see and understand their place from the standpoint of the other: birds and their habitats, the environment, the local bird-watchers, Aboriginal elders. The students encounter multiple perspectives, and come to see themselves, their place, and the environment differently in their immediate and day-to-day world. She recognizes that students need to have access to curriculum that takes them beyond appreciating the environment and its "special places" to engagement with critical questions and issues about the impact of human activity on the very ecosystems that we need for survival.

Conclusion

Through examining one teacher's critical pedagogy of place and her advocacy for conserving and improving the natural environment for future generations, the politics of teachers' work are highlighted. There are risks attendant in being proactive. Environmental work in a rural setting is quite visible and open to contestation by the local community in which one lives and works. The teacher's positioning as farmer and conservationist, as well as her professional identity, makes for a complicated negotiation of the politics of the utilization and deployment of place and its resources. Hannah does not sidestep such challenges. Indeed it is because she is a teacher that she sees the need to model for her students how to stand up for her beliefs and the rights of the environment and future generations who will inherit it. She demonstrates the need for careful research in order to take up a defensible position, but eschews a "radical greenie" identity.

Hannah invited a range of people with different expertise, including local Indigenous elders, to work with her class. Her place-based pedagogy is not the result of teacher and students working with a "textbook"; rather, it is a situated, multivoiced pedagogy, interested in issues that matter to the students, to herself, and to communities in the MDB. In bringing together literacy practices and a study of the environment, Hannah is intent on exploring and developing environmental knowledges that are personally and socially meaningful for the students she perceives as the "future custodians" of the MDB.

Along with her active role as a community member and farmer, Hannah develops a pedagogy of place and an environmental communications curriculum that opens up possibilities for her primary school students. In learning to research their everyday outdoor world, as bird-watchers, the students not only begin to see "places" differently, for instance, as habitats, they assemble the discursive practices of "twitchers" and an ecological vocabulary. Yet Hannah does not restrict them to scientific genres, as she encourages the production of a wide range of artifacts and genres, including photographs, sketches, poetry, i-movie, PowerPoint, public presentations, and bids for project funding. Place, and in this case, local birds and their habitats, became the object of study and, as students' knowledge grew, they were invited to share their expertise in a range of media and modes and in a variety of situations. In this work we can begin to see how a critical pedagogy of place and critical literacy can mutually inform each other and provide a strong basis for a proper education for rural-regional sustainability.

Notes

1. *Special Forever* began in 1993 as part of a broad literacy-environmental education strategy in the Murray-Darling Basin, located in eastern inland

Australia. It was funded by the Murray-Darling Basin Commission and managed by the Primary English Teaching Association of Australia (PETAA). Up to 2010, PETAA published high-quality annual anthologies of children's writing and artwork. Participation from around 800 primary schools in the MDB means that approximately 20,000 students engage in school and community-based *Special Forever* projects each year (http://www.petaa.edu.au).

2. Pseudonyms have replaced place names and teacher identities.

3. *River Literacies* is the plain language title for "Literacy and the Environment: A Situated Study of Multi-mediated Literacy, Sustainability, Local Knowledges and Educational Change," an Australian Research Council (ARC) Linkage project (No. LP0455537) between the University of South Australia, Charles Sturt University, and the Primary English Teaching Association (PETA) as the Industry Partner. Chief investigators were Barbara Comber, Phil Cormack, Bill Green, Helen Nixon, and Jo-Anne Reid. The project was undertaken between 2004 and 2007.

4. Camp drafting is a competitive time trial event where cattle and horses are steered through a series of barricades.

5. The bird routes are an initiative promoted by "Mr. Twitchers" to protect the few vital remnants of the Grassy White Box Woodlands, which had previously stretched from Victoria to the Queensland border. It is one of the few places along the North West slopes of NSW where birds might survive. According to CSIRO's Plant Industry Communication Group, only 0.001 percent of this woodlands survives in a relatively unmodified condition. The bird routes include old cemeteries and villages in the area and for the most part they follow the old stock routes used by cattle drovers (Watts 2000).

References

Bishop, S., 2003, "A Sense of Place," in R. Brooke (ed.), *Rural Voices: Place-Conscious Education and the Teaching of Writing*, Teachers College Press, New York.

Bowers, C. A., 2001, "Toward an Eco-Justice Pedagogy," *Educational Studies,* vol. 32, no. 4: 402–416.

———, 2003, "Can Critical Pedagogy Be Greened?" *Educational Studies*, vol. 34, no. 1: 11–36

———, 2004, "Comments on David Gruenewald's 'A Foucauldian Analysis of Environmental Education," *Curriculum Inquiry*, vol. 34, no. 2: 223–232.

———, 2005, "Toward a Culturally Informed Eco-justice Pedagogy," in *The False Promise of Constructivist Theories of Learning: A Global and Ecological Critique*, Peter Lang, New York.

———, 2008, "Why a Critical Pedagogy of Place Is an Oxymoron," *Environmental Education Research*, vol. 14, no. 3: 325–335.

Cameron, J., 2003a, "Educating for Place Responsiveness: An Australian Perspective on Ethical Practice," *Ethics, Place and Environment*, vol. 6, no. 2: 99–115.

————, 2003b, "Responding to Place in a Post-colonial Era: An Australian Perspective," in W. Adams and M. Mulligan (eds.), *Decolonizing Nature: Strategies for Conservation in a Post-colonial Era*, Earthscan, London.

Comber, B., 1994, "Critical Literacy: An Introduction to Australian Debates and Perspectives," *Journal of Curriculum Studies*, vol. 26, no. 6: 655–668.

Comber, B., H. Nixon, and J-A. Reid, 2007, *Literacies in Place: Teaching Environmental Communications*, New South Wales, Primary English Teaching Association, Newtown.

Connell, R. W., 1993, *Schools and Social Justice*, Our Schools/Our Selves Education Foundation, Toronto.

Cormack, P. and B. Green, 2007, "Writing Place in English: How a School Subject Constitutes Children's Relations to the Environment," *Australian Journal of Language and Literacy,* vol. 30, no. 2: 85–101.

Cormack, P., B. Green, and J-A. Reid, 2007, "Children's Understanding of Place: Discursive Constructions of the Environment in Children's Writing and Artwork about the Murray-Darling Basin," in F. Vanclay, M. Higgins, and A. Blackshaw (eds.), *Senses of Place: Exploring Concepts and Expressions of Place Through Different Senses and Lenses*, National Museum of Australia Press, Canberra, pp. 57–75.

Donehower, K., C. Hogg, and E. Schell, 2007, *Rural Literacies*, Southern Illinois University Press, Carbondale.

Edmondson, J., 2001, "Prairie Town: Rural Life and Literacies," *Journal of Research in Rural Education*, vol. 17, no. 1: 3–11.

Fairclough, N., 1989, *Language and Power*, Longman, London.

————, 1993, *Discourse and Social Change*, Polity Press, Cambridge.

————, 1995, *Critical Discourse Analysis*, Longman, London.

Freire, P., 1972, *Pedagogy of the Oppressed*, Seabury, New York.

Freire, P. and D. Macedo, 1987, *Literacy: Reading the Word and the World*, Bergin & Garvey, Westport, CN.

Gilbert, P., 1993, "(Sub)versions: Using Sexist Language Practices to Explore Critical Literacy," *Australian Journal of Language and Literacy*, vol. 16, no. 4: 323–331.

Gore, J., 1993, *The Struggle for Pedagogies: Critical and Feminist Discourses as Regimes of Truth*, Routledge, New York.

Green, B., 2010, "Education and Rural-Regional Sustainability," paper presented at the Educational Practice and Rural Social Space Symposium, the Annual Conference of the American Educational Research Association (AERA), Denver, Colorado, United States, April 30–May 4.

Green, B., P. Cormack, and H. Nixon, 2007, "Introduction: Literacy, Place, Environment," *Australian Journal of Language and Literacy,* vol. 30, no. 2: 77–81.

Gruenewald, D., 2003a, "The Best of Both Worlds: A Critical Pedagogy of Place," *Educational Researcher*, vol. 32, no. 4: 3–12.

————, 2003b, "Foundations of Place: A Multidisciplinary Framework for Place-Conscious Education," *American Educational Research Journal*, vol. 40, no. 3: 619–654.

Gruenewald, D., 2004, "A Foucauldian Analysis of Environmental Education: Toward the Socio-ecological Challenge of the Earth Charter," *Curriculum Inquiry*, vol. 34, no. 1: 71–107.

Gulson, K. and C. Symes (eds.), 2007, *Spatial Theories of Education: Policy and Geography Matters*, Routledge, New York and London.

Hall, S., 2003, "The Work of Representation," in S. Hall (ed.), *Representation: Cultural Representations and Signifying Practices*, Sage, London.

Janks, H., 1993, *Language and Identity*, Hodder & Stoughton and Wits University Press, Johannesburg.

———, 2010, *Literacy and Power*, Routledge, New York and London.

Kerkham, L., 2011, "Embodied Literacies and a Poetics of Place," *English Teaching: Practice and Critique*, vol. 10, no. 3: 9–25.

Kerkham, L. and B. Comber, 2007, "Literacy, Places and Identity: The Complexity of Teaching Environmental Communications," *Australian Journal of Language and Literacy*, vol. 30, no. 2:. 134–148.

Lupton, R., 2005, "Social Justice and School Improvement: Improving the Quality of Schooling in the Poorest Neighbourhoods," *British Educational Research Journal*, vol. 31, no. 5: 589–604.

Martusewicz, R. and J. Edmundson, 2005, "Social Foundations as Pedagogies of Responsibility and Eco-ethical Commitment," in D. W. Butin (ed.), *Teaching Social Foundations of Education: Contexts, Theories and Issues*, Lawrence Erlbaum Associates, Mahwah, NJ.

Mellor, B., A. Patterson, and M. O'Neill, 1991, *Reading Fictions*, Chalkface Press, Western Australia.

Nixon, H., 2007, "Expanding the Semiotic Repertoire: Environmental Communications in the Primary School," *Australian Journal of Language and Literacy*, vol. 30, no. 2: 102–117.

Reid, J-A., 2007, "Literacy and Environmental Communications: Towards a 'Pedagogy of Responsibility," *Australian Journal of Language and Literacy*, vol. 30, no. 2: 118–133.

Seddon, T., 2003, "Framing Justice: Challenges for Research," *Journal of Education Policy*, vol. 18, no. 3: 229–252.

Smith, G., 2002, "Place-Based Education: Learning to Be Where We Are," *Phi Delta Kappan*, vol. 83, no. 8 (April): 584–594.

Soja, E., 2011, *Seeking Spatial Justice*, University of Minnesota Press, Minneapolis.

Somerville, M., 2007, "Place Literacies," *Australian Journal of Language and Literacy*, vol. 30, no. 2: 149–164.

Stables, A., 1996, "Reading the Environment as Text: Literary Theory and Environmental Education," *Environmental Education Research*, vol. 2, no. 2: 189–195.

———, 2001, "Language and Meaning in Environmental Education: An Overview," *Environmental Education Research*, vol. 7, no. 2: 121–128.

———, 2004, "On Teaching and Learning the Book of the World," in S. Mayer and G. Wilson (eds.), *Ecodidactic Perspectives in English Language, Literacies and Cultures*, Rodopi, Amsterdam and New York.

Stables, A. and K. Bishop, 2001, "Weak and Strong Conceptions of Environmental Literacy: Implications for Environmental Education," *Environmental Education Research*, vol. 7, no. 1: 89–97.

Stables, A., A. Reid, R. Soetaert, S. Stoer, K. Bishop, and M. Lencastre, 1999, "The Development of Environmental Awareness through Literature and Media Education," a project sponsored by DGXI of the European Commission, http://www.bath.ac.uk/Departments/Education/eu/project.htm.

Watts, R., 2000, "National Awards for Innovation in Local Government, 10th November 2000," Presentation, Canberra, http://www.loc-gov-focus.aus.net/editions/2000/may/green/award.shtml.

Weiler, K., 1991, "Freire and a Feminist Pedagogy of Difference," *Harvard Educational Review*, vol. 61, no. 4: 449–474.

CHAPTER 11

The Making of "Good-Enough" Everyday Lives: Literacy Lessons from the Rural North of Finland

Pauliina Rautio and Maija Lanas

Introduction

Successful lives tend to be led and defined through vocabularies of material possessions, economic growth, social connections, and increasing mobility. This approach emphasizes standards of living, the level of which is commonly measured in terms of gross domestic product. As a result, the everyday lives of people in rural areas (by definition faraway and scarcely populated, and typically less economically vibrant than their urban counterparts) are often considered unsuccessful and unproductive by the standards of the wider society.

The fact remains, however, that there are people who lead balanced and satisfying lives in rural areas of the world *in spite of* what some would view as material shortcomings. The ways in which these people make their lives "good-enough" need to be acknowledged in order to diversify understandings of what counts as a successful life. To bring people in rural areas into this conversation about desirable living conditions within a nation-state is important in terms of recognizing and inviting previously unheard perspectives to contribute to the dialogical and critical reflection about a society:

> I think about a young author, who once in some TV show claimed that he becomes anxious the minute he ends up in the country. [...] I find it somehow healthy to think that we are different, us humans, and that what is beautiful to me, is not beautiful to someone else. But now I allow myself

to enjoy this beauty. I will go back to my garden to be with the mosquitoes and my flowerbeds. The beds are flourishing with all kinds of weeds as well as hardy perennial plants. There it is I who decides what is beautiful. I take out the weeds I don't like and plant and sow what I like.[1]

In order to understand the variety of possible lives led in diverse environments, there is need for a lateral focus on continuous *making* of what we describe as a good-enough life, rather than a focus on consumption and the accumulation of readymade, measurable elements of a good life (see also Bauman 1998). The former is an open-ended project that is essentially never complete. We propose, drawing on our fieldwork and research in the villages of Finnish Lapland (Rautio 2010; Lanas 2011), that one of the ways in which people in remote villages keep making their lives worthwhile is what can be understood as a particular literacy. We will call this "aesthetic literacy."

Literacy, understood as ranging from being a basic activity of decoding print, to being an ability to engage in a variety of activities required for functioning in one's community, has been traditionally considered as a more or less technical skill possessed by individuals (Kalman 2008). This so-called autonomous model of literacy (e.g., Street 1984) has since been challenged by socioculturally oriented theories of literacy that emphasize a diversity of literacies through a focus on situatedness and social relations (e.g., the New London Group 1996; Cazden, Cope, and Kalantzis 1996; Gee 1996; Street 2003). As a result, multiple and multimodal literacies (e.g., Heath and Street 2008) are flourishing, and literacies are now considered in their everyday life contexts (Kalman 2008).

However, whether it is the autonomous or the sociocultural model of literacy, it seems that literacies remain in the sphere of human culture, as opposed to, and as if external to, nature or the nonhuman material world. Being literate is often defined as an ability to use language to participate in the explicitly *human* world. While scholars who subscribe to broader definitions of what counts as literacy are critically-minded and quick to point out the embedded power relations in conventions surrounding literacy (Brandt and Clinton 2002; Street 2003), they often fail to address the nature-culture relationship, or indeed the lack of such relations in conceptualizing literacies. With a focus on a human being as the literate subject, research on literacies—and poststructural social scientific research in general (see Alaimo and Hekman 2008)—tends to be centered on human meaning-making and discourse constituting our (social) reality. Little attention is paid to how elements in our material surroundings possess agency essentially overlapping with and generating human subjects (see especially Bennett 2010).

We propose aesthetic sensibilities as a way of conceptualizing literacy that can bridge the human/nonhuman gap and address the simultaneous interconnectedness and uniqueness of people and our material world, as text. By this, we mean *that the ability to communicate one's apprehensions and understand those of others*, traditionally seen as literacy, in aesthetic literacy refers to one's dialogical existence with a material world in its entirety. It refers to the ability to read one's surroundings and respond to them cognitively, bodily, consciously, and unconsciously. This we think is accomplished in ways that increase the harmony—positive aesthetic value—between an individual and his/her surroundings.

It is evident, in our research, that rural people take active agency in crafting good-enough lives relative to their immediate material surroundings, rather than buying into predefined standards of living that are articulated on a national or regional scale. We identify this as an aesthetic literate tendency that is about imaginative interest in and toward the sensory qualities of everyday life. Being aesthetically literate indicates not only recognizing existing relations to one's material environment;[2] it also involves seeking and creating new relations and responding imaginatively in ways that also challenge normative expectations. We perceive aesthetic literacy as a continuous, more or less acknowledged state of being, a thought position, or an orientation to be initiated into, rather than a straightforward skill to be learnt or taught.

Rurality, in this chapter, is seen as based in a particular biophysical condition, and thus, a concrete framework for aesthetic literacy in everyday life. It is due to this particular condition, entailing sparse population, often harsh climate, abundance of relatively untouched nature, limited infrastructures, and great distances, that the articulation of sensory relations to one's material surroundings is a necessity, rather than a luxury. We do not claim that all rural inhabitants possess aesthetic literacy, nor do we insist that urban dwellers lack it categorically.

Our take on well-being and the standards or quality of life is to propose a notion of a good-enough everyday life. We emphasize the particularity and diversity of what is perceived, and what is possible to perceive as "enough." It is also to conceive of the production of meaningful everyday life as a rhizomatic process without a definitive end point or a clear objective. To talk about a good-enough life is to discuss the phenomenon of everyday life as relative to one's environment; daily life keeps on unfolding and challenging us in diverse ways, depending on one's location. An ability to make do, and to lead a successful life where you are, requires relations to your surroundings that are good-enough.

Aesthetic Literacy in Two Villages in the Rural Finnish North

> I think that it is a privilege to live in such a beautiful place, it is a privilege to get used to beauty. I cannot help thinking that it affects us all the time, even if we do not think about it consciously or focus intentionally on all that surrounds us. You can't after all hide your eyes, ears and sense of smell being outside.

The empirical basis of this chapter is a research project entitled "Life in Place" (2007–2012),[3] conducted by Syrjälä and Rautio at the University of Oulu, the second most northern university in Finland. Within this project, various substudies exist, including the two inquiries upon which this chapter draws. A shared objective of Life in Place has been to explore the lives of rural northern villagers as they perceive them, and to focus on hearing the voices of people who actively choose to stay. The villages are both small and are located north of the Arctic Circle in Finnish Lapland. The villages boast populations of approximately 150 and 30 respectively.

In both of the two subprojects on which this chapter builds, the participants conveyed the same kind of aesthetic literacy, but in different ways. While the participants in Rautio's research relied on verbal language when describing their lives, the participants in Lanas's research relied on sharing experiences. Rautio's PhD research (2010) addresses perceived beauty in everyday life. In this research, four women of the smaller village engaged in writing letters about beauty. In addition to exchanged letters, the data comprises individual as well as group interviews prior to and after the phase of correspondence. All in all, 44 letters were exchanged by four people within the time frame of one year. In these letters, the participants communicate aspects of their everyday lives that they find to be of aesthetic worth. The second subproject that contributes to the empirical basis of this chapter is Lanas's PhD research, based on two years of ethnographic visits and interviews conducted in northern Finnish villages, as well as an ethnographic study, over four months, in one village (Lanas 2011).

The inarticulable is not necessarily noncommunicable. The participants in Lanas's research told Lanas about their lives by inviting her to share experiences that they perceived as meaningful and descriptive of their lives, such as personal celebrations, reindeer roundups, walks, meetings with municipal officials, visiting favorite Internet sites or games such as Grand Theft Auto (these last two were shared by youth). The first invitations Lanas received after a participant had failed to explain something with words: "I can't explain it, you have to come there to experience it for yourself." Later, it became a regular, inarticulated way of communicating. The participants ultimately left it for Lanas to verbalize, in her research, the experiences that they couldn't.

When aesthetic aspects of everyday life—that which is found to be in balance and valued as good-enough—do get articulated into language and end up on paper, the process is one of aligning world with words (Winston 2010). There is always residue, however, especially when it is multisensory experiences that one wishes to communicate in writing. This residue causes a need for reiteration and produces a practice that is essentially open-ended. Writing becomes as much about conveying subjective feelings to others as an aesthetic practice in its own right. Aesthetic literacy, in its conventional form, is about refining one's ability to (re)produce a communicable sensory world and to (re)create discursive reality that is of aesthetic worth.

Aesthetic literacy is, however, not only about translating felt world into language. Being aesthetically literate does not necessarily have to do with conventional reading and writing. In this, we refer to Bakhtinian dialogism in which a dialogue is seen as a state of existence and the utterances exchanged go beyond written or spoken language (Bakhtin 1987; Holquist 1990; Lanas 2011). For instance, one's decision to remain in the rural North—that is, one's actual physical existence in the North—can be considered as itself indicative of a particular literacy, eminently relevant to and communicating about leading a meaningful life in a given context.

Aesthetic literacy is often exemplified in processes of negotiating the aspects that are usually rendered as problems of rural life, such as sparse population, isolation, and so on. One example of this kind of challenge and an aesthetically literate way of living with it is the lack of social contact, an aspect often articulated as a down-side of rural life in remote small villages. While nobody we worked with referred to the amount of social contact as satisfying, let alone a beautiful thing in their everyday life per se, it is their creative adaptation to this condition that bears beauty. The letters are abundant with writing about the diversity and richness of life in their village. The relative solitude of these people allows them to observe and appreciate interaction in terms of beings, rather than only humans. Life, to those writing, is not equal to social contact between humans but includes, for example, the sounds, tracks, and sights of nonhuman animals as indicative of coexisting beings (see Rautio 2011). The popular and political discourse of "dying villages," based on declining number of human habitants, is contested:

> A bright star (Venus, says my husband) and a sliver of moon wander all night from the southern sky towards west. I see how the sky slowly turns darker, trees in the horizon become darker, the star and the moon approach the ground. Here, we follow our fellow travelers, on the road and in the skies. It is a habit that makes everything seem smaller and homier. Nature is close, the passers-by in nature are part of our village, even in the skies [stars]. When I lived in Helsinki I used to love rain and storms because they broke the illusion of humans being on top of the world.

Emergence in a Relational Field

Both of the authors conduct research within the discipline of Education, approaching and defining educational phenomena widely and through other disciplines as well. Our interest, as educationalists, lies in the understanding of a variety of possible everyday lives and the ways in which people craft these in various surroundings. Rather than seeking to explicitly arrive at pedagogical implications, our insights are directed at a grounded level of what it means to grow and live as a human being, coexisting with a particular environment, not only molding that environment to one's liking but also being continuously molded by it.

Why partly inarticulable material surroundings should be considered both in research of education and of literacies can be argued through a Deleuzean understanding of *difference* as generative and as the basis of existence rather than as a by-product of our existence as individuals (Deleuze 1994; Lehtinen 2010, pp. 51, 55–56). Difference, in this sense, is not located in individuals, nor in their biophysical surroundings. Rather, it *generates individuals* in continuous, unique, and unpredictable *encounters* with each other and with surrounding material elements. Understood like this, it becomes pivotal that we have orientations toward these encounters that help us to manage and understand the ways in which we are generated: how we become simultaneously interdependent and unique beings.

A multimodal and multisensory literacy, such as aesthetic literacy, can be taken as an orientation toward identifying and working with encountered elements, bringing momentary coherence, meaning, or sense, into the world. If so-called traditional literacy is about an ability to function and understand one's place in a given society, aesthetic literacy is a component in our understanding of ourselves as part of the world. Furthermore, aesthetic literacy is not just about aesthetic sensitivity or responsiveness, such as perceiving and imaginative understanding of multisensory information. The literacy component is needed exactly to emphasize an active, generative relation to surroundings. Living a good-enough life is a continual act of reading and writing with one's body.

Methodologically, the influence of Deleuze and Guattari (1987; see especially Hultman and Taguchi 2010) yields an approach in which we, as researchers, focus on continuities rather than oppositions: we look at ways in which people differentiate in continuous encounters with other bodies, human and nonhuman, and the ways in which this differentiation is perceived as meaningful and affirming. Human beings are bound to their unique contexts—including but not limited to language as a context. Yet it is not the context per se, rather the intra-activity[4] of the human being and the elements of a particular context that interests us. A woman from the village of Suvanto, jumping in muddy puddles, articulates delightfully where we might direct our interest. We look neither at the woman alone, nor the puddles (or at her boots) but, rather, at the intra-action of the two, the negotiation of bodies and entities as if in play: we see the woman as emergent in a relational field:

> I step from one puddle to the next in my new white rubber boots. [. . .] My boots dive enthusiastically into the same brown muddy water that my dog is slurping with as much delight, as if he did not get enough clean water at home. Something in these puddles draws me to them. Kids love them too. You cannot say that a puddle is beautiful as such. Or can you? Maybe its beauty lies in the joy of splattering in the muddy water. Beauty is a feeling: joy. And it has to do with freedom. I can jump in a puddle all I want, nobody tells me not to. If someone did, I would jump anyway in secret and feel free anyway, for I would be doing what I want regardless of other people's opinions.

That which interests us lies in-between two bodies: a child and a dog, a woman and a muddy puddle, a young man and an older man. Our focus is in the ways in which these encounters become perceived as good-enough, affirming, marking a contribution to a feeling of simultaneous connectedness and uniqueness (Bai et al. 2010; Hultman and Taguchi 2010).

Aesthetic Literacy in Negotiating a Relational Field

In critiquing the anthropocentric approaches prevalent in social scientific research, it is common for advocates of environmental issues to seek to diminish or abolish such human-centeredness altogether (e.g., Hultman and Taguchi 2010; Russell 2005; Naess 1989; see also Calarco 2008). One of the main reasons that we choose to approach human-environment relations in the Finnish rural North through the notion of aesthetic *literacy,* in particular, is to maintain a default level of anthropocentrism in our research. In line with a basic posthumanist principle of "openness from closure" (e.g., Wolfe 2010, p. xxi), we suggest that there is a need to realize that we experience and make meaning of the world necessarily as human beings, with all of our species-specific biophysical limitations and possibilities. We cannot but be anthropocentric in this sense. It is through this realization, exhibiting a default level of anthropocentrism (as distinct from hierarchical, value-laden anthropocentrism), that we can then begin to acknowledge the heterogeneity of nonhuman ways to coexist and communicate with us (Martinelli 2008; see also Bonnett 2006).

We propose, based on our encounters with our data, that aesthetic literacy is a notion that can accommodate human engagement with the totality of his/her surrounding material world, without reducing the world into consumable objects or reality into being constructed with human discourse alone. Aesthetic literacy can, at best, address the generative agency of our material world as constitutive of us. As such, it can highlight the self-environment relations that are required for functioning in everyday life, for the making of a good-enough life as it unfolds.

Importantly, aesthetic literacy does not only assign us as being passively generated, but renders our role as active—without delusions that this role would be omnipotent. Being aesthetically literate is being able to affect one's life, to make it worthwhile and render it with worth. While washing the windows of her old house, a participant of Rautio's research is explicitly insightful, weaving together parts of her material surroundings and creating continuity between herself and her environment. She concludes that her surroundings constitute her self-portrait— *at the moment*:

The window [. . .] reflects my whole world: in the low right corner there is a woman wearing an old blue scarf and an army-green hunting jacket, behind her there is the yard and the barn with its white lining boards around windows and the door. Down in the middle there is a light blue saintpaulia in full bloom [...] In the midst of all this there is an old, partly decaying mountain rowan, the branches of which reach towards the grey sky. [...] The old window refracts light and distorts parts of the image [...] The window is beautiful to me because it evokes something in me, it tells me things about myself, about my life. It feels in me, and it feels important and true. It is my self-portrait at the moment.

Aesthetic literacy has a history of being defined as familiarity with various artistic modes of expression (Sykes 1982; Hamblen 1986) and the development of this familiarity as a type of cultural literacy, rather than a functional one (Greene 1981; Smith 1991). In line with recent developments in aesthetics, particularly in the fields of environmental and everyday aesthetics (Saito 2007; Irvin 2009b; Light and Smith 2005; Melchionne 2007; Berleant 2010), we approach aesthetic literacy as imaginative interest in one's material surroundings in everyday life. By imaginative interest, we mean an approach to environment that utilizes the Deleuzian notion of difference as generative: a tree in the distance is not a tree, as such, but a possibility for an encounter in which something new and meaningful could arise:

I reached for branches from a tall willow that grew by a field. I bent my neck to look up the branches. They were straight, sturdy, deep mahogany colored, with dark blue sky as the background. I looked with disbelief. It was as if I had entered a different world of colors. I looked around, and up again. It took me a while before I realized that my sunglasses were playing tricks on me. [...] Another time I was lying on the sled of a snowmobile, by Oravakumpu, on a mattress with my son. We played with colors, looking at pine branches against the sky wearing different sunglasses, or not wearing any. My son's glasses made the colors change depending on whether you looked through the upper or the lower part of the lens. We saw four different versions of blue sky and green branches.

Emerging from our data and refined through our theoretical approach, we have come to assign aesthetic literacy the following character for our purposes here (figure 11.1).

Aesthetic literacy emerges in our data as a positive orientation and interest toward the beings and entities one coexists with. The hallmark signs of this orientation are almost a light-hearted approach to the world as if riddles and an explicitly sensory attentiveness to events in everyday life. Aesthetic literacy is an orientation that contributes to the making of a good-enough life in highlighting the potential for growth and well-being that our interconnectedness with our world provides.

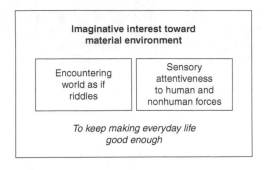

Figure 11.1 Aesthetic Literacy.
Source: By author.

In an interview, Cora Diamond (2000, p. 70) discusses riddles much in the same way that we mean to discuss aesthetic literacy. It is when one views daily surroundings as though it were a riddle. There are a multitude of familiar objects, events, sights, and sounds about. There are also a multitude of combinations of these elements and interpretations/applications, each with a slightly different outcome mostly unknown to us beforehand:

> [With riddles] we don't have the identity of the words delivering to us what we're trying to do. One of the examples I used in that riddle paper was from the upbringing of my niece, when she was eighteen months or so, when my sister told her [...] "kiss your ear." Now what my niece did was kiss her hand and put it to her ear. There the identity of the piece does not tell her at all how to interpret the command. And so she invents a solution to the riddle. (Diamond 2000, p. 70)

An aesthetically literate person has a keen interest in connecting the "dots," making sense of the endless riddle surrounding him/her through relating to his/her surroundings as potentially rewarding and transformative. In line with the "air" of riddles, Jane Bennett (2010) grounds her thinking on the vitality of matter in our lives. Bennett illustrates a space that, in our view, is a form of aesthetic literacy: a space in which familiar things collide and differentiate into new meanings, into new combinations of relations, a space in which good-enough life is continuously generated:

> I will turn the figures "life" and "matter" around and around [...] in something like the way a common word when repeated can become a

foreign, nonsense sound. In the space created by this estrangement, a vital materiality can start to take shape. (p. vii)

Bennett (p. xiv) proceeds to describe a human orientation toward the vitality of matter as "a cultivated, patient, sensory attentiveness to non-human forces operating outside and inside the human body." This is akin to the orientation that we see required in aesthetic literacy. In the following quote from Rautio's research data, a woman writes about a winter evening stroll. Albeit expressed in a deliberately poetic style, the writing is exemplary of much of our data where the boundaries of the body and the self begin to dissolve into the environment:

> The world had changed. The year had changed and the world had changed. An air of winter was hovering over me, after first having disappeared somewhere far into Siberia. It had returned. I took a deep breath. Cold air traveled through my nostrils, slightly filtered, towards my lungs and what did I feel! My chest widened. My pose straightened. My eyes brightened. My mind revived and rose to the rooftops. It was winter again. I enjoyed the moment. [...] It felt as if everyone in the entire universe was making content sounds. As if things had fallen into place. I sighed and smiled.

A similar experience was shared, albeit unverbalized, by Lanas and her young research participants on a winter walk. The air glittered, the youth hugged Lanas, wrestled each other, ran with her, showed her various houses, and laid in the snow with her, looking at their breath making statues in the air. The experience was not communicated through words but in movement and in laughter.

Consistent with our approach, comprising in part everyday language philosophy (e.g., Cavell 1969; Wittgenstein 1966), we direct our attention not only to the kind of literacy that aesthetic literacy represents but also what it *does*. What do we do when we rephrase our sensory surroundings, into either words or actions, with the intent of sharing our experiences with others?

Stanley Cavell (1969) discusses aesthetic claims as a specific kind of claim for which we cannot produce empirical evidence so as to convince anyone of anything. There is no evidence for our assertion that a breath of cold air is beautiful. These claims are then often regarded as a matter of individual taste, and thus relative. Beauty, then, is in the eye of the beholder (Armstrong 2004). For Cavell (1969) and Wittgenstein (1966), however, aesthetic claims are neither relative nor irrational. Both pay attention to what it is that *we do* when we feel the need to share an aesthetic judgment. If these aesthetic claims were purely subjective and relative, why would we bother expressing them to others? Cavell (2000) suggests that it is about initiation: a process of negotiation over our modes of life, over our shared understandings of the world in which we live.

The woman telling us that a breath of cold air is beautiful is not asking us to agree blindly without evidence. Nor are the youth proposing, with their actions, that we join them in jumping into the snow. For the evidence needed, we need to look at our own lives, our own conceptions and experiences, and see whether we can agree. The way Cavell (1969) explains this is that the work of an art critic or a philosopher (of everyday language) is to express, the best "he" can, "his" world, in order to make others pay undivided attention to *their worlds*. The assertion that a breath of cold air is beautiful is an act of making life: of exploring one's relation and conceptions of the world, translating this relation into an aesthetic claim and opening it up for negotiation and reiteration, both by herself and by others. The Deleuzian notion of difference as generative is truly at play here.

The practices with which we make our lives good-enough, one of which we suggest to be aesthetic literacy, can be taken as autotelic in nature (see Donehower, this volume [Ch2]). This is to say that we do not make aesthetic assertions for the sake of any external motive or a definitive end. Our aesthetic literacy sustains a life perceived as good-enough, and is thus internally motivated. Practices exhibiting aesthetic literacy rely on material surroundings, yet are immaterial and unmeasurable in essence. On the level of everyday life, the good-enough has to be made by us—it will not be offered by anyone else for us to consume and accumulate.

The Making of a Good-Enough Life

Research in rural education, as well as place-based education, suggests that particular lived-in contexts are relevant to education (e.g., Schafft and Youngblood Jackson 2010; Corbett 2008; for practical insights, see also Brooke 2003). David Sobel (2004) warns us of falling out with lived-in beauty in our surroundings, stating that if it happens, "educational biodiversity falls prey to the bulldozers of standardization." In the insightful words of Gregory Smith (2002), education that takes the notion of place seriously is about "learning to be where we are." Pedagogies based on emphasis of proximity or situatedness (e.g., that are lococentric—see Garrard 2010) tend to be quite literally focused on learning about one's immediate natural environment and do not fare without due criticism (Knapp 2005; Ball and Lai 2006; Nespor 2008).

We choose to direct criticism toward the implied normative binaries that foci on place bring forth: proximity over distance; and place over space. A pedagogical objective of learning about nature, at the core of many ecologically-oriented place-based studies, implies a further binary, that of human/nature, in which nature is as if a separate entity from us (see also Somerville, this volume [Ch9]). What is implied is that we exist outside of nature and are in danger of falling out of touch with it, unless we make an effort to teach and learn about it. Our own existence, as always already with nature and *as nature,* remains to be discussed.

Furthermore, the heterogeneity of our material, biophysical world, not limited to so-called natural environments, remains to be given agency in generating human subjectivity (e.g., Bennett 2010; Soja 2010). Education that takes the notions of place, situatedness, or context seriously is education that does not reduce our interest toward the world to remain on either side of the binaries—human/nonhuman, discourse/matter, place/space (see also Hultman and Taguchi 2010, p. 526). Rather, such education seeks to if not eradicate these binaries altogether, at least to introduce them through the Deleuzian idea of a generative difference: either side of any binary is constantly generative of the other and there are no clear-cut borders or stable positions.

People taking part in both of our research projects produced data, in writing, talking, or behaving. We have interpreted these encounters as communication about their lives in the making. In the data, countless accounts of diverse events or thoughts all convey a strong sense of ownership of one's life. But ownership is understood in a way that allows and anticipates a generative role for both human agency and material surroundings. To get a fresh viewpoint on everyday life and to feel delighted about life requires attention and playfulness toward the material world:

> On one trip to the shops in Sodankylä, I managed to buy a new wax cloth for our kitchen table. It is light, maybe faded rose in color. It has little white flowers on it, some with full white petals, some with only white outlines of petals. Our everyday white ceramic kitchenware looks beautiful on it. For weeks now I have played with making the most diverse of small arrangements on a plate on that table. Light green domestic apples or dark plums and nectarines are beautiful on there. The new cloth brought with it a new world of colors that I find nice to play with. It is lovely when everyday things become beautiful. The kitchen table is so central, always used and constantly viewed. The old table cloth was also beautiful, but time and wear took their toll on it. New colors and new experiences

arrived with the new cloth. On that cloth, old things look new again. Maybe that is also important: that one gets a fresh viewpoint, finds novelty in everyday life. That is beautiful.

We adopt the notion of good-enough from D. W. Winnicott (1971) and his work on creativity and play. For Winnicott, the aspect of enough was crucial to the freedom and space required for playing and creative life. His core example, as a psychoanalyst, was the mother-infant relation, in which the mother's imperfection was in fact a desired element in this relationship. A mother needs to be good-enough, rather than "perfect," to allow her child the potential space in which to develop into a balanced self. What we take from Winnicott's thinking is not so much the psychoanalytic approach, rather, the idea that sometimes the best approach to the making of one's everyday life, at any age, is one that is always in a sense lacking, unfinished, and yet in the process of becoming and being made. This is something that is not easily verbalized. A man in Lanas's research data makes an effort to verbalize what we call lateral attention to the making of everyday life:

> I always remember that you try, you must always try. If you don't try you have nothing. It doesn't matter if you live in the city or here or anywhere, it doesn't matter, you must try, whether you live in the city or in the country.

To others, what he articulates may read as struggling, but he is, in fact, describing a triumph: a good-enough life in the making. He fares well in his village and he does not feel a need to go anywhere else. The "trying" he refers to is the kind of lateral, unceasing, and reiterative making of everyday life that we identify at the core of a good-enough life. The same villager goes on to explain what one does to make do and be well in his village: "one must think of something, if nothing else, one does something, one can always think of something to do." The "something to do" here refers to activities and tasks such as skiing, hunting, picking berries, caring for reindeer, looking for firewood, building things, helping someone else build things, fishing, contacting the municipality to demand streetlights, arguing against closing the school or for hunting privileges. Although doing such things comes naturally for him, articulating it is not as natural. This is precisely why we cannot solely focus on how people describe their lives in words but must also be able to discern how they communicate their lives through what they do, and what they thus invite us to consider worthwhile as well.

The good-enough life involves a continuous tending to horizontal, rhizomatic relations and meaningfulness, rather than accumulating finite experiences, possessions, and calculable milestones. It is a difference in perspective that the notion of the good-enough proposes to us: one toward horizontality and momental diversity of life, rather than life as causal, cumulative, and linear. A lateral perspective to aesthetic literacy, in the making of everyday life in the rural north of Finland, emphasizes three main aspects:

- The diversity of what is possible to be perceived as good enough at a given time, in a given society;
- The making of meaningful life as a process without a definitive end-point or a clear objective; and
- The orientation toward everyday life as characterized by playfulness and openness.

Conclusion

Through an emphasis on what we call aesthetic literacy, we are able to challenge the notion of material possessions as indicative of successful life. It is a common view that rural villagers have fewer resources available to make do, to increase their material wealth, and thus, their well-being. However, if we consider meaningful everyday life as made, rather than consumed, it is human capacities, orientations, and tendencies, rather than human possessions, that we need to think about as resources. Rural villagers, then, have no fewer resources at hand than do urban dwellers. Our sensory and cognitive capabilities are roughly the same regardless of where we are. It is how we use these resources in relation to our diverse material surroundings, every day, that matters.

Overall, an aesthetic view to literacy is about continuous attempts to articulate one's inarticulable existence in the midst of a material world. Being aesthetically literate is about being able and *interested in* relating to what surrounds one in an imaginative way, and to create meaning with the heterogeneity of the bodies and beings (not only human) with whom we coexist. This is one practice of making everyday life good-enough.

Notes

1. All block quotes in this chapter are by the villagers who participated in the authors' study in 2007–2010 in the Finnish Lapland.

2. In using "material environment," we refer, in this chapter, to the entirety of one's surroundings: human, nonhuman, and inanimate.
3. Funded by the Academy of Finland and led by Professor of Education, Leena Syrjälä.
4. For the distinction between "interactive" (e.g., two independent entities taking turns in affecting each other) and "intra-active" (e.g., two interdependent entities coemerging through simultaneous activity), see especially Karen Barad (2007).

References

Alaimo, S. and S. Hekman, 2008, "Introduction: Emerging Models of Materiality in Feminist Theory," in S. Alaimo and S. Hekman (eds.), *Material Feminisms*, Indiana University Press, Bloomington.

Armstrong, J. 2004, *The Secret Power of Beauty: Why Happiness Is in the Eye of the Beholder*, Penguin, London.

Bai, H., D. Elza, P. Kovacs, and S. Romanycia, 2010, "Re-searching and Re-storying the Complex and Complicated Relationship of Biophilia and Bibliophilia," *Environmental Education Research*, vol. 16, nos. ¾: 351–365.

Bakhtin, M. M., 1987, *The Dialogic Imagination: Four Essays*, M. Holquist (ed.), C. Emerson and M. Holquist (trans.), University of Texas Press, Austin, Texas and London.

Ball, E. L. and A. Lai, 2006, "Place-Based Pedagogy for the Arts and Humanities," *Pedagogy: Critical Approaches to Teaching Literature, Language, Composition and Culture*, vol. 6, no. 2: 261–287.

Barad, K. 2007, *Meeting the Universe Halfway: Quantum Physics and the Entanglement of Matter and Meaning*, Durham, Duke, NC.

Bauman, Z., 1998, *Work, Consumerism and the New Poor*, Open University Press, Buckingham.

Bennett, J., 2010, *Vibrant Matter: A Political Ecology of Things*, Durham, Duke, NC.

Berleant, A., 2005, *Aesthetics and Environment: Variations on a Theme*, Ashgate, Aldershot.

———, 2010, *Sensibility and Sense: The Aesthetic Transformation of the Human World*, Imprint Academic, Exeter.

Bonnett, M., 2006, "Education for Sustainability as a Frame of Mind," *Journal of Environmental Education Research*, vol. 12: 265–276.

Brandt, D. and K. Clinton, 2002, "Limits of the Local: Expanding Perspectives on Literacy as a Social Practice," *Journal of Literacy Research*, vol. 34, no. 3: 337–356.

Brooke, R., 2003, *Rural Voices: Place-Conscious Education and the Teaching of Writing*, Teachers College Press, Columbia University, New York and London.

Calarco, M., 2008, *Zoographies: The Question of the Animal*, Columbia University Press, New York.

Cavell, S., 1969, *Must We Mean What We Say?* Scribner, New York.

————, 2000, "Excursus on Wittgenstein's Vision of Language," in A. Crary and R. Read (eds.), *The New Wittgenstein*, Routledge, Oxon.

Corbett, M., 2008, *Learning to Leave: The Irony of Schooling in a Coastal Community*, Fernwood, Black Point.

de Certeau, M., 1984, *The Practice of Everyday Life*, S. Rendall (trans.), University of California Press, Berkeley.

Deleuze, G., 1994, *Difference and Repetition*, P. Patton (trans.), Columbia University Press, New York.

Deleuze, G. and F. Guattari, 1980/1987, *A Thousand Plateaus: Capitalism and Schizofrenia*, Continuum, London.

Diamond, C., 2000, "What Time Is It on the Sun?" *Harvard Review of Philosophy*, vol. 8, no. 1: 69–81.

Garrard, G., 2010, "Problems and Prospects in Ecocritical Pedagogy," *Environmental Education Research*, vol. 16, no. 2, http://bathspa.academia.edu/GregoryGarrad/Papers/168920/Problems_and_Prospects_in_Ecocritical_pedagogy.

Gee, J., 1996, *Social Linguistics and Literacies: Ideology and Discourses*, Falmer Press, Bristol, PA.

Greene, M., 1981, *Aesthetic Literacy in General Education*, National Society for the Study of Education, Chicago, Illinois.

Hamblen, K. A., 1986, "Exploring Contested Concepts for Aesthetic Literacy," *Journal of Aesthetic Education*, vol. 20, no. 2: 67–76.

Heath, S. B. and B. V. Street, 2008, *On Ethnography: Approaches to Language and Literacy Research*, Teachers College Press, New York.

Hultman, K. and H. L. Taguchi, 2010, "Challenging Anthropocentric Analysis of Visual Data: A Relational Materialist Methodological Approach to Educational Research," *Qualitative Studies in Education*, vol. 23, no. 5: 525–542.

Irvin, S., 2009a, "Aesthetics and the Private Realm," *Journal of Aesthetics and Art Criticism*, vol. 67: 226–230.

————, 2009b, "Aesthetics of the Everyday," in S. Davies, K. Higgins, R. Hopkins, R. Stecker, and D. Cooper (eds.), *A Companion to Aesthetics*, 2nd ed., Wiley-Blackwell, Malden.

Kalman, J., 2008, "Beyond Definition: Central Concepts for Understanding Literacy," *International Review of Education*, vol. 54: 523–538.

Knapp, C. E. 2005, "The 'I-Thou' Relationship, Place-Based Education, and Aldo Leopold," *Journal of Experiential Education*, vol. 27, no. 3: 277–285.

Lanas, M., 2008, "Oikeus paikkaan—kuinka koulu ja pohjoinen pienkylä kohtaavat" [The Right for a Place—How Do School and a Northern Small Village Meet?], in M. Lanas, H. Niinistö, and J. Suoranta (eds.), *Kriittisen pedagogiikan kysymyksiä 2*, Tampereen yliopiston kasvatustieteiden laitos, Tampere.

Lanas, M., 2011, "How Can Non-verbalized Emotions in the Field Be Addressed in Research?" *International Journal of Research & Method in Education*, vol. 34, no. 2: 131–145.

Lanas, M. and M. Corbett, 2011, "Disaggregating Student Resistances—Analysing What Students Pursue with Challenging Agency," *Young—Nordic Journal of Youth Research*, vol. 19, no. 4: 415–432.

Lehtinen, J., 2010, *Encounters with the Virtual: The Experience of Art In Gilles Deleuze's Philosophy*. PhD thesis, University of Helsinki, Faculty of Arts, Department of Philosophy, History, Culture and Art Studies, May 12, 2011, http://urn.fi/URN:ISBN:978–952–10–6458–6.

Light, A. and J. Smith (eds.), 2005, *The Aesthetics of Everyday Life*, Columbia University Press, New York.

Martinelli, D., 2008, "Anthropocentrism as a Social Phenomenon: Semiotic and Ethical Implications," *Social Semiotics*, vol. 18, no. 1: 79–99.

Melchionne, K., 2007, "Living in Glass Houses: Domesticity, Interior Decoration, and Environmental Aesthetics," in A. Berleant and A. Carlson (eds.), *The Aesthetics of Human Environments*, Broadview Press, Plymouth.

Naess, A., 1989, *Ecology, Community and Lifestyle,* Cambridge University Press, Cambridge.

Nespor, J., 2008, "Education and Place: A Review Essay," *Educational Theory*, vol. 58, no. 4: 475–489.

The New London Group, 1996, "A Pedagogy of Multiliteracies: Designing Social Futures," *Harvard Educational Review,* vol. 66, no. 1: 60–92.

Rautio, P., 2010, *Writing about Everyday Beauty in a Northern Village: An Argument for Diversity of Habitable Places*. PhD thesis, Acta Universitatis Ouluensis, E 109, http://herkules.oulu.fi/isbn9789514263194/isbn978951426.

————, 2011, "Writing about Everyday Beauty. Anthropomorphism and Distancing in Relating to Environment," *Environmental Communication: A Journal of Nature and Culture*, vol. 5, no. 1: 104–123.

Russell, C. L., 2005, "'Whoever Does Not Write Is Written': The Role of 'Nature' in Post-approaches to Environmental Education," *Environmental Education Research*, vol. 11, no. 4: 433–443.

Saito, Y., 2007, *Everyday Aesthetics*, Oxford University Press, Oxford.

Schafft, K. A. and A. Youngblood Jackson, 2010, *Rural Education for the Twenty-First Century: Identity, Place, and Community in a Globalizing World*, Penn State Press, University Park, PA.

Smith, R. A., 1991, *Cultural Literacy and Arts Education*, University of Illinois, Chicago.

Smith, G. A., 2002, "Learning to Be Where We Are," *Phi Delta Kappan*, vol. 83, no. 8: 584–594.

Sobel, D., 2004, *Place-Based Education. Connecting Classrooms and Communities,* Orion Society, Great Barrington, MA.

Soja, E., 1989, *Postmodern Geographies: The Reassertion of Space in Critical Social Theory*, Verso, London.

————, 2010, *Seeking Spatial Justice*, University of Minnesota Press, Minneapolis.

Street, B., 1984, *Literacy in Theory and Practice*, Cambridge University Press, New York.

————, 2003, "What's 'New' in New Literacy Studies? Critical Approaches to Literacy in Theory and Practice," *Current Issues in Comparative Education*, vol. 5, no. 2: 77–91, http://www.tc.columbia.edu/cice/Issues/05.02/52street.p.

Sykes, G., 1982, "The Case for Aesthetic Literacy," *Educational Leadership*, vol. 39, no. 8: 596–598.

Syrjälä, L. and P. Rautio, 2007–2012, "Life in Place," University of Oulu, http://lifeinplace.wordpress.com/.

Tuan, Y., 1977, *Space and Place: The Perspective of Experience*, University of Minnesota Press, Minneapolis.

Winnicott, D. W., 1971, *Playing and Reality*, Routledge, London.

Wittgenstein, L., 1966, *Lectures & Conversations on Aesthetics, Psychology and Religious Belief,* C. Barrett (ed.), Blackwell, Oxford.

Wolfe, C., 2010, *What Is Posthumanism?* University of Minnesota Press, Minneapolis.

PART IV

Mobilities and Futures

CHAPTER 12

Reading Futures: Exploring Rural Students' Literacy Practices in Neoliberal Times

Kate Cairns

Over the low hum of the projector, Mrs. Sullivan reads aloud the role profile for Hotel Desk Clerk, which is displayed on the screen at the front of the classroom. She moves slowly through the job description, income breakdown, and educational preparation, highlighting key terms in each section and inviting students to explain their meaning. Following "gross monthly income" and "transferable skills," they reach "full time," and Johnathon's hand shoots into the air. He appears excited to see a vocabulary term he's heard before. "My dad works for a truck company and his full time is 12 hours a day," he says, turning around in his chair to watch for his classmates' reactions. When Paul says, "Whoa!" Johnathon smiles and turns back to the front.

It is no surprise that most of these vocabulary terms are new for the Grade 7/8 students in Mrs. Sullivan's class. The first Friday of September, this is only the third lesson within a career studies program called *The Real Game* (RG), which will be a major focus during the first two months of the school term. RG is promoted as a way to make schooling more "real," and to help students begin thinking about their futures. Earlier this week, students discussed the idea of a "career" as one's path through life, encompassing education, family, and hobbies, in addition to work. They then designed wish lists for their ideal future home, creating collages to represent the lifestyle of their dreams. This afternoon's vocabulary lesson is preparing them to meet their very own RG "character," an occupational profile that will become their role for the rest of the program (e.g., Photographer, Mechanic, Lawyer, etc.). From this position, they will balance budgets, plan vacations, and negotiate the struggles of job loss. Each of these role-play activities is preparation for the final task of looking toward the future from their own embodied locations, as young, mostly white, working-class boys and girls in a rural Ontario community that I call Fieldsville.

As students become acquainted with this new set of concepts, I negotiate a different set of introductions. Seated at the back of the classroom, I watch quietly as the lesson unfolds, a small notebook in my lap. Having been raised in an Ontario town much like this one, I can identify with many aspects of being a young person growing up in a small rural community. Now, as a graduate student at the University of Toronto, I bring a different set of lenses to this sociospatial context. Equipped with the tools of feminist poststructural ethnography, I am eager to explore how students negotiate the multiple discourses through which they are constituted, as they embrace certain categories and resist others in the process of crafting selves and futures. I have arrived at the question of imagined futures by way of critical scholarship on neoliberalism and education. This body of work has raised concerns regarding the ways in which schooling is being defined in this historical moment, with particular focus on the kind of person that students are encouraged to become. What studies of the neoliberal subject tend not to ask is *where* young people locate their futures, and how this question of the "where" fits into practices of self-making more broadly. As I sit at the back of the classroom during my first week in Fieldsville, it is this collection of questions that shapes my own sense-making.

This chapter explores how rural students construct readings of the future in neoliberal times. Based on the larger study *Mapping Futures, Making Selves: Subjectivity, Schooling, and Rural Youth* (Cairns 2011), I examine how rural young people read possible futures from the contradictory discourses available to them, and then write themselves into narratives of adulthood that attempt to mediate these contradictions. The analysis demonstrates how students draw upon a range of texts beyond the formal curriculum to construct readings of the future, including discourses of rurality, popular culture, and narratives of the "good life." Tensions emerge where local identifications meet dominant discourses of mobility, as students read conflicting representations of rural space alongside images of "success" that encourage them to locate their futures elsewhere. I argue that by examining these tensions, we may better understand not only the complexities of young rural lives, but also the literacy skills required to read competing future narratives *in place*.

Reading and Writing Futures in Neoliberal Times

Developed in Canada in 1994, and now implemented internationally, RG (http://www.realgame.com/) attempts to prepare young people for their futures as adults in a changing world.[1] Highlighting the unpredictability of current economic realities, the introduction to the RG Facilitator's Guide situates the program in relation to a particular sociohistorical context:

> *The Real Game* career and life exploration program is a response to the new and emerging challenges the evolving working world is relentlessly throwing at young people, indeed all citizens. It not only introduces them to everyday realities of the future upon which they are embarking, but helps them learn the competencies they will need to find meaning, purpose, satisfaction and fulfillment in both their present and their future. (Barry 2005, p. 13)

As seen here, the program is promoted as a necessary intervention to help students make themselves into the type of person who can succeed in an uncertain world. In this way, RG may be interpreted as one manifestation of a historically specific vision of schooling, in which a successful education produces future-oriented, enterprising citizens who can adapt to constant change. In the words of Australian education scholar Lyn Yates (2009, p. 22),

> Almost universally, today the task of schooling is not only addressed in terms of knowledge or skills, but also in terms of what kind of person (or at least what kind of worker) students should become: what learners will need to be able to do and who they will need to be to manage their future lives.

As a curricular program that stresses the importance of flexibility, mobility, and entrepreneurial capacity for success in a changing world, RG fits within a set of discourses that have been widely critiqued by critical scholars who view them as technologies of neoliberalism (e.g., Apple 2001; Bradford and Hey 2007). In an article entitled "Neoliberalism and Education," Davies and Bansel (2007, p. 248) characterize neoliberalization as the shift to "a state that gives power to global corporations and installs apparatuses and knowledges through which people are reconfigured as productive economic entrepreneurs of their own lives." Studies in North America, Europe, Australia, and New Zealand have shown how neoliberal shifts alter the discursive terrain in literacy

(Davies and Saltmarsh 2007), media education (Dehli 2009), vocational programming (Yates 2006), and notions of student success (McLeod and Yates 2006), as they produce a student-subject that reflects the ideals of risk-management and entrepreneurship (Demerath and Lynch 2008). In the context of discourses of choice and self-invention, Petersson, Olsson, and Popkewitz (2007, p. 49) argue that the future operates as "a technology to shape and nurture the 'future oriented' subject." They explain that while this emphasis on the future is not new to Western modernity, what is produced through neoliberal discourses is the conception of the individual as an "agent of the future" (p. 49), so that "the making of the present and of the future thus becomes an individual project" (p. 53). Critical scholars show how discourses of neoliberal self-hood obscure enduring structural inequities, presenting particular challenges for young women, working-class, and racialized individuals, who are encouraged to interpret structural constraints through the lens of individual agency (Francis and Hey 2009; Goodkind 2009).

These critiques provide insight into the dominant discourses currently shaping systems of education, yet they tell us little about how these discourses become meaningful in the context of schooling (Yates 2009). In this way, RG provides a fascinating site through which to explore how dominant educational discourses are connected to local classroom contexts and the everyday practices of embodied learners. My overall study asks: How do young people interpret and respond to this invitation to become enterprising citizens of the future? What discourses do they draw upon to envision their futures, and how is this process shaped by their sociospatial location?

My approach to these questions is grounded in the assumption that location matters. The young people at the center of this research encounter the invitation to imagine their futures from particular positions in social and geographical space: namely, as girls and boys experiencing schooling with varying access to resources, and within the context of a rural community that is predominantly white and working class. To attend to the significance of locality, I draw theoretical tools from the productive intersection of feminist poststructural theory and cultural geography. Together, these two approaches provide a framework from which to theorize subjectivity as discursively constituted (Davies 2003), yet embodied, felt, and embedded within particular histories, places, and social structures (Massey 1994; Walkerdine, Lucey, and Melody 2001). Given the project's focus on imagined futures, I conceptualize place through Massey's relational notion of a "lived world of a simultaneous multiplicity of spaces" (1994, p. 3), and view rural social space as both a sociospatial construct and lived geography (Little 2002; Reid et al. 2010). Conceiving of spaces and subjects as relationally constituted, I explore how rural youth produce their own sense of place alongside, or in relation to, constructions of "others" located "elsewhere" (Leyshon 2008).

The study involved three months of ethnographic research in the Grade 7/8 classroom (ages 12–14) in Fieldsville Public School, a small school of just over 100 students spanning Kindergarten to Grade 8. I attended school three full days each week, observing and participating in classroom activities, recesses, and afterschool events. At three critical points of the program, I led small focus groups in which students discussed recent activities in the RG and raised related issues that were meaningful to them. During my final month at the school, I conducted semistructured interviews with each participant, exploring students' backgrounds, schooling experiences and imagined futures. In total, 18 focus groups and 20 interviews were completed with the study's 20 participants (which included 10 boys and 10 girls).

Future Literacies

It was only after preliminary analysis that I began to consider how Fieldsville students' readings of the future might be productively engaged in relation to literacies research. As students made sense of the discourses available in the RG in order to narrate their own imagined futures, they engaged in situated practices of meaning-making (Barton, Hamilton, and Ivanîc 2000). In their book, *Rural Literacies*, Donehower, Hogg, and Schell (2007, p. 4) define literacy as

> the skills and practices needed to gain knowledge, evaluate and interpret that knowledge, and apply knowledge to accomplish particular goals. In this sense, "reading" refers to the ability to gather and process knowledge from a variety of "texts"; "writing" means the ability to transform knowledge to achieve a particular purpose, just as writers transform ideas and information to accomplish rhetorical goals.

Throughout my research in Fieldsville, I was frequently struck by the agility with which students manoeuvred across various texts as they crafted their imagined futures. The interactive and open-ended focus groups allowed me to observe how young people coconstruct meaning by weaving together narratives of personal experience, popular culture, and community knowledges, alongside insights they've drawn from lessons in the classroom. Recent literacy research that engages with questions of power can provide insight into this interplay of discourse and subjectivity (Collins and Blot 2003; Janks 2010). Discussing how Foucauldian theories of discourse can inform literacies research, Hilary Janks (2010, p. 55) writes that "it is important to think about how who we are and how we think is profoundly influenced by the discourses we inhabit." Literacy scholars have highlighted the persistent gap between the "school literacies" that tend to be legitimated within formal education, and those that students use regularly in their out-of-school lives (Hicks 2005). In response, critical scholars advocate for pedagogical approaches that incorporate students' diverse literacies into classroom practice (Nixon and Comber 2006).

In keeping with this broader project, I suggest that Fieldsville students actively engage in this kind of interdiscursive practice as they negotiate competing discourses of the future. RG's claim to foster within students "the competencies they will need to find meaning, purpose, satisfaction and fulfillment in both their present and their future" (Barry 2005, p. 13) references a historically specific set of literacy practices that is deemed necessary for one to become a contributing member of today's society. While Fieldsville students draw upon the RG's language of choice and self-invention in their readings of the future, they also incorporate local insights that undermine central tenets of this neoliberal ideal, such as the enduring significance of an attachment to place. Thus, I explore how students negotiate the relationship between their own "situated literacies" (Barton et al. 2000) and the "neoliberal literacies" (Edmondson 2003) promoted in their schooling experiences.

Like Jane Kenway and colleagues, I found that young people "learn about the future, their futures and themselves through contradictory and shifting webs of discourses" (1994, p. 199). In their analysis of girls' experiences of gender reform in Australian schools, Kenway et al. (p. 199) conclude that girls "read their futures from the gendered and other narratives in which they are immersed and then . . . write their future's script variously constrained and enabled by the narratives' conventions." This chapter uses the frame of reading and writing futures—literally and metaphorically—to explore Fieldsville students' participation in RG. In doing so, it builds upon Kenway et al.'s feminist poststructural approach to discourse and subjectivity by incorporating a spatial analysis. I argue that many of the contradictions that Fieldsville students must manage in their future narratives arise from competing ideas of place and movement. In the chapter's remaining sections, I show how students draw upon a range of texts to envision and locate their futures, and discuss the tensions that arise when place-based narratives are confronted with dominant discourses of mobility. In closing, I suggest that these very tensions constitute a potential starting point from which to read against the grain of neoliberal discourse.

Reading and Writing Futures in Place

Narratives of the rural landscape provide a key organizing text within Fieldsville students' readings of the future. One of the first activities in RG requires students to compile a "wish list" for their future home—a seemingly straightforward task. In practice, however, the task of envisioning a "dream home" raises questions of belonging that force students to articulate fundamental assumptions about where they "fit" in the world. At the beginning of our first focus group, Hilary announced definitively: "I wanna live in the country cuz I wanna have a barn and I don't want all the traffic." Beside her, Jessie pulled a worksheet from her thick binder and slapped it down in the middle of the table where her friends could see. "I'm in the country," she declared. Among the many homes pictured on the sheet, Jessie had circled the image of a white farmhouse on the left-hand side of the page. "I couldn't afford that house!" cried Rebecca, pointing toward Jessie's sheet.

Reflecting upon the initial RG activities, our discussion touched on many aspects of students' futures—work, family, romance, leisure—but the conversation consistently returned to issues of place. Within five minutes of sitting down together, each of the five girls had aligned herself with a future in "the country" or "the city," with only Kristin choosing the latter. I asked them to elaborate on these preferences:

KC: So I'm curious, why the country? Like, when you think about living in the country/
Rebecca: Maybe cuz like, we've lived here.
Hilary: We've lived in the country.
Amanda: I don't like, I like to be able to look out my window and there not to be anyone else, like, right there. [Murmurs of agreement around the table].
Hilary: You can see like, you can see nature [Stretches her arms in front of her as if visualizing a vast landscape].
Jessie: [With disdain] In the city you can see like, cars goin' by and/
Kristin: See, that's why I want to live in a neighbourhood because there's not a lot of cars going by, and like, you [All talk at once].
Hilary: I want to live in the country cuz I'm used to it.

During this first focus group, I began to notice how students read possible futures in RG with a sense of themselves as situated in place. The task of creating wish lists is not simply about what kinds of possessions they desire for their adult homes, but *where* these homes will be located—the physical landscape, community context, associated lifestyle, and proximity to particular people and places. Thus, while compiling a collage to characterize their dream home, students negotiate questions of belonging that reveal a great deal about how they understand the spaces that give shape to their lives.

Rooting their identities within their local community, many Fieldsville students invest in the "rural idyll," a discourse characterized by themes of nature, safety, and community (Matthews et al. 2000; Rye 2006). When asked to describe their local community, they said things like, "It's nice and peaceful"; "there's lots of room for bike riding"; "we live in a small town so it's not like anyone's gonna come in and shoot people"; and "everybody knows everybody. It's like that country song." Students sometimes described experiences that contradicted this rural imaginary—hinting at inequities within the community, or lamenting the boredom of small-town life. But despite the existence of negative elements, they continued to identify with an idealized depiction of the local landscape.

Cultural geographers have problematized the categories of "rural" and "urban" by revealing the diverse meanings ascribed to these spatial constructs, yet research suggests that rural/urban distinctions constitute a meaningful difference for young people in rural communities (Vanderbeck and Dunkley 2003). In describing their local community, Fieldsville students often defined rural space in opposition to urban living, depicting the city as a crime-ridden, polluted, and overpopulated space. In addition to lamenting the heavy traffic and crowded city streets, many students depicted urban spaces as rife with danger. "You can't go for bike rides cuz there's scary people in the city," says Cody. Paul agrees, adding "you go for a bike ride and gangsters jack your bike." These narratives of city life draw on a combination of lived experience and urban imaginaries, which are heavily informed by popular culture. This was particularly evident in students' use of language like "the ghetto" or references to "Compton, LA" when describing the dangers of urbanity. The fact that Fieldsville students easily call to mind these images when discussing the perils of urban living demonstrates the power of urban imaginaries as a resource that informs their own sense of place (Green and Letts 2007). Ultimately, these spatial representations of danger and decay serve to solidify their claims about the positive aspects of country living, as they write their futures into a rural imaginary characterized by a picturesque, safe, and close-knit community. I was struck by the consistency with which students incorporated these spatial representations into their readings of the dislocated futures on offer in the RG, a literacy practice that appeared to satisfy their own investments in a sense of place.

An approach to literacy as a situated social practice draws attention to the ways in which students actively draw upon, combine, and revise the discursive resources that inform their futures. From this perspective, the interplay between dominant discourses and students' emerging identities may be understood as a form of cultural production (Barton et al. 2000). Indeed, in addition to situating themselves in rural social space, Fieldsville students also used popular texts to bridge their own experiences with the abstract discourses available in the RG. When reflecting upon recent RG activities, students sometimes struggled to articulate the gendered, classed, and place-based constraints that structure their lives—struggles that were not reflected in RG narratives of the individuated economic actor. Faced with this gap, students sometimes drew upon movie or television narratives in order to illustrate their own situated struggles. For example, when Christie mentions that the popular students tease her and her friends for being the "low-class people," I ask her to explain further. Faced with the formidable challenge of deconstructing classed boundaries, she crafts her response through a popular text:

> *Christie*: It means like, at fancy schools, cuz there's a movie I watched, it's called *The Legally Blondes*, they're two twins. They're not high class, like, they're not rich. They don't have limos and stuff. [While Christie speaks, Arbor, who is seated beside her, pretends that she is a "high-class" person, pushing out her chest and making a snooty face. She whispers, "I've got a limo," in a snooty voice.] The high class, they're popular, they think they're everything. And the low class are the people that have a scholarship. And the high class people make fun of them because they have a scholarship.
>
> *KC*: Okay. And you think that happens here? That groups get set up that way?
>
> *Christie*: Ya. There's like, there's groups kinda in our class, eh?
>
> *Tanya*: Ya.

Christie narrates her own class oppression through the movie *Legally Blondes*, despite the apparent distance between the main characters' lived experience and her own. Her use of this text creates an opening for us to discuss the power dynamics within peer social hierarchies in Fieldsville.

This interaction illustrates how students look to popular representations for explanatory frameworks through which to make sense of their own lives and futures. With its emphasis on personal choice and individual motivation, RG does not provide discursive resources through which to make sense of classed boundaries. The erasure of class within neoliberal discourse obscures the "distinctive ways in which particular landscapes of poverty are formative of thought, feeling, imagination, and identity" (Hicks and Jones 2007, p. 57). Christie and her friends creatively fill this void through insights from popular culture.

By attending to students' situated practices of meaning-making, a literacies analysis reveals how young people transgress the discursive boundaries of formal curriculum, popular culture, and place-based knowledge, as they integrate disparate texts within narratives of the future. This holds theoretical implications for studies of neoliberalism in education, for it challenges researchers to engage with dominant discourses as they are taken up and interpreted within local contexts of schooling. This approach also holds implications for studies of young people's imagined futures. Australian scholars Julie McLeod and Lyn Yates (2006) criticize the persistent divide between studies of youth "pathways" and "daydreams," as scholars reproduce an artificial distinction between career and education plans on the one hand, and fantasies and fears on the other. Similarly, Janks (2010, p. 212) calls for a critical literacy of the future that moves "beyond logical reasoning and argument" to actively embrace "the territory of desire and identification." By exploring the various discursive fields in which young people forge identifications and envision futures, a literacies analysis offers a means of moving beyond this enduring division within the literature.

While Fieldsville students frequently drew upon popular culture and rural/urban imaginaries within their situated readings of the RG, these texts were not always integrated seamlessly. Instead, tensions sometimes arose among the various discourses through which students read their current and future lives. Emerging out of each student's particular living situation, these tensions often centered on conflicting attachments to place and movement. In her book *Prairie Town*, Jacqueline Edmondson (2003) explores how rural residents negotiate the pressures of what she calls "neoliberal literacy," which promotes an individualized, competitive ethos rooted in the promise of efficiency and prosperity. She observes that "neoliberal literacy frequently works to the demise of the community as it leads the young people away from rural areas" (p. 106; see also Corbett 2010). Indeed, even as Fieldsville students identified strongly with rural imaginaries, they were also drawn toward stories of movement and improvement that surround dominant narratives of "success." Social and spatial mobility are deeply intertwined within popularized success stories, as classed fantasies of self-improvement map onto spatial discourses of moving "elsewhere." Students struggled to reconcile these sociospatial mobility narratives with their own situated literacies and place-based identities.

One of the most striking examples of this conflict can be seen in students' efforts to write themselves into futures that integrate positive aspects of both rural *and* urban imaginaries. For instance, after self-identifying as a "country girl" and insisting that she will build her adult life in or around Fieldsville, Hilary shares her dream of becoming a fashion designer traveling around the world attending fashion shows, just like the designers do on television. These kinds of contradictory narratives were not uncommon—especially among girls—as students wrote themselves into futures that preserved their attachments to the rural idyll, while also mirroring popular images of success that tend to be coded urban.

Alongside conflicts surrounding their rural location, an additional tension emerged through stories of class mobility, as many students were drawn toward narratives of moving outward and upward through higher education. Fieldsville students often spoke about their educational futures in terms of their parents' desire for their children to exceed their own educational and career trajectories. Some expressed hesitations about continuing schooling after high school, but said their parents insist they do so. As Jessie explains,

> I said "Mom, do I really have to go to university and all that?" cuz I wasn't sure about going. And she said, "Well if you don't wanna end up like me and not having a full education and all that, then ya I'd consider going to college or university." So I'm like, alright, it might be kinda fun, like, getting more knowledge of what you actually want to do.

Here, Jessie's mom's life story is presented as a reference point from which to construct a narrative of mobility through higher education. Valerie Walkerdine (2003) has highlighted the tensions at the heart of such mobility narratives, which tend to assign a negative value to people, practices, and places that are central to one's identity. At another point in the interview, Jessie speaks with pride regarding her mom's work as a painter:

> Me and [my sister] actually went to one of her houses that she was painting and it was like ginormous. She had to do, like, the basement... and then the main floor and then the upstairs, so she had to paint so much.

And so I was like, "Mom, this is really cool." And she was like, "Ya, I enjoy it."

Jessie sees value in her mother's work, and her mother describes this work as personally rewarding. I place these two excerpts alongside each other in order to highlight the potential struggles that young people may encounter when invited into "improving narratives" of bettering the life experiences of their parents (Skeggs 1997). In her study of working-class women's struggles to become "respectable," Beverley Skeggs (p. 82) writes that "class was configured through the improvement discourse because in order to improve they have to differentiate themselves from those who did not or could not improve." While Jessie has access to the encouragement of a supportive mother, I wonder how she negotiates the tensions within this vision of educational success. That is, how does one write her own future "mobility" if it is premised upon a reading that devalues those she loves and admires?

Becky Francis and Valerie Hey highlight numerous studies that show how "neo-liberal discourses of meritocracy and individuality project responsibility for failure away from social structures and institutions and onto individuals" (2009, p. 226). Indeed, many Fieldsville students invest in individualized stories of success in which they alone are responsible for their futures. This is particularly evident in my interview with Jonathon:

> *KC*: What are you most looking forward to? Like, in terms of being older.
> *Jonathon*: Owning a boat and being able to fish whenever I can.
> *KC*: Ya.
> *Jonathon*: And that's really about it.
> *KC*: And then is there anything that you're kind of worried or nervous about?
> *Jonathon*: [pause] Being poor.
> *KC*: Okay. And why do you say that?
> *Jonathon*: Just because a lot of people now are being poor, or ending up poor because they don't plan out how they're gonna live when they're young. And that's [pause] I guess how, what happens.
> *KC*: Huh. So you think that that's one of the main reasons why people are poor, is because they haven't planned well?
> *Jonathon*: Well, they don't get a good enough education which leads them to not a very good job and eventually that can't be very good.
> *KC*: Hmm, okay. And so that's something that you're worried about?
> *Jonathon*: Ya. Makes me wanna stay in school as long as I can. And I think I'm going to.

It's helpful to contextualize Jonathon's concerns about future poverty in relation to his current living situation. Jonathon's dad works as a truck driver and his mom commutes to the city to work at a fast food restaurant. During my time in Fieldsville, their family spent several weeks staying with neighbors because their own house had no electricity. I share these details not to essentialize complex lives, but in order to give some context for his stated fear of "being poor." Jonathon encounters poverty not simply as an abstract "bad" that threatens narratives of the good life, but as a very real experience of material insecurity and constraint. That said, the interpretation that one brings to such circumstances is always mediated by discourse. Jonathon's account of poverty as something that happens to people who "don't plan out how they're gonna live when they're young" draws upon an individuated narrative of inequality that blames poor people for their own hardship.

Given the emphasis on future planning and personal responsibility in RG, his use of this explanatory framework is not surprising. But consider the tensions that emerge where these discourses and materialities collide. How does Jonathon reconcile this reading of poverty as a product of individual failure with his lived experiences of material hardship? In response to the threat of being poor, Jonathon constructs a narrative of educational mobility that works to secure a future outside of poverty. For many young people in Fieldsville, these individuated futures require a double mobility that moves across both geographical *and* social boundaries, as they are positioned as solely responsible for transcending the constraints of their rural and classed location.

Future Literacies in Place

This chapter has explored how students in one rural community make sense of the discursive resources available to them in order to create narratives of the future. Following the lead of rural scholars like Donehower, Hogg, and Schell (2007), the analysis counters deficit models of rural literacy by highlighting students' creative engagement with a variety of texts, as young people incorporate narratives of rurality and popular culture alongside the neoliberal discourses of mobility and self-improvement on offer in RG. At the same time, I have demonstrated how these literacy practices operate in the context of powerful structural constraints.

My hope is that this analysis of Fieldsville students' future narratives highlights the potential for pedagogies that recognize and value the practice of reading futures in place. Such an approach would extend to rural young people "identities as critical and resistant readers of the cultural forces [that] shape their lives" (Kenway et al. 1994, p. 204). Deborah Hicks and Stephanie Jones model this kind of pedagogy in their work with girls in a Midwestern American community where many working-class students have learned to view literacy education as something that happens apart from (and often, contrary to) their out-of-school lives. Hicks and Jones work with girls to develop an afterschool literacy program that "creates the possibility for a pedagogy that is *answerable* to the students' life language, experiences, imaginations and hopes for their futures" (2007, p. 81).

Building upon students' readings of their local community, teachers can work with young people to develop literacies that "read hope, rather than despair, in the current rural condition" (Edmondson 2003, p. 104). Such hope is not rooted in a nostalgic celebration of rurality, but rather in creating the conditions in which to engage young people critically and constructively with their lived geographies. In the words of Gruenewald (2003, p. 7), "a critical pedagogy of place ultimately encourages teachers and students to reinhabit their places, that is, to pursue the kind of social action that improves the social and ecological life of places, near and far, now and in the future." Fieldsville students' future narratives highlight tensions at the very heart of their schooling experiences, illuminating the competing attachments to place and mobility that structure their current and future identities. Rather than dismiss these tensions by inviting students into neoliberal discourses of movement and improvement, I want to suggest that we (as scholars and educators) take these very tensions as our starting point. What possibilities are opened if we interpret the contradictions within students' future narratives as the makings of a counterreading? How might we build upon these tensions in order to support students in reading against the grain of neoliberal discourse? We have much to learn from, and with, young people, as they negotiate the difficult task of reading competing futures in place.

Note

1. The official website for *The Real Game Series* provides links to versions used in Australia, Canada, Denmark, France, Germany, Hungary, The Netherlands, New Zealand, the United Kingdom, and the United States.

References

Apple, M. W., 2001, "Comparing Neo-liberal Projects and Inequality in Education," *Comparative Education*, vol. 37, no. 4: 409–423.

Barry, B., 2005, *The Real Game Facilitator's Guide*, The Real Game, Inc., St John's, Newfoundland, Canada.

Barton, D., M. Hamilton, and R. Ivanîc (eds.), 2000, *Situated Literacies: Reading and Writing in Context*, Routledge, London and New York.

Bradford, S. and V. Hey, 2007, "Successful Subjectivities? The Successfication of Class, Ethnic and Gender Positions," *Journal of Education Policy*, vol. 22, no. 6: 595–614.

Cairns, K., 2011, "Mapping Futures, Making Selves: Subjectivity, Schooling and Rural Youth," Unpublished doctoral dissertation, Ontario Institute for Studies in Education, University of Toronto.

Collins, J. and R. K. Blot, 2003, *Literacy and Literacies: Texts, Power and Identity*, Cambridge University Press, Cambridge.

Corbett, M., 2010, "Standardized Individuality: Cosmopolitanism and Educational Decision-Making in an Atlantic Canadian Rural Community," *Compare: A Journal of Comparative and International Education*, vol. 40, no. 2: 223–237.

Davies, B., 2003, *Shards of Glass: Children Reading and Writing beyond Gendered Identities* (Revised edition), Hampton Press, New York.

Davies, B., and P. Bansel, 2007, "Neoliberalism and Education," *International Journal of Qualitative Studies in Education*, vol. 20, no. 3: 247–259.

Davies, B. and S. Saltmarsh, 2007, "Gender Economies: Literacy and the Gendered Production of Neo-liberal Subjectivities," *Gender and Education*, vol. 19, no 1: 1–20.

Dehli, K., 2009, "Media Literacy and Neo-liberal Government: Pedagogies of Freedom and Constraint," *Pedagogy, Culture & Society*, vol. 17, no. 1: 57–73.

Demerath, P. and J. Lynch, 2008, "Identities for Neoliberal Times: Constructing Enterprising Selves in an American Suburb," in N. Dolby and F. Rizvi (eds.), *Youth Moves: Identities and Education in Global Perspective*, Routledge, New York.

Donehower, K., C. Hogg, and E. E. Schell, 2007, *Rural Literacies*, University of Southern Illinois Press, Carbondale.

Edmondson, J., 2003, *Prairie Town: Redefining Rural Life in the Age of Globalization*, Rowman & Littlefield, New York.

Francis, B. and V. Hey, 2009, "Talking Back to Power: Snowballs in Hell and the Imperative of Insisting on Structural Explanations," *Gender and Education*, vol. 21, no. 2: 225–232.

Goodkind, S., 2009, "'You Can Be Anything You Want, but You Have to Believe It'": Commercialized Feminism in Gender-Specific Programs for Girls." *Signs: Journal of Women in Culture and Society*, vol. 34, no. 2: 397–422.

Green, B. and W. Letts, 2007, "Space, Equity and Education: A 'Trialectical' Account," in K. N. Gulson and C. Symes (eds.), *Spatial Theories of Education: Policy and Geography Matters*, Routledge, London and New York.

Hicks, D 2005, "Class Readings: Story and Discourse among Girls in Working-Poor America", *Anthropology and Education Quarterly*, vol. 36, no. 3, pp. 212–229.

Hicks, D. and S. Jones, 2007, "Living Class as a Girl," in J. A. Van Galen and G. W. Noblit (eds.), *Late to Class: Social Class and Schooling in the New Economy*, SUNY Press, Albany, NY.

Janks, H. 2010, *Literacy and Power*, Routledge, New York and London.

Kenway, J., S. Willis, J. Blackmore, and L. Rennie, 1994, "Making 'Hope Practical' Rather Than 'Despair Convincing': Feminist Post-structuralism, Gender Reform and Educational Change," *British Journal of Sociology of Education*, vol. 15, no. 2: 187–210.

Leyshon, M., 2008, "The Betweenness of Being a Rural Youth: Inclusive and Exclusive Lifestyles," *Social & Cultural Geography*, vol. 9, no. 1: 1–26.

Little, J., 2002, *Gender and Rural Geography: Identity, Sexuality and Power in the Countryside*, Prentice Hall, Harlow, England.

Massey, D., 1994, *Space, Place and Gender*, Polity Press, Cambridge.

Matthews, H., M. Taylor, K. Sherwood, F. Tucker, and M. Limb, 2000, "Growing-Up in the Countryside: Children and the Rural Idyll," *Journal of Rural Studies*, vol. 16: 141–153.

McLeod, J. and L. Yates, 2006, *Making Modern Lives: Subjectivity, Schooling, and Social Change*, State University of New York Press, New York.

Nixon, H. and B. Comber, 2006, "Differential Recognition of Children's Cultural Practices in Middle Primary Literacy Classrooms," *Literacy*, vol. 40, no. 3: 127–136.

Petersson, K., U. Olsson, and T. Popkewitz, 2007, "Nostalgia, the Future, and the Past as Pedagogical Technologies," *Discourse: Studies in the Cultural Politics of Education*, vol. 28, no. 1: 49–67.

Reid, J., B. Green, M. Cooper, W. Hastings, G. Lock, and S. White, 2010, "Regenerating Rural Social Space? Teacher Education for Rural-Regional Sustainability," *Australian Journal of Education*, vol. 54, no. 3: 262–276.

Rye, J. F. 2006, "Rural Youth's Images of the Rural," *Journal of Rural Studies*, vol. 22, no. 4: 409–421.

Skeggs, B., 1997, *Formations of Class & Gender: Becoming Respectable*, Sage, London.

Vanderbeck, R. M. and C. Morse Dunkley, 2003, "Young People's Narratives of Rural-Urban Difference," *Children's Geographies*, vol. 1, no. 2: 241–259.

Walkerdine, V., 2003, "Reclassifying Upward Mobility: Femininity and the Neo-liberal Subject," *Gender and Education*, vol. 15, no. 3: 237–248.

Walkerdine, V., H. Lucey, and J. Melody, 2001, *Growing Up Girl: Psychosocial Explorations of Gender and Class*, Palgrave, London.

Yates, L., 2006, "Vocational Subject-Making and the Works of Schools: A Case Study," *Australian Journal of Education*, vol. 50, no. 3: 281–296.

———, 2009, "From Curriculum to Pedagogy and Back Again: Knowledge, Person and the Changing World," *Pedagogy, Culture & Society*, vol. 17, no. 1: 17–28.

CHAPTER 13

Mediating Plastic Literacies and Placeless Governmentalities: Returning to Corporeal Rurality*

Michael Corbett and Ann Vibert

I n this chapter, we take up three contemporary problematics in the space encompassed by literacy, rurality, and social justice. We are educational researchers who collaborate but who also manage distinct, yet related research projects located in Atlantic Canada. The focus of one project is social justice educators and the way their practice is influenced by the standards/accountability movement and changes to the nature of teacher professionalism and the governance of education. The focus of the second project is on how teachers, parents, and students manage competing expectations in literacy curricula around standardization and generic skills, on the one hand, and creativity and new literacies, on the other.

Here, we isolate three distinct tensions and the ways that teachers and parents resolve them as they think about supporting children in their care. Each of these tensions represents a different way that teachers, parents, and students, living and working in a rural place, create space, manage, mediate, and make sense of their lives and work in the face of positivist/managerial attempts to regulate their lives. The first of these tensions focuses on teachers' work, and it relates to the way that they handle questions of social justice in the context of abstract expectations for educational "performance" emanating from the state. The concrete act of feeding children is central to this response. Second, we examine parents' efforts to navigate a challenging and even threatening world of online literacies. They do this, we demonstrate, by invoking what we call a hierarchy of text that places concrete, "hard-copy" text in a privileged position within school curriculum. Parental discourses of safety and teachers' discourses around concrete action in support of social justice both point to a transformation of rural communities in Atlantic Canada away from convivial face-to-face, tight-knit communities to diverse and connected nodes in a networked risk society. In our final section, we turn to an analysis of a new diversity in one rural village in Nova Scotia. Each of these three discussions, in different ways, points to the parallel transformations of rural contexts and literate contexts, instantiating in concrete ways the nature of these changes.

What we hope to achieve here is an analysis that demonstrates the increasing complexity of what has been called "rural social space" (Green and Letts 2007; Reid et al. 2010), which is a way of thinking about rurality that combines the materiality of rural locations with diverse and sometimes contested cultural constructions of what rurality means. This level of analysis allows us to look beyond productivist notions of rurality (Woods 2006, 2011) and structural associations, in rural places, between allegedly essential characteristics of people and place (e.g., "fishing villages" or "agricultural communities") toward more complex postproductivist understandings of the multilayered nature of life places that are transforming rapidly and incessantly. There are a number of implications for education here, not the least of which is that rural youth require an education that is as outward-looking and broad as youth living in urban and suburban locales.

Diversity of Contexts: Literacies, Rurality, and Placeless Governmentalities

Recent scholarship in new literacies and multiliteracies establishes a view of literacies as sets of social practices situated in particular communities, practices arising out of intersections of place, form, and purpose (Gee 1999; Knobel and Lankshear 2007). Multiliteracies work challenges "traditional" print-based conceptions of literacy, underlining the emergent, provisional, and dynamic character of twenty-first-century literacy conventions and practices, as visual and digital forms emerge to interact with and transform print-based conceptions (Corbett and Vibert 2010). In a similar vein, work in rural and place-based/sensitive education challenges generic, placeless views of curriculum, positing a vision of curriculum as arising from the purposes of particular communities engaging in literate activities for real-world uses (Donehower, Hogg, and Schell 2007; Comber, Nixon, and Reid 2007). At the same time, teachers in rural Nova Scotia find themselves operating within a system policy scape dominated by accountability discourses that by their very nature promote pedagogies grounded in a view of literacy, and curriculum, as generic, static, and technical (Vibert 2009).

Here we draw upon interview data generated in the context of two recent qualitative studies to explore ways in which rural teachers attempt to negotiate tensions and competing demands produced through intersections of rurality, literacies, and accountability. The first study, titled *Pedagogies at Risk: Teaching for Social Justice in an Age of Accountability* (Vibert 2005), did not primarily deal with questions around literacy or rurality; instead, it focused on documenting how teachers in three Canadian provinces negotiated social justice pedagogies, broadly defined, in the context of increasingly neoliberal, accountability-focused educational bureaucracies. However, the study included teacher participants working in rural Nova Scotian sites alongside participants from three urban sites, and in the process of analyzing data across sites we saw how our plan to identify emergent "national" themes might sideline, diminish, or distort the narratives of the rural teachers. Here we explore one example of those "glazes" or "ellipses." The points we raise below are concerns for the particular teachers in this study, in their particular rural settings; they are not attempts to generalize about social justice pedagogies in rural versus urban settings. But as Corbett (2009, p. 4) has observed, "All education is place-based and there is an ongoing struggle over which places will be represented in curriculum." And a critical pedagogue would point out that accounting for our centricisms, metro- or otherwise, entails examining gaps and anomalies in representation.

For us, one of those anomalies arose in the *Pedagogies at Risk* project around the meaning of food and feeding students in schools. All schools represented in our study provided free meals for students in the form of breakfast clubs, hot lunches, and nutritious snacks. In our national analysis, we recognized this reality and moved on, choosing not to code references to food and food provision as indicative of a robust justice pedagogy. As a consequence, the research team failed to take up ways in which the meanings of food and feeding might differ across contexts, both materially and symbolically.

Interestingly, the rural teachers and schools in this project are located in one of the food-producing regions of the province. At any meeting we attend in our capacity as teacher educators, academics, or as interested community citizens there is always food on offer. As we reviewed focus group and interview transcripts, we saw that almost all of the teachers made references to food; it may be that where access to food banks is limited, the pedagogical agenda *is* significantly about feeding people. In the following three instances, food becomes a central symbol both of the challenges that participants face as educators and as a concrete human act of caring that they can accomplish in the face of these challenges.

Food makes the idea of social justice concrete, and, as Weaver-Hightower (2011) points out, it is an understudied and underappreciated topic in educational research. We think that there is a great deal of potential for the analysis of rural place and space through the lens of food. Not only does food partially define cultural place meanings, but also food practices represent the intersections and hybridities marked by contemporary understandings of social space (Massey 2005; Cresswell 2004). The way that teachers link food to questions of social justice is also an everyday material aspect of life, lost in the drive for data-fixated, positivist understandings of school in particular (Corbett 2008) and human life in general (Abrams 1996). The need to feed children is also an instance drawn upon by the teachers to illustrate the regulatory effects on pedagogy of encroaching data-fixated accountability regimes, in all their many aspects. The following quotes illustrate this:

> *RD*: That's what bothers me, the head counting, or number counting— the kids that were involved, doesn't really matter. My Christmas dinner, I have 140 volunteers show up, but it's the guy sitting with his son peeling the carrots in the back room, was the one that made that whole dinner for me, and that doesn't come out in data.
>
> *LC*: In my guidance capacity, sometimes I deal with kids that are, you know, wrestling with highly emotional issues, that needs to be expected, and I was thinking, what do I do with an adult? I would offer them a cup of tea, or a cup of coffee, to, you know, as just a bridge. So I thought, it was such a great idea, I went out and bought hot chocolate, and some mugs for my students, so that if they were having a difficult time, I could offer them a warm drink. To me, that is the most natural thing, it's just so much a part of our culture . . . And I was, reprimanded . . . cautioned that that didn't fit into the nutritional policy. Honestly . . . there were issues around, I call it the nutritional police, but there were people whose job it was to ensure that the nutritional policies were being implemented. I just thought that that was so far overboard.

We want to make three points about these examples: (1) in all cases, food is shared rather than provided; (2) in each case the sharing of food has a distinct pedagogical purpose; (3) these teachers offer up the regulation of *food and food sharing* as one of the most *vivid* available symbols of the absurd effects of accountability regimes in education. The preparation and sharing of food in school, for these teachers, is a potent symbol of an authentic and human pedagogy ("natural" is the word LC uses), constrained and distorted by various placeless governmentalities.[1] We are suggesting that these particular meanings have something to do with the places these teachers inhabit. And we further suggest that they are meaning differences made easy to overlook in the metro-centric and/or placeless habits of educational discourses, including discourses of social justice. Indeed, the focus on food by rural educators can be positioned by "critical" educators as a shallow reading or even as a misunderstanding of social justice principles.

In the examples above, we have claimed that for the teachers in question, accountability discourses "displaced" their local pedagogical practices, introducing absurdity as standardized policy and practice bump up against actual places. In the case of literacies curriculum, these ruptures are further intensified by the proliferating and dynamic character of twenty-first-century literacies. One of the faces of accountability is a growing centralization of policy and authority. Standardized assessment has moved definitions of literacy away from the classroom and community, out of the hands of teachers and students, toward a complex of faceless provincial, national, and international governance bodies. At the same time, students and communities are redefining for themselves actual literacies-in-use through the proliferation of digital and visual literacies and social media. Teachers negotiate this murky terrain, as they attempt to account for the literacies of their actual students in actual places, and simultaneously, to meet preordained outcomes proscribed from somewhere else. In the context of our filmmaking project, *A Lens on Community* (Corbett and Vibert 2008–2011), we spoke with teachers about how these competing claims played out in their work.

Briefly, this was a two-year action research project set in a small-town school in rural Nova Scotia. The project introduced video documentary to teachers, student teachers, and students at the school in an attempt to support the development of a broader literacies curriculum. At the same time, a team of university-based researchers documented and analyzed the way that teachers, parents, and students understood this work. Here we want to focus primarily on the teachers' experiences with the project.

ST: It certainly created lots of excitement with the students. It gave them something different to concentrate on and a different format for them to express themselves which was really neat to see. It's just outside of the mainstream curriculum is what it is. It is not prescribed by the Department of Education, although it meets a huge amount of our curriculum outcomes, it is a different way to approach our curriculum outcomes. It is a different way to approach literacy and it gives the kids a different perspective . . . No, they did not see it as curriculum . . . they didn't feel like they were being taught all the time.

All participants (students, parents, and teachers) attested to the excitement and engagement the project engendered. Nevertheless, different "players" configured that engagement in distinct ways. Parents tended to value the project for its engagement possibilities, above all. While they recognized the centrality of digital literacies in their own lives, and, therefore, framed such textual practices as an appropriate component of a school literacy curriculum, they tended to see the project as a worthwhile and even necessary release from the "real" literacy practices involving print conventions and authorized texts.

Students tended to see the project as did their parents in some ways, though they valued the competing literacy forms very differently. While they maintained that they had learned valuable things through the project, they did *not* see it as school curriculum; students in fact argued passionately for these literacies *not* to be included as part of their regular school subjects. Their position suggests that their view of curriculum is similar to that of their parents, and that their fear is that schooling such innovations through insertion in the curriculum will only tame and distort them. Ultimately they welcomed a space in school that allowed them to improvise with new technologies, but they resisted losing control of the agenda to teacher-controlled engagements. Teachers, on the other hand, appreciated unpredictable and uncontrollable aspects of visual and digital literacies in the curriculum, while simultaneously struggling with a variety of constraints:

> GH: I think in a lot of ways we are learning as kids are learning when it comes to technology or anything new. We are aware of it and we see it in our classrooms on a daily basis. It is not just in our homes, it is in our classrooms. But we are hired to complete the Department of Education curriculum. We are hired to deliver that curriculum. Bottom line is our clients are the parents just as much as the kids. So we have a tension between all three . . . I think that is where the Department of Education is missing out on things. Curriculum takes, like we all know, 15 to 20 years to develop, to introduce and all that stuff. With something like technology, as soon as the Department of Education introduces a

curriculum outcome, regarding technology they are behind the times. But the teachers, I'd been working with my kids about that kind of thing. We talk about cyberbullying in my classes and we've talked about those privacy settings and why it is important to set them.

Here we begin to see a number of splits between centralized curriculum, the tracks of the larger phenomenon of accountability, and the lived curriculum that inevitably arises with flesh-and-blood students and teachers in particular places and times. These splits mirror the complaints of teachers, in the former project, about the distorting effects on their pedagogies of regulations around food. Competing conceptions of curriculum are at work here. On the one hand, there is curriculum as document, the fixed and generic official curriculum; and on the other, there is curriculum as verb, the continuously improvised curriculum that must take place where and when actual teachers and students go to school. And while this teacher sees the official curriculum as inevitably out of date and out of place, especially where twenty-first-century literacies are concerned, she does not reject it. In fact, she sees that curriculum as centrally comprising her work. What these teachers reject is not so much the existence of an official curriculum, but the ways that curriculum has grown static and authoritarian, insensitive to the necessarily located and provisional nature of teaching and learning. Effectively, these teachers enact a place-sensitive curriculum in the emerging hybrid spaces in a changing rural space. At the same time, they recognize that new technologies enter schools not as game changers, but as tools that are taken up by young people who use them in ways that are largely unpredictable and built upon their out-of-school experience with technologies (Prinsloo 2005). Furthermore, they see the potential of new media to help them manage multiple tensions in their work as teachers, while at the same time creating new tensions, expectations, and problematics for them.

There are other tensions that arise for these teachers presaged in the transcript fragment above. One of them is in GH's reference to her discussions of cyberbullying with her students, which she offers as an example of how the lived curriculum eclipses the official. We have discussed, in another context, issues of danger and safety arising from these risky literacies, and how teachers, parents, and students in this community framed and approached those issues (Corbett and Vibert 2010). This teacher also refers to tensions arising from parental expectations, the historic and ongoing negotiation between emerging literacies and the adult generation's often nostalgic view of academic capital. What we raise for consideration here is the teachers' plight in this nexus of changing land-scapes of risk (Beck 1992), place, literacies, and accountability frames. GH captures it when she articulates a variant of the students' strong desire to play creatively and improvise with new technologies to create their own literate spaces in school against pressures to follow official scripts (Au 2012; Eppley and Corbett 2012):

> *GH*: I think that the sin of it is we are moving away from improvisation in teaching in a lot of ways. We are, as teachers, being pushed to have our yearly plans and daily plans... our prescribed plans and there are best practices that are created by the school board and presented to us as this is the template for the classroom. We all know that the reality of it is, you give anybody a prescribed lesson and the kids will take it and change it... we have our overall ideas and goals and curriculum and whatever. But in terms of what happens in the classroom, a lot of it for me is improvised because it [pause] really does depend on what's going on in the lives of the kids on any given day.

Any attempt to open curriculum to emergent literacies and to reframe it in terms of sensitivity to place will need to grapple with these increas-ingly powerful and constraining accountability moves and their conse-quences for teachers' lives and work. We have found teachers enacting a balancing act, attempting to respond to the abstracted expectations of contemporary standards-based governmentalities while at the same time responding in an improvisational way to the multiple concrete challenges they face in a complex rural space.[2] They want to make a difference in increasingly challenged rural communities and they respond with the concrete offer of food, a fundamental human response.

Diversity and Plasticity: The Hierarchy of Text and the Literate Body

If the theme for teachers is to situate their practice as a balancing act between the abstract expectations of the state and the concrete needs of their students, parents are motivated by what we describe elsewhere as issues of safety (Corbett and Vibert 2010). They see emerging literate environments as potentially dangerous spaces that need to be controlled and regulated in school. Literacy education practices are important com-ponents of this regulatory practice. Parents seem to be watching their children develop literacies that are both fascinating and exciting, and at the same time challenging and even frightening in many ways. In this world of expanding "acquired" literacies, parents want their children be engaged in the not-so-automatic and engaging learned literacies. A part of parents' understanding of literacies that matter have to do with what we have called an implicit hierarchy of text. We begin with the following transcript from an interview with a parent conducted by a student assistant:

> Q: What do you think a school reading and writing program should look like?
> A: Hmmm. Reading and writing. Well, definitely hard-copy reading, so books they take home, books they have in the classroom, um, writing, gosh it really depends on the age.

What we see here is a clear articulation of the hierarchy of text. A school reading program has as its proper foundation the hard-copy book. The book is the fundamental tool for engaging the child in the structured discourse of formal literacy and it opposes more "plastic" and ordinary text children encounter and engage in their online activities. These texts are ethereal and unstable; they are plastic in the sense that they are subject to manipulation (indeed they invite and even require response and manipulation), and in the sense that they look shiny and polished, betraying their questionable durability. Plastic text is insubstantial, unlike the word printed on paper. As for writing, a similar distinction is made. The parent continues:

> I know that with my daughter who's seven, there is practice printing, practice writing, she has had in the past and will have in the future, so that's good. Um, with Grade 5, 6, 7 there hasn't been a lot of practice writing.

Writing, in this articulation, is the physical act of printing, which is inferior to the physical act of cursive writing. This parent actually laments the fact that her child no longer "practices" writing, which is understood to be the ability to transpose clearly and neatly by hand. In tandem with the hard-copy text is the physical trace represented by penmanship and cursive style. When asked about writing instruction, several parents lamented the lack of attention to cursive writing in the school program. In this community at least, the fundamental business of writing is about producing readable cursive script and not about making meaning for self-directed purposes. Without prompting, the interview continued with a juxtaposition of the informality of plastic, electronic text with the handwritten script and one of its quintessential representations, the formal letter:

> Q: OK.
> A: I know a lot of it is technology, sending e-mails through the internet, but I also think that they should definitely learn how to write, and learn how to format a letter.

Implicit in this comment is that children are communicating through relatively "informal" kinds of textuality, but what they lack is the ability to create structured texts. The plasticity and ethereality of the "fired off" social media text falls at the lower end of the textual hierarchy, insignificant because of its informality and ubiquity. At this point, the interviewer does not press the issue but, rather, returns to the question of literacy and what exactly it means to this parent. The answer, once again, brings things back to the physical. Writing is a physical act, the construction of words on paper mimicking the hard-copy book. High-status literacy is represented for this parent as words written on paper, either by an author, or by a child in school. Literacy is not a "technological term" for this parent, who contrasts books with the rapid-fire, off-the-cuff, emoticon- and acronym-peppered, inventive ramblings of peers. Rather, it is a question of producing and penetrating the meaning of formal, structured, safe hard-copy texts. The distinction made here situates the literate child's body in front of a book or with pen in hand:

> Q: What does the term "literacy" mean to you?
> A: Um, I think that it encompasses writing, um, I see it more as a physical than a technological term, just understanding, reading and books writing stories, understanding what is read and what is written.

The juxtaposition of the technological and the physical in this account is interesting. Mediated literacies are clearly lower down the hierarchy of text for this parent. At the same time, they represent vernacular forms of communication that are seductive and relatively risky. The dangerous anarchistic literacy spaces of informal, networked communication, in this sense, also resemble nonstandard oral language. The interviewer then turned to orality and the importance of the spoken word. Spoken language too is understood as a pedagogical tool to support decoding:

> Q: What role do you think talk or spoken language plays in learning to read and write?

A: I think it plays a very high role, especially expression when you're reading to a child cause if they can't recognize a word, they can sometimes
understand its meaning with the expression that you give the word,
um, and well I think just to answer it, it's very important and for that
purpose, memory helps recognition of words and understanding.

Finally, when asked about the school's promotion of literacy, the parent
brought things back to the hard-copy book and to the promotion of
reading through a commercial book order distributed in the school. It is
interesting that she did not address literacy practices in the classrooms
or in the school. She also noted how the book order contains not only
the hard-copy book, but also new forms of text like video games. The
parent then expresses nostalgia for apparently similar practices in her
own schooling:

Q: Do you think that your child's school is doing a good job of promoting literacy? Tell me about that.
A: Yes. They send home book orders continually and we love books. And
within these book orders there are Nintendo DS games, PC games;
there's one brochure with all the orders (choices?). I'm spitting a ton of
money out on these things, but I myself, I loved them when I was in
school, so when I see them I just can't say no.

The school book order is a space that brings together literacies of pleasure and literacies of the school, and indeed this parent's own positive
memories of the blending of formal and informal literacies connects with
the similar tastes of her daughter. The interview moved on to questions
about on-screen engagements and literacy. This parent commented that
these literacies support reading but not writing. In fact, writing and the
"physical act of writing," as she puts it, are not supported by plastic
online literacy practices:

Q: Do you feel that IT's makes your child a better reader and writer?
A: Reader, yes, I think it helps because for a child who doesn't like to
sit down with a book, they see a screen in front of them a website
that would be a lot more colorful and interactive and more entertain-
ing so that can inspire them to read. So whatever interests a child in
reading and gets them to read, not necessarily what format the words
are in front of them, they are there and if it interests them they are
going to do it. But as far as writing, the physical act of writing, no;
but the formation of letters or something, the actual composition of
writing, not particularly cause there isn't anyone over their shoulder

proofreading it and they don't, some of the e-mails I see come in, even from university students you can tell the ones that are used to social networking, because nothing is capitalized, grammar is poor; so writing not so much.

Most parents noted that the reading of hard-copy text is something that has to be literally forced on children. So while new literacies are acknowledged as important in terms of engagement and interest, important, consequential, and higher status literacies of the book are what is important to most parents. For this parent, the "reading program" signified the paper novel and the prescribed roster of questions at the end of each chapter:

I think there should definitely be a reading program because at the last school Laura was at, she had to do at least a half hour of reading every night. They would pick their books, like a novel or some type and read and then you would have to do questions after that and do a little book report after each chapter. I would like to see that because I find ... unless you force them to read, they won't pick up a book.

When we attempted to connect literacy to the idea of community and indeed, of rurality, parents spoke about the way things are changing rapidly around them in their home places, and how networked living erodes a traditional sense of community while at the same time transforming the actual experience of living in community. For instance, this parent speaks to the way that online engagements have created a community of visual networked loners (Turkle 2011):

Everyone sees everyone's pictures now. I think it's made everyone a little bit more nosy [laughs]. I think it can just zap up time that you don't put into a community. Again, socially, I think people need to just talk to one another. I think it can really isolate families. There is one house up the street that all summer you never see them outside, they spend all their time on the computers. I don't know what's going to happen with this generation that's coming up.

At the same time, though, traditional imagery of the rural community as a convivial small society (Redfield 1955, 1956) is notably absent. The quote above illustrates the sense in which life online has eroded the physical proximity that was the foundation of the traditional notion of the face-to-face community. There is the "nosiness" that online networks have generated and the phenomenon of traditional rural gossip moved online has been the subject of attention in some publications recently (Sulzburger 2011).

Whatever the case, it is clear that emerging literacy practices are constructed as threats to community as it has been traditionally understood. The isolation, physical inactivity, and gossip that are thought to be promoted by networked communication is constructed as a threat to children's safety (Corbett and Vibert 2010), literate development, and indeed even physical health. All of this is thought to have potential to disrupt bonding social capital that has characterized popular images of rurality. Literacies, even schooled literacies, have always been controversial, illustrating the fault lines within and between communities as texts have been banned and added/removed from approved lists. But what is new is the way that parents now recognize certain forms of text, particularly unregulated, unsupervised plastic, Internet-based text, as potentially dangerous. Indeed, children's facility with social media and the literacies developed in the process represent what might be termed dangerous literacies. The multiple threats implicit in the social network and the online globalized world (often represented by urban social problems) are presented in opposition to the safe, school-approved hard-copy book (ibid.) and the face-to-face safety in the locale of the traditional rural community. What is clear is that the nature of rural community has changed and that changing literacy practices are part of this change.

Diversity in Contexts: A Short Journey through a Contemporary Atlantic Canadian Rural Place

The foregoing section illustrates the way that the proliferation of texts, textual environments, and textual practices cause parents to juxtapose concrete and allegedly stable forms of text with the instability and plasticity of lower-status electronic text in a hierarchy. At the same time, teachers strive to concretize social equity in the context of educational standardization and a preoccupation with generic standards and testing through the medium of food. In both parents' and teachers' discourse about community, there is a recurrent sense that older forms of community have disappeared and been replaced by emergent online textual environments and economically challenged rural places in which older forms of survival have become obsolete. They also speak to a transformation of formerly convivial spaces of community where "everyone knew everyone else," to distributed matrices of networked communities that may or may not exist in physical space.

Many Canadian rural communities, particularly those that have coastal views or that are close to major centers, have become newly attractive to immigrants, many of whom are escaping what they perceive as the anonymity and diversity of urban and suburban places. The irony here is that these very developments make rural communities more diverse in themselves. We conclude here by illustrating this emerging diversity with an account of the transformation of one residential street containing 12 houses in a rural village. One of the authors (Corbett) moved onto this street in 1987 when the entire population, with one exception, had lived in on the street for at least two generations. By 2011, when Corbett moved from the neighborhood, he was, with one exception, the most senior resident of this street that now contains a diversity of residents.

On the east side lived a social researcher who telecommutes to Halifax. She recently sold the house to a couple from Saskatchewan who appeared to be looking for a better place to raise children where they can enjoy a simple, rural life. Next-door is a family that originates in Alberta. The main breadwinner in the household works with regional governments to develop hiking, cycling, and recreational trails in the region. Further east is an English woman who married an Inuk man from Nunavik in high northern Quebec, and who moved her children to the south for schooling as well as to enable her son to have a higher level of competition in ice hockey. Coming back down the hill to the east is the home of the longest tenured resident of the street: a retired couple who raised their family in the village.

If you still move east down the hill on the opposite side of the street from Corbett's house, you will find the home of a man from Montana who met a woman from Newfoundland while stationed at a military base in Goose Bay Labrador. Both are retired. Next is the Baptist church parsonage that is now rented to a salesman from the Annapolis Valley of Nova Scotia and his family. Further down on this side of the street is the family of a man who grew up in the village in the 1950s and who spent his career in southern Ontario, and retired to the village in the early 1990s. At the end of the street lives a mysterious family or person the villagers seldom see. At the end of the street is a clergyman who from the 1980s and into the 2000s ran one of Nova Scotia's first gay and lesbian bed-and-breakfast accommodations. On the opposite side of the street is a house that was previously owned by a multigenerational resident, one of the first families of the village who settled after the American revolutionary war. The current owner is the former fire chief who worked at the local military base decommissioned in 1994.

Next to this house, toward the west, there is the property of an American philanthropist, artist and arts patron who owns houses all over the world. He uses this house rarely himself but keeps it for the use of his artistic protégés and friends. A number of these temporary residents have been HIV/AIDS sufferers near the end of their lives or in treatment. Next to this house is the home of a store clerk and hairdresser from the local service center village of around 2500 residents. Finally, a Japanese luthier who attempted unsuccessfully to immigrate to Canada in the late 1990s, to build guitars, owns the house next to Corbett's former home on the west side. Since the early 2000s he has rented the house to a variety of people, including a British couple who are craftspeople (a potter and a stone-builder), a South African podiatrist and his English partner, and an Aboriginal woman who works with the local First Nations Band for cultural preservation and indigenous spirituality and knowledge.

The diversity on this particular street represents a marked transformation of the community in part facilitated by emerging digital literacies. The real estate market has become global, facilitated by online websites that allow better visibility for rural Nova Scotian properties. Within the past five years, broadband Internet has been made available in this part of rural Nova Scotia making it possible for immigrants to live the "rural idyll" while at the same time remaining connected through digital networks to their work and social and family lives, no matter where they exist physically. Cheap air travel has also made it easier to move between geographies for those who have the capital and the connections. Furthermore, the relatively low cost of rural properties, in the context of inflated and increasingly precarious urban markets of the past decade, have spurred an interest in the area. And indeed an increased concentration of diverse residents in a rural village tends to increase the attractiveness of the village to potential immigrants.

Ironically, these transformations are caught up in the same forces that parents see challenging the stability and safety of the spaces that they have known previously as "community." These are emerging spaces of risk in contemporary capitalism (Harvey 2010). These transformations also introduce, into the established distribution of wealth in rural communities, a new dimension of privilege. While this is not universally true, the newcomers tend to have a good deal more capital than many of the established residents, as well as different expectations for services including education. All of this creates new challenges for the schools, for teachers, and for parents and children. Like the community, these rural schools become increasingly diverse places, and in yet another ironic twist, this is so even if new immigrants think they are escaping urban and suburban diversity for their rural idyll.

We suggest this emerging diversity as a phenomenon to watch as rural communities develop in part on the strength of new mobilities, and as information and transportation networks shrink global spaces and introduce new elements into rural spaces. We also suggest that these developments introduce into contemporary rural communities both new literate challenges and new literacies with which to meet them, all of which creates a novel and ever-changing space whose character challenges established rural stereotypes and notions of the kind of education needed in the countryside.

Notes

*We would like to thank the Social Sciences and Humanities Research Council of Canada for supporting the research on which this chapter is based.

1. We suggest that the located nature of disciplinary technologies represents a key feature of governmentality, about which Foucault became increasingly concerned in his own theoretical trajectory from normalization and the means of correct training in *Discipline and Punish* (1979) to the spatial and indeed individualized analysis in his later analysis of sexuality and lectures on governmentality and biopolitics (2010).

2. While we will not take it up explicitly in this chapter, we are now developing a framework of understanding rural literacy practices among youth using the idea of "improvisation" as a central concept (Sawyer 1997, 2011). The framework at its most basic level points to different preoccupations among different players in the rural schools we have studied. Parents' fundamental preoccupation is with safety and the idea of school as a space of safe passage between the parental home, postsecondary education, and their children's future living spaces. The fundamental preoccupation of teachers tends to be one of striking a balance between competing and often contradictory commitments and expectations. So balance and tension characterize teachers' response to contemporary educational challenges. Finally, students use the idea of improvisation as a central framework for organizing their educational experience as they learn to creatively navigate and negotiate the multiple expectations of their parents, their teachers, state testing requirements, peer pressure, and online/multimedia engagements in their lives.

References

Abrams, D., 1996, *The Spell of the Sensuous: Perception and Language in a More Than Human World*, Vintage, New York.

Au, W., 2012, "Playing Smart: Resisting the Script," *Rethinking Schools*, vol. 26, no. 3: 30–31.

Beck, U., 1992, *Risk Society: Towards a New Modernity*, Sage, London.

Comber, B., H. Nixon, and J. Reid, 2007, *Literacies in Place: Teaching Environmental Communications*, Primary English Teaching Association, Australia.

Corbett, M., 2008, "The Edumometer: The Commodification of Learning from Galton to the PISA," *Journal for Critical Education Policy Studies*, vol. 6, no. 1, http://www.jceps.com/?pageID=article&articleID=125.

———, 2009, "Assimilation, Resistance, Rapprochement, and Loss: Response to Woodrum, Faircloth, Greenwood, and Kelly," *Journal of Research in Rural Education*, vol. 24, no. 12: 1–7.

Corbett, M. and A. Vibert, 2008–2011, *A Lens on Community: Video Ensemble Practice in a Rural School. Research Grant,* Social Sciences and Humanities Research Council.

———, 2010, 'Curriculum as a Safe Place: Hierarchies of Text, Improvisation and New Literacies in a Rural Small Town School," *Canadian Journal of Educational Administration and Policy,* no. 114, http://www.umanitoba.ca/publications/cjeap/pdf_files/comm2-Corbett-Vibert.pdf.

Cresswell, T., 2004, *Place: A Short Introduction*, Blackwell, London.

Donehower, K., C. Hogg, and E. F. Schell, 2007, *Rural Literacies*, University of Southern Illinois Press, Carbondale.

Eppley, K. and M. Corbett, 2012, 'I'll See That When I Believe It: A Dialogue on Epistemological Difference and Rural Literacies," *Journal of Research in Rural Education*, vol. 27, no. 1, http://www.jrre.psu.edu/articles/27–1.pdf.

Foucault, M., 1979, *Discipline & Punish: The Birth of the Prison*, Vintage Books, New York.

———, 2010, *The Government of Self and Others: Lectures at the College de France, 1982–1983,* Plagrave, New York.

Gee, J. P., 1999, *The New Literacy Studies and the "Social Turn,"* ERIC Opinion Paper, http://www.eric.ed.gov/PDFS/ED442118.pdf.

Green, B. and W. Letts, 2007, "Space, Equity and Rural Education: A Trialectical Account," in K. N. Gulson and C. Symes (eds.), *Spatial Theories of Education: Policy and Geography Matters,* Routledge, London and New York.

Harvey, D., 2010, *The Enigma of Capital and the Crisis of Capitalism*, Oxford University Press, Oxford and New York.

Knobel, M. and C. Lankshear, 2007, *A New Literacies Sampler*, Peter Lang, New York.

Massey, D., 2005, *For Space*, Sage, London.

Prinsloo, M., 2005, "The New Literacies as Placed Resources," *Perspectives in Education*, vol. 23, no. 4: 87–98.

Redfield, R., 1955, *The Little Community*, University of Chicago Press, Chicago.

———, 1956, *Peasant Society and Culture*, University of Chicago Press, Chicago.

Reid, J., B. Green, M. Cooper, W. Hastings, G. Lock, and S. White, 2010, "Regenerating Rural Social Space: Teacher Education for Rural-Regional Sustainability," *Australian Journal of Education*, vol. 54, no. 3: 262–276.

Sawyer, R., 1997, *Pretend Play as Improvisation: Conversations in the Preschool Classroom*, Lawrence Erlbaum, Mahway NJ.

———, 2011, *Structure and Improvisation in Creative Teaching*, Cambridge University Press, Cambridge.

Sulzburger, A., 2011, "In Small Towns, Gossip Moves to the Web, and Turns Vicious," *New York Times*, September 19, http://www.nytimes.com/2011/09/20/us/small-town-gossip-moves-to-the-web-anonymous-and-vicious.html?pagewanted=all.

Turkle, S., 2011, *Alone Together: Why We Expect More from Technology and Less from Each Other*, Basic Books, New York.

Vibert, A., 2005, *Pedagogies at Risk: Teaching for Social Justice in an Age of Accountability*, Funded by Social Sciences and Humanities Research Council of Canada research project.

———, 2009, "Painting the Mountain Green: Discourses of Accountability and Critical Practice," in C. Levine-Rasky (ed.), *The Sociology of Education in Canada*, Oxford University Press, Don Mills, ON.

Weaver-Hightower, M. B., 2011, "Why Educational Researchers Should Take School Food Seriously," *Educational Researcher*, vol. 40, no. 1: 15–21.

Woods, M., 2011, *Rural*, Routledge, New York and London.

———, 2006, "Redefining the 'Rural Question': The New 'Politics of the Rural' and Social Policy," *Social Policy and Administration*, vol. 40, no. 6: 579–595.

Contributors

Kate Cairns is a Postdoctoral Fellow in the Department of Sociology at the University of Toronto. Her primary areas of interest include feminist theory, sociology of education, critical geography, and cultural studies. Kate's doctoral research explored how rural youth envision their futures in neoliberal times. Her work has appeared in journals such as *Gender and Education*, *Gender & Society*, *Ethnography and Education*, *Education and Urban Society*, and *Journal of Consumer Culture*.

Barbara Comber is a Research Professor in the Faculty of Education at Queensland Institute of Technology, Brisbane, Australia. Her interests include critical literacy, social justice, teachers' work, and place-based pedagogy. She has done a number of ethnographic studies, and collaborative research with teachers, in high poverty schools. Among her publications are the coedited volumes *Literacies in Place: Teaching Environmental Communications* (Primary English Teachers Association, 2007) and *Negotiating Critical Literacies in Classrooms* (Lawrence Erlbaum, 2001).

Michael Corbett is Professor of Education and Director of the Acadia Centre for Rural Education and Sustainability in the School of Education at Acadia University in eastern Canada. His research is focused on the sociology of education, literacies, mobility, and rural education. He has published the monograph *Learning to Leave: The Irony of Schooling in a Coastal Community* (Fernwood, 2007) and a body of book chapters and journal articles based on research in rural schools and communities in Atlantic Canada.

Phillip Cormack is Adjunct Associate Research Professor of Education in the School of Education at the University of South Australia, Australia. His research interests include the history of adolescence, contemporary and historical perspectives on literacy policy, curriculum, and pedagogy. He currently works on projects on the history of reading education in Australia and the impact of contemporary standardized testing reforms on teachers' work.

Kim Donehower is an Associate Professor of English at the University of North Dakota, United States, where she researches literacy in rural communities. She is the coauthor of *Rural Literacies* (Southern Illinois University Press, 2007) and coeditor of *Reclaiming the Rural: Essays on Literacy, Rhetoric, and Pedagogy* (Southern Illinois University Press, 2012).

Karen Eppley is an Assistant Professor of Language and Literacy Education at Penn State Altoona, United States. She received her PhD from Penn State University. Her research interest is the intersection of literacies and rural education. Specifically, she is interested in rural teacher preparation, situated and multiple literacies, place-based pedagogy, and the textual representations of rural life. She has published in the *Journal of Research in Rural Education*, *Teaching and Teacher Education*, the *Rural Educator*, and *Pedagogies: An International Journal*.

Bill Green is Professor of Education in the Faculty of Education and formerly (2006–2012) Strategic Research Professor in the Research Institute for Professional Practice, Learning and Education (RIPPLE) at Charles Sturt University, New South Wales, Australia. His research interests include literacy studies and curriculum inquiry, English curriculum history, doctoral research education, and education for rural-regional sustainability. His recent publications include the edited volumes *Understanding and Researching Professional Practice* (Sense, 2009) and *Literacy in 3D: An Integrated Perspective in Theory and Practice* (Australian Council for Educational Research, 2012).

Kathryn Hibbert is an Assistant Professor of Adolescent Literacy at the Faculty of Education, University of Western Ontario, Canada. She has taught in rural, urban, and virtual spaces and is the creator of *The Salty Chip: A Canadian Multiliteracies Collaborative* (http://www.saltychip. com). Her recent publications have explored the affordances of multiliteracies practices as a means of expanding identity options and engaging learners marginalized by traditional literacy pedagogies and practices.

Craig Howley, Adjunct Associate Professor in the Patton College of Education and Human Services at Ohio University, United States, is the coauthor of 15 books and book chapters and 50 peer-reviewed research articles. He currently directs the research initiative of a federally funded center devoted to rural mathematics education (ACCLAIM). Earlier, he directed an ERIC Clearinghouse and worked as a research and development specialist at a Regional Educational Laboratory. Howley is particularly interested in connections between education and everyday life in rural places and cultures. Recent publications (with Aimee Howley) include two book chapters, one dealing with social class and rural identity, and the other analyzing the Gates Foundation's hasty abandonment of small schools (both published in 2010).

Ursula Kelly is Professor in the Faculty of Education at Memorial University of Newfoundland, St. John's, Newfoundland, Canada. Her most recent book is *Migration and Education in a Multicultural World: Culture, Loss and Identity* (Palgrave, 2009). She is also the author of *Marketing Place: Cultural Politics, Regionalism and Reading* (Fernwood, 1993) and *Schooling Desire: Literacy, Cultural Politics and Pedagogy* (Routledge, 1997). She is the coeditor of two collections, *Narrating Transformative Learning in Education* (Palgrave Macmillan, 2008) and *Despite This Loss: Essays on Culture, Memory, and Identity in Newfoundland and Labrador* (ISER Books, 2010). Her teaching, research, and writing interests are critical education, cultural studies, and literacies and language studies.

Lyn Kerkham is a research fellow for the Australian Research Council project "Educational Leadership and Turnaround Literacy Pedagogies." She also teaches undergraduate and postgraduate teacher education courses at the University of South Australia after a career of teaching in disadvantaged primary schools in regional South Australia and in metropolitan Adelaide. She has recently received her PhD from the University of South Australia. Her research interests include literacy, sustainability, and teachers' lives and work.

Maija Lanas is a postdoctoral researcher in University of Oulu, Faculty of Education, Finland. In her PhD she conducted ethnography in an arctic Finnish reindeer-herding village, where people live in the borderline of localization and globalization, constructing their identity in a dialogue with Othering national representations. In her own work, she looks for alternative inscriptions for agency traditionally seen as student resistance.

Pauliina Rautio is a postdoctoral research fellow at the Department of Teacher Education at the University of Helsinki, Finland. She is also affiliated with the University of Oulu, Finland, working as a part-time PhD program coordinator. Her broad research interests include everyday life and child-matter intra-action within the frameworks of posthumanism, new materialism, and postqualitative methodology.

Jo-Anne Reid is Professor of Education and Associate Dean, Teacher Education, in the Faculty of Education at Charles Sturt University, New South Wales, Australia. Her research and teaching interests include teacher education, primary literacy education, Indigenous education, and rural education. Her publications include the coedited volume *Literacies in Place: Teaching Environmental Communications* (Primary English Teachers Association, 2007).

Margaret Somerville is a Professor of Education in the School of Education and Director of the Centre for Educational Research at the University of Western Sydney, Australia. Her research and teaching interests are in place and sustainability education, literacy, arts-based research, and the nature of Indigenous knowledges. Her recent publications include two coedited volumes, *Landscapes & Learning: Place Studies for a Global World* (Sense, 2009) and *Place Pedagogy Change* (Sense, 2011), and two books, *Singing the Coast* (Aboriginal Studies Press, 2010—with Gumbaynggirr knowledge holder Tony Perkins) and *Water in a Dry Land* (Routledge, 2013).

Ann Vibert is Director of the School of Education at Acadia University in Canada. Her work has spanned the broad fields of literacy education and social justice education. Ann is principal investigator in a major research project funded by the Social Sciences and Humanities Research Council of Canada entitled *Pedagogies at Risk,* which looks at the experience of Canadian educators committed to social justice working through a decade of neoliberal educational reform.

Index

Printed in the United States of America